The Art of Not
Falling Apart

The Art of Not Falling Apart

Christina Patterson

Atlantic Books
London

First published in trade paperback in Great Britain in 2018 by Atlantic Books,
an imprint of Grove Atlantic Ltd.

10 9 8 7 6 5 4 3 2

A CIP catalogue record for this book is available from the British Library.

Trade paperback ISBN 978 1 78649 274 6
Ebook ISBN 978 1 78649 275 3

Printed and bound by CPI Group (UK) Ltd, Croydon, CR0 4YY

In fact, may you be dull –
If that is what a skilled,
Vigilant, flexible,
Unemphasised, enthralled
Catching of happiness is called.

Philip Larkin,
'Born Yesterday'

Contents

Prologue

I was writing up an interview when I got the call. Five minutes later, I felt as if I was falling off a cliff. The letter had been bad enough. The letter had used words like 'synergies' and 'integration', and the 'synergies', it said, would 'reduce costs'. The letter had been followed by a meeting with a young blonde from HR who talked about 'consultation' while she gazed at her nails. But now what the man in front of me was saying didn't seem to make any sense at all. When I asked him to explain, he started fiddling with his pen. 'You'll have,' he said, 'to see the editor.'

When I walked into the editor's office, he was hunched behind his desk. Something about his mouth made it clear he was raring for a fight. I had, I told him, accepted the 'synergies', but I had been promised a contract to sugar the pill. Now the promise seemed to have been broken and I didn't understand what was going on. The editor, who is fat and bald and looks as though he should be wearing a nappy, stared out of the window as he told me that he had decided to 'freshen the pages up'.

It's quite hard to swallow when the boss has just made it clear that your older, male colleagues are still 'fresh', but you are not. I tried to keep my voice steady as I told the editor that readers liked my work. I told him that I couldn't have worked much harder. I told him that I had given ten years' loyal service to the paper and I did not deserve to be treated like this.

Now the editor looked at me and his cold, grey eyes made me think of a fish. 'And what,' he said, and he seemed to be smiling as he said it, 'is so special about you?'

When someone asks you why you're special, there isn't really anything you can say. You could, I suppose, say that some people think you're special, but it isn't easy to say that to someone who's looking at you as if you're a stain on the carpet they would like to blast with bleach.

I told him that I didn't like his tone. I told him that I didn't like the way he was treating some of the senior women on his staff. The editor looked away and then back at me. He said I didn't know what I was talking about. I was surprised to hear myself shouting that I did. And then he threatened to call security. This big bull of a man actually threatened to call security.

When I walked out of the office, for the last time, after ten years, nobody even looked up.

I always dreamt of being a journalist, but never seriously thought I could be. I grew up in a family of teachers and public servants and was brought up to believe that saying you wanted to write for a living was very much like saying you wanted to be a punk. At university, I had vague dreams of sitting on a frontline, looking like Martha Gellhorn, bashing out pieces that 'spoke truth to power'. But the only things I wrote, as dawn broke and the birds in the college grounds shattered the silence of the night, were essays about alliteration in *Sir Gawain and the Green Knight* or the use of allegory in *The Faerie Queen*.

I was thirty-eight, and running a small arts organization called the Poetry Society, when I got a call from the literary editor of *The Independent*, saying that his deputy was leaving and asking if I wanted to apply for the job. I had been reviewing books for the national papers since I was twenty-six, but had given up all dreams of journalism as anything other than a sideline to a full-time job. I loved my job, and my colleagues, and I also quite liked being the boss. But I knew that if I wanted to work on a national paper, this was my chance.

A newspaper, my new boss told me, was like a medieval fiefdom. At first I didn't understand what he meant. In the arts world, bosses pretended to be interested in getting the views of their staff. In the arts world, you got sent on courses on 'diversity' and talked about things like 'continuing professional development'. I once even got sent on a course to learn the Alexander Technique. I thought it was very nice of the taxpayer to let me lie with my head on a cushion, 'allowing my neck to be free'.

Newspapers were not like this. On a newspaper, or at least on my newspaper, no one cared about your 'continuing professional development'. You didn't get training for anything except IT. There was only really one item on your job description: do whatever the hell your boss says. On the books desk, we would sweat over each semi-colon and piece together the pages as if they were the fragments of a Ming vase. At five o'clock on press day, the deputy editor would stroll down to look at the proofs. He would glance at the pages, grab his pen from his pocket and slice it through the air as if it was a machete hovering over a neck. When he handed the proofs back, we would gaze at the marks like gashes on the pages and wonder how to salvage something from the wreck. My boss said it was just 'willy waving', but dealing with 'willies' seemed to be quite a big part of the job.

When I moved upstairs, to be an editor on the comment desk, I learnt more about stress. It started with the tension in the faces of the section editors as they tried to put together their morning list. A list on a newspaper isn't like a list you write on a notepad, where you might or might not tick some of the items off. A list on a newspaper is a miracle you have snatched out of air. You have got up, you have listened to the *Today* programme, you have read, or at least flicked through, all the papers, and tried to grasp the latest developments on quantitative easing in the Eurozone and the Nigerian government's shift in policy on Boko Haram. You have strained every neuron in your brain to put together a list of ideas that will make editors on other papers feel sick that they didn't come up with them first. But when you see the editor's PA opening the door to his office, you know that there is only one view that counts.

A 'conference', according to the dictionary, is 'a formal interchange of views'. Perhaps, in some places, it is. In conference on a newspaper – not 'a conference', because there's no time to mess around with indefinite articles – the 'interchange of views' is just one-way. The editor asks you to read your list, and then stares at you as if you had just projectile vomited on to his new Damien Hirst. If he's in a good mood, he might nod. If he's in a bad mood – and editors are in bad moods quite a lot – he will pick out something on your list, and repeat the words back to you as if you had just suggested a front-page story on Jane Austen's use of the quadrille. He will then ask you about a tiny news item on page 36 of the one paper you didn't get a chance to skim.

It's hard to explain why we all love it, but we do. Perhaps we all like to think we really are in a war. The relief that it wasn't you in the firing line, or that it was you, but that the bullet somehow missed your heart, sends some chemical flooding through your veins. It makes you want to climb up on your desk, raise your arms as high as you can get them and bellow that you're still here, you are actually still alive. After that, all you have to fear is the later prowl round the office. That, and the ticking clock. If you're editing, you get on the phone. You talk, you wait, you hone, you chop. If you're writing, you do as much googling as you can squeeze into the minutes before you have to get that first mark on that blank page. At the start of the day, there is nothing. At the end of the day, there are a hundred pages of what you hope is sparkling copy. This happens every day and it makes you feel as if you are, or are working with, God.

When I was asked to write a regular column, I felt like singing an aria. When I was told I could drop the editing and write full-time, I felt like singing the Hallelujah Chorus.

As well as my column, which I now did twice a week, I did a weekly interview. I had been interviewing writers for years. Jeanette Winterson had given me the number of her psychic. Jacqueline Wilson had told me that she sometimes only just managed to 'get her knickers on' when people asked for her autograph at the gym. Philip Pullman had talked about a satire he had written on journalism called *I Was a Rat!* He seemed to think that being a journalist was something that should make you feel ashamed. I wanted to tell him that nothing in my life had ever made me feel as proud.

And nothing had. The truth is, nothing ever had. It was certainly stressful. Writing two columns a week and finding someone famous to interview, and doing the research on them, and going to meet them, and transcribing the tape, and writing it up, meant that I ended up working nearly all the time. Sometimes the interviews were interesting. Sometimes they weren't. Alice Cooper told the same anecdotes he had been trotting out for thirty years. Eddie Izzard compared himself to Nelson Mandela. Carlos Acosta complained about being a sex symbol. I told him that it might be a good idea to do up the buttons of his shirt.

Candace Bushnell, who wrote *Sex and the City*, gave me some advice on dating. I thought I could do with some advice on dating, because my so-called romances never seemed to last more than a few weeks. 'The people I know who are happily married,' she said, jabbing her finger, 'don't expect their husbands to bring home the bacon. If you're very wedded to a narrow idea of what life should be like,' she added, 'you're going to run out of time.' When I realized she thought I was trying to find a rich man to support me, I had to make an effort not to laugh. I thought of the date with the man with buck teeth who had shouted to the whole restaurant that I was 'a cunt' and left me to pay the bill. Never mind bacon, I wanted to tell her. I'm thrilled if someone buys me a drink.

When I was asked to write the lead column in the paper once a week, I started reading newspapers all the time. A lead column can't just be about some little thing you find quite interesting, like the return of the legging, or the fact that men seem to think they should get a medal for saying that Helen Mirren is still 'quite hot'. A lead column has to be about a big item in the news that day. It could be a change to the definition of child poverty, or a cut to tax credits, or whether you should try to extradite a radical preacher with a hook for a hand. I started to feel as if my life was a twenty-four-hour viva for a PhD in current affairs. I went to bed with the news and woke up to the news and felt like yelling at the presenters of *Newsnight* that the news they were discussing was now rather old.

Every Tuesday, when I heard people stumbling over their interviews with John Humphrys, I wanted to tell them that they should count themselves lucky. *They* should try to think of a 'fresh' argument about a piece of news they'd only just heard about, wait for the comment editor to take the idea to conference and wonder if you might then have to write about something else that has just leapt into the editor's head. And then churn out 1100 words of interesting, thought-provoking, editor-pleasing prose by 3 p.m.

When the emails started pouring in, they sometimes made me laugh. '*If* you had done your research, Miss Patterson' was a fair sign that what followed would make me smile less. Yes, I wanted to say. Yes, if I'd had time to do research I might well have come up with a different argument. If I'd had time to do research, I would have had a different job. I sometimes wondered whether readers thought columnists sat in libraries, rifling through Socrates and weighing up arguments like a judge. A columnist, I wanted to say, was someone who showed up. You licked a finger, stuck it in the air and hoped to catch a breath of wind. What you did next was fill a page. Whatever else you did, you had to fill that page. And your photo and name would be stuck over it whether what you produced was Plato or Russell Brand.

Freud talked about love and work. He said they are 'the cornerstones of our humanness'. Most people have taken that to mean that if we want to be happy, we need work we like and someone to love. As Candace Bushnell pointed out, my search for love wasn't going well. Work I could do. Work was what I had. And then a new editor arrived on the paper, and a junior member of staff was given my boss's job, and then I got a letter about 'synergies', and then a bald, fat man asked me why I was special and threatened to call security, and then I walked out of an office on Kensington High Street knowing that I had lost the thing I had spent my whole life building up.

It's interesting what happens to the body when it's in shock. Shock, according to the medical definition, is 'a life-threatening condition of low blood perfusion to tissues resulting in cellular injury and inadequate tissue function'. But this, it says, is not the same as 'the emotional state of shock'. When you're in emotional shock you're not likely to die. You're just likely to feel that some-one has tried to kill you.

What you experience in emotional shock is an 'acute stress response'. This is triggered by something called the 'sympathetic nervous system', which is specially designed to respond to phrases like 'I don't love you any more' or 'what's so special about you?' You might think that a sympathetic system would be trying to calm you down, wrapping you in a nice chemical blanket and offering you a choice between Green & Black's cocoa and a whisky sour. It doesn't. The sympathetic nervous system has decided that what you need when you're really, really upset is to be flooded with hormones that set your whole system on fire. It thinks that what you need, when you're trying to keep upright as you walk out of an office on Kensington High Street, is to be able to gallop over a savannah.

It's actually quite hard to do anything when your heart is thumping in your chest like a mad prisoner trying to hammer a way out. And when your whole body is trembling, like one of those Power Plates you never use at the gym. You think, at first, that it's quite interesting that you can actually see your body shaking. You wonder if this is what it's like when people say they have 'the shakes' and can't do anything until they've had a drink. You think that the shaking will surely soon stop. You honestly don't see how it can carry on. But your heart keeps hammering and your body keeps shaking and you still find it hard to swallow, while you're still gulping air and wondering why you seem to have forgotten how to breathe.

I was still shaking the next day when I got a phone call from Harriet Harman's chief of staff saying that they were keen to fix the interview she had agreed to do for my planned series on 'women and power'. I had to explain that I wouldn't be doing any interviews on 'women and power' because I didn't seem to have any power any more. I didn't, in fact, seem to have a job. A few minutes later, the phone rang again. 'I've got Harriet on the line,' the voice at the end of it said. 'She wants to speak to you.'

I was wearing torn leggings and a stripy Primark top as I paced around my study and told the shadow deputy prime minister what had happened. Harriet Harman had started something called the Commission on Older Women. Three days before, on the Sky News press preview on which I was a regular guest, I had talked about her commission. Now she said she wanted to understand *The Independent*'s policy towards women. Why, she wanted to know, was a national newspaper that had a reputation for being liberal forcing out quite a few of its forty-something women?

I wanted to be helpful, but I couldn't tell her why. I knew I couldn't have worked much harder. I didn't think I could have done a much better job. I had, for example, recently done a big campaign to raise standards in nursing that had had a record response from readers and been mentioned in a debate in the House of Commons. I wanted to tell her that I wasn't so naïve as to think that hard work would always be rewarded, but that nothing in my life had prepared me for this.

I had a wild urge to tell her about my father's seventieth birthday dinner, some years before. He had cancer and we knew he was dying and my mother made a speech. My mother talked about my father, and some of the things he had done. She also talked about the guests. She talked about how they had met, and what their friendship had meant.

There were six couples round that table and they all met their partners when they were young. Like my parents, they got married in their early twenties, had a baby and bought a house. Like my parents, they then had more babies, in most cases another two. They didn't have to worry all that much about how they were going to pay the mortgage, since they had jobs – in teaching, the civil service or the NHS – that were theirs for life. They didn't need to worry about retirement, either. When they hit sixty, or, if they weren't quite so lucky, sixty-five, they would have the kind of pension that meant they could carry on living pretty much as they had before. They could still go to the theatre, and eat out. They could still have foreign holidays. And they would have plenty of time to spend with the grandchildren, because that, as they all say, is one of the big joys of getting old.

In my parents' world, I wanted to tell Harriet Harman, you knew what you should be doing. You had to feed your children and you had to pay your bills. To do these things, you had to go to work. It was important to do your work well. You should do your work so well that you get promoted every few years without ever having to boast about yourself on Twitter. But a job was how you showed your responsibility to your family. A job was not a bridge over a void.

In my parents' world, you didn't wake up on a Saturday morning in your forties thinking that if you wanted to speak to a human being in the next two days, you'd better try to make an arrangement. You didn't think that, if you ever wanted to have sex again, you'd better force yourself to do some internet dating, and then hear a man say, on your fifth date, just after you've had really rather adventurous sex, that he's 'determined to hold out for something good'.

I had, I wanted to tell Harriet Harman, faced plenty of difficulties before. I had had to deal with illness. I had had to cope with sudden death. I had never thought I would face my middle years without a family or a man to love, but I had tried very hard to make the best of it. I had my career. At least I had my career. But now I didn't.

In a corner of my study, behind the filing cabinet and the printer, there's a secret shelf. On it are the kinds of books that sprang up on the Amazon page of a computer I once shared with a colleague.

He, it was clear from the 'Related to items you've viewed' section, was ordering books on Eastern European poets. I, it was clear from the same section, was ordering books with titles like *Men Who Can't Love* and *I Can Make You Thin*. When I realized he was getting my recommendations, I went hot, then cold.

It started with a book I begged my mother to buy me when I was thirteen. It was written by Vidal Sassoon and his glowing wife Beverly, and called *A Year of Beauty and Health*. Vidal and Beverly said you should start the day with hot water and lemon and continue it with a run. Then, after 'dry-brushing' your skin in the shower, you were meant to have a breakfast of egg whites or oatmeal, and then prepare a packed lunch of raw vegetables and sprouted seeds. I didn't do any of this, of course. I had toast and marmalade for breakfast, school lunch, with spotted dick or jam roly poly for pudding, and a Dayvilles ice cream or a Twix on the way home. As an adult, I've bought *The Hip and Thigh Diet*, *The Red Wine Diet*, *The Food Doctor Diet*, *The Easy GI Diet*, *Dr Atkins New Diet Revolution*, *The South Beach Diet*, *6 Weeks to Super Health* and *Stop the Insanity!*, which probably sums up the rest of them. And I'm not even fat.

The diet books, which I usually read with a cup of coffee and a big slab of cake, aren't hidden behind the filing cabinet. They're next to the cookery books, which look as if they've hardly been opened, because they haven't. The diet books aren't hidden, because women are supposed to worry about their weight, even if they hate cooking, don't weigh themselves, and eat whatever the hell they like. And because there's only one shelf behind the filing cabinet, and it's pretty jam-packed.

People judge you by your bookshelves, and I don't really want any of my guests to see *Wanting Everything, Instant Confidence* and *Awaken the Giant Within*. I particularly don't want them to see *How to Meet a Man After Forty*, and particularly since the jacket is pink. I wouldn't want to explain why I'd bought a book called *You Can Heal Your Life*, or one called *Happiness Now!* I think I'd be embarrassed by the exclamation mark.

If any of my guests did peer behind the filing cabinet, I'd have to explain that the self-help books, like the diet books, hadn't changed anything, but it probably didn't help that I hadn't followed any of the instructions. I'd have to say that you couldn't actually read *War and Peace* or *The Waste Land*, and then pick up a book with a title like *Change Your Life in 7 Days* with anything like a straight face. These books weren't about solving anything. Like an action movie, or a rom com, they were about escape. They were about taking you, for a couple of hours, with a nice glass of Sauvignon and a bowl of Kettle Chips, to a simpler, perkier place.

I have never yet found a book called *I Feel So Awful I Don't Know What to Do*. If I had, on a few occasions in my life I might have snapped it up. Instead, I have bought books with titles like *A Grief Observed* and *Prisoners of Pain*. I have read books about people in refugee camps, and people who live in slums, and children who have been abused. I have certainly learnt a lot about how other people live their lives, but have ended up feeling ashamed that I sometimes seem to be making such a mess of mine.

I was once jealous of someone who was at Auschwitz. I'm not proud of this, but I'm afraid it's true. I was lying on a hotel bed in Turkey, drinking a cup of tea, and reading about a man who was trying to stay alive in a place where people were being starved, and tortured, and made to dig railway tracks in frozen ground, in a place, in fact, where people were sent to be slaughtered, and I actually thought, at least for a moment: it's all right for you.

I had ordered *Man's Search for Meaning* on Amazon, because I felt my own search for meaning wasn't going well at all. I had met a man who had promised to be my 'rock', but turned out to be more like one of those houses in the Bible that are built on sand. After he left, I felt as though my life had turned into the lyrics of one of those soul songs where everyone wears a tight satin suit. 'What becomes of the broken-hearted?' sings a man with an Afro and a *very* big collar. 'I know I've got to find,' he sings, 'some kind of peace of mind.' Unfortunately, he doesn't tell us how he does it.

The days that followed after my lover left were bad enough, but what happened two weeks later was much, much worse. I stopped even thinking about 'peace of mind' and wondered how I would get through it without cracking up. I thought it might help to hear how other people had got through things that would make the things I had to face look like a walk in the park. So I ordered *Man's Search for Meaning*, and on page 49 I found the answer. What had kept him going, said Viktor Frankl, through the hunger, and the pain, and the screams of anguish from the bunks around him, was the thought of the woman he loved. He had found his strength, he said, in the 'contemplation of his beloved'. And I thought, perhaps just for a moment, but a moment is enough: it's all right for you.

When a book about a concentration camp makes you feel a cold thud you have learnt to recognize as envy, take it from me, that doesn't make you feel good at all.

*

'What will survive of us', said the poet Philip Larkin, 'is love.' He says this in his poem 'An Arundel Tomb', about a stone knight and his lady who, even in death, are holding hands. The tone of the poem is ironic, but the simple beauty of the words is stronger than the tone. Even Philip Larkin – miserable, moaning Philip Larkin – can't help agreeing with Viktor Frankl. In the end, what matters is having someone to love.

Most of us want love. Most of us want satisfying work. Most of us want a family. We want a place, and people, to call home.

So what do you do if you haven't got it? Or if you had it and lost it? What do you do when you've made the best of what you have and then lose the thing you care about most? How do you 'search for meaning' when so many of the traditional ways of finding it seem to have gone? And how on earth do you keep picking yourself up when life keeps finding ways to knock you down?

Life, as Boris Pasternak said, 'is not so easy as to cross a field'. It never has been, but for many of us there are fresh challenges now. Nearly a third of us live on our own. More of us are single than ever before. And if you do get married, you have almost a fifty–fifty chance that your marriage will fail.

You could throw yourself into work, but the digital revolution is wiping out jobs. Some economists say that about half of us will lose our jobs in the next twenty years. Some of us – particularly in areas like journalism where the business model is failing – might struggle to get a job again. We can, of course, all become 'entrepreneurs', but the average annual income of a self-employed person in Britain is about £10,000. You try having a lovely life on £10,000.

If this was a self-help book, I could tell you what to do. I could be the teacher and tell you all about success. I am not a teacher, and for big chunks of my life I have felt I have failed.

At the end of that phone call with Harriet Harman, I said that I didn't think there was anything much that could be done about my lost column and my lost job. If someone doesn't think you're 'fresh', I said, you're not likely to change their mind.

But no one can stop me from being a journalist. However I earn my living, I will always be a journalist. I know how to ask questions. I know how to listen. And in the weeks following that phone call I decided it was time to ask different kinds of questions and to listen in a way I had never listened before.

I can't tell you what to do when your heart is broken and your spirit has been crushed. I can tell you what I learnt, and what I did next.

Part I

Falling

'If you want to make God laugh, tell him about your plans'

Woody Allen

Kafka, eat your heart out

I have never had a heart attack, but I think I now have some idea what it's like. For days after I walked out of that office on Kensington High Street, I felt as if I had something crouching on my chest. I'm normally keen to lose a pound or two, but even I was shocked to lose eight pounds in three days. The day after the editor threatened to call security, I got an emergency appointment with my doctor. I told her that I couldn't stop shaking. My heart, I said, felt like a bomb that was about to go off.

I never thought losing a job would be easy, but I always thought so many things would be worse. I had been through quite a few of the things that are meant to be so much worse. They didn't seem all that much worse now.

It was the psychologist Abraham Maslow who came up with the idea of a hierarchy of needs. He talked about life as a pyramid, where your need for food and shelter come first. After that, there's a need for safety and then for 'love, belonging and esteem'. Shelter I had, at least for a while. Food, for once, I didn't want. And love? Love was a luxury I couldn't worry about now.

When mice go through changes in status, it affects their immune system and their ability to move. No wonder humans can't stop shaking when they're suddenly pushed from a perch.

One moment, you're being invited to go on *The One Show* and speak in seminars at the House of Commons. The next, you start talking about work in the past tense. It makes you feel as though you have been knocked down by a bus, and are somehow still functioning even though you have been technically certified as dead.

In John Lanchester's novel *Mr Phillips*, a man sets off with his briefcase, in a suit. Instead of going to the office, he sits on a bench in the park until it's time to go home. He doesn't know how he's going to tell his wife or sons that he has lost his job. Not long after I shouted at the editor, I met someone who did something similar. After he lost his job as an executive editor of a national newspaper, Grant Feller rushed out of the house before his children got home from school, and then strode in with his briefcase, telling them that 'Daddy was home early again'. It took him three days to pluck up the courage to tell them that he had been marched out of the office with his things in a cardboard box.

'I can remember every single moment of it happening,' he told me. 'I can remember being approached by the managing editor and tapped on the shoulder. I can remember the walk. I remember being sat down. I remember the look on his face and the sun coming through the shutters on the window overlooking the Thames. He said, "The editor has lost faith in your ability and we no longer want you to work here." I went cold.

'It was,' he admitted, 'a brutal environment, but secretly I loved it. I loved being pushed to my limits. The adrenaline, the testosterone, the thing you feel when you get that great pat on the back when you've done a great column, or even when you've written a great headline, that's the most amazing gift.' Oh yes, that thing you feel. That terror. That excitement. That thrill. But the pressure mounted, he said, as the budgets were slashed. 'I never, ever, ever put in a bad day's work,' he said, 'but I just didn't fit any more. My wife says, "Didn't you see it coming?" And the reason I didn't was that I was good at the job.'

When Grant walked out of that meeting with the managing editor, he found security guards waiting outside the door. Newspaper editors love the grand exit with security guards. It's a way of showing the whole office that you have turned, on the flash of a whim, from friend to foe. 'I said to the managing editor that I'd appreciate it if we didn't have any security guards,' Grant told me. 'We shook hands. I left. It must have been about ten-thirty in the morning. I got on the train. It was a completely empty train, full of old people and students and tourists. There was a kind of numbness and a sort of feeling that you're not quite in this world, almost as if all people had disappeared and you were just on your own, like in those westerns when that tumbleweed rolls across the desert.'

The next day, he said, was the worst. 'I just couldn't tell the children. I walked them to school, came home, did stuff in my T-shirt, then put my suit on at about quarter to five and went for a walk and then came back when I knew the children were there. And they said, "Daddy, home early again?" And I said, "Easy day."'

Grant took another sip of his wine and then he gulped. 'When you don't have work, and you look into your children's eyes at breakfast time . . . they don't quite understand what losing a job means. But when they start worrying about money, it's just the worst thing. Being the provider that society deems a man to be, that was right at the core of things for me.'

I nodded, as if I knew exactly what he meant. I knew I should have thought that I was lucky not to have had to worry about having other mouths to feed. I didn't feel lucky. I felt as if worrying about my own livelihood, home and future was something a woman's magazine might tell you to do when you've had a hard day with the kids. Like a bubble bath, with a scented candle and perhaps a tiny glass of wine. 'Me time'. Because I'm worth it. Even if I now have a horrible feeling I'm not.

'I was fortunate,' he said, 'to live in an affluent part of London, but it makes things difficult. You start to measure your life in terms of what you possess or own. And also how you define yourself: I am a doctor, I am a lawyer, I am a journalist. And then there was a time when it was: I'm looking for something else to do, and you can't walk into a room and say that.'

Well, you can, but the trouble is that other people don't know what to say. I am an ex-journalist. I am a recovering journalist. I am a journalist who may no longer be able to carry on living in my home. 'There was a period,' said Grant, 'when there was a "for sale" sign outside the house, two or three months after I lost my job. That was awful. One morning,' he said, and he seemed to be half wincing at the memory, 'I pulled it out of the ground. I looked at it and thought "no way", and told the estate agent, "It's not for sale."'

I first met Grant at a professional networking dinner organized by someone we both knew. We were each asked to say something about ourselves and he said that losing his job was the best thing that ever happened to him. At the end of the dinner I rushed up to him and told him that for me it had felt like one of the worst. I couldn't understand how he had managed to be positive and upbeat and all the things the self-help books tell you to be when you lose your job, while I had been staggering around as if I was carrying a corpse. When we finally met for a drink to swap stories of newspaper battlefields, he set me right. 'I was monumentally depressed,' he said. 'And I was angry, so angry and so bitter and so full of poison. Honestly, there were days when I wanted to do the most terrible things to the people I felt had wronged me.'

I poured us both another glass of wine and had to fight the urge to cheer. I had been talking to a radio producer about making a programme about compassion, following some work I'd done on nursing and the NHS. 'To be honest,' I told the producer, 'I'm currently more interested in making a programme about revenge.' I was joking, and was quite surprised when he said it was 'a great idea'. We put together a proposal. We would, we said, look at the history and psychology of revenge, from Medea to the contemporary armed forces and the judiciary. We would ask whether the import of 'honour' codes from the South and East had affected Britain's traditional Christian/liberal humanist idea of turning the other cheek. But all I really wanted to do was plunge *The Independent*'s management in boiling oil.

The producer's bosses weren't, it turned out, very keen on compassion or revenge. But the producer was so upset by what had happened to me that he cancelled his subscription to *The Independent*. His act of loyalty cheered me up when not all that much else did.

Ken Olisa sounded very cheerful when I heard him talk at an event on 'finding your balance'. I was invited to it by someone I met at a conference, one of many people I bored with the tale of my dramatic departure, and who listened and was kind. The event was in a wood-panelled hall. There were candles. There was champagne. But there was not very much champagne. Like most journalists, I have been programmed to expect a nice glass of something chilled to be quickly followed by a second. So when I listened to three leading businessmen talk about a turning point in their life, I was a bit distracted by my empty glass.

It was Ken Olisa who broke through. He is short. He wears a bow tie. I'm usually filled with irritation at the sight of a man in a bow tie, but after a while I didn't notice the bow tie because Ken Olisa is very funny. He was telling us about the dilemma he faced when the company he worked for collapsed in 'internecine fighting', the boss he liked got cancer and died and his new boss was 'as close to evil as I've found'. I'm rarely gripped by tales of corporate infighting. In fact, when the earlier speaker talked about his struggles to 'make partner' in a major accountancy firm I had to hide my yawns. But Ken talked about his childhood as the mixed-race son of a single mother in a two-up two-down in Nottingham with an outside loo. He told us how the head teacher of his state junior school had played his pupils Mozart and given them each a tiny taste of caviar, so they would know there was a world beyond the one they lived in, a world where the appointment of a black bus conductor made the front page of the *Nottingham Evening Post*. He talked about the thrill, after Saturday jobs doing night shifts at factories and painting toilets, of getting a job, and university scholarship, with IBM. He talked about his time at Cambridge, where he 'initially didn't know how to use the array of knives and forks, but sucked it all in'. And he talked about getting fired from the international computer company Wang.

Ken made getting fired sound like fun. I did not think that getting fired was fun. I thought getting fired was less fun than a cervical smear, less fun than a biopsy, less fun even than foreplay with a man who has just made you a lovely stir fry, but unfortunately got bits of chilli stuck under his nails.

'I couldn't work for him,' said Ken, when I met him in his office in Regent Street to find out more. He was talking about the 'evil' boss at Wang in America. 'I decided to think about how my mother would handle this, and you don't just say: well, that's it, I'm going to get another job. You go with a bang and not with a whimper. So I conceived this idea of a management buy-out, on the principle that you either get fired or you get to run the business. I got a promise of the money in the City and made an offer – and he fired me.'

Ken still sounded jaunty. I think he nearly always sounds jaunty. But he didn't, it turns out, feel jaunty at the time. 'It was awful,' he said. 'It was a very low moment. He fired me in his office. I remember seeing images of my children and the garden in England floating before me.'

He was offered a job with another software company. 'Same salary, same car, same everything. I sat looking at the offer, and thought: that's great – self-esteem saved! The neighbours will never know that I was fired. I'll just say I moved to another company. So I'm looking at this job offer and I'm looking out of the window. I'm still at Wang doing my gardening leave bollocks, so it's a terrible time and I look at this piece of paper and my inner imp – the one that only appears at moments of great importance – said, "So, you're going to spend the rest of your life working for great businesses that someone else has started?"

And I think: if I'm ever going to start my own business, it has to be now.'

Ken started a boutique technology-focused merchant bank, as you do when you're a hotshot City type who knows about things like computers and banking, which make money, and not things like poetry and journalism, which don't. He got a string of board roles and chairmanships. He was the first black man to serve on the board of a public UK company and has been voted the most influential black person in the country. But the strapline he chose for his current enterprise, another technology boutique merchant bank, is 'Entrepreneurs never travel smoothly'. After talking to him, you can see why.

From 2008 to 2011 he was a director of a mining company controlled by Kazakh oligarchs. I was tempted to swap stories of oligarchs and tell him that I'd had a nice chat about Russian poetry with the one that owned *The Independent*, in the days when I was part of the editor's inner court. But my own falling out with an oligarch, or at least an oligarch's puppet, wasn't plastered all over the *Sunday Times*. 'It's a really tragic story,' said Ken. The short version of it is that ENRC, a Kazakh-based multinational focused on mining and metals, wanted to be listed on the Stock Exchange, which meant it had to conform to British governance. Ken and some of the other non-execs helped launch 'a really big due diligence exercise', but somebody produced a dossier accusing them of 'all kinds of dodgy things' and sent it to every British newspaper. 'The *Sunday Times* published a full-page article on us and how evil we were,' said Ken. 'It was a terrible story.'

Ken managed to persuade the board to undergo an independent governance review. The reviewer concluded that it was the worst board it had ever seen. On the week of the AGM, the Kazakh government, which owned 11 per cent of the company, said it would support the directors. On the Tuesday, it changed its mind and the oligarchs followed their lead. Later that day, Ken became the first non-executive director of a FTSE 100 company to be publicly fired at its AGM. Ken published his farewell letter, saying that the whole situation was 'more Soviet than City'.

Even when being publicly ousted, Ken kept his sense of humour. But it was, he said, 'a horrible experience' and for a while he felt his reputation was in shreds. In an interview a few weeks after it all happened, he said that 'technically' everything the shareholders did was 'completely correct, like all great show trials in Moscow in the Communist regime'. Everything, he said, 'is done according to the book, it's just that the book wasn't fair. Kafka, eat your heart out.'

It's surprising how often Kafka comes up in stories of redundancy. You don't have to be a big fan of German literature to recognize the feeling he describes of a man arrested and put on trial, but never told what crime he is meant to have committed. You don't have to have read his novel *The Castle* to have that sense of reporting to officials whose jobs and actions are never explained. You don't have to have read *Metamorphosis* to know what it's like to wake up feeling like a creature that no longer recognizes its world.

Most people I know do not found boutique merchant banks. Most people I know work in the arts or journalism, because these are the fields I have worked in. They are not professions that make management buy-outs a good option for going out with a bang. They are not, in fact, even professions. Most of us feel proud if we've raised the cash to buy a sofa. Most of us get redundancy deals that would make a business person laugh. But our managers seem to be as keen on Kafka, or on re-enacting Kafka, as everyone else.

It's quite a few years since I worked with Claire. She is kind and funny and conscientious and has always been very good at whatever job she has done. Claire is not her real name. Because of the gagging clause in her poxy redundancy deal, I can't give her real name. But when Claire told me about what had happened with her employer I felt like calling a big strong friend of mine who was once banged up for GBH.

'There was,' she told me, in the café where we nearly always meet, 'talk of a restructure. The seed of anxiety was sown four years ago and it continued to build and build. So there was this anticipation that we might all have to apply for our jobs or lose them.' Ah yes, that HR favourite, 'restructure', which nearly always seems to lead to all kinds of other pseudo-scientific words. 'There was a sense,' she said, 'that what had been before was wrong, and then there was talk of being "fit for purpose". From very early on, there was a sense of those people who were safe and those people who were unsafe, and those people in the unsafe camp were set up to fail.'

After the talk of being 'fit for purpose', there were appraisals. But not the kind of appraisals that were meant to make you better at your job. 'Basically, within those appraisals,' said Claire, after taking a bite of the mini biscuit they give you free with your cup of coffee, 'twelve months before the redundancy, a narrative was being created. You could be told, for example, that you were over-conscientious, that you panicked. Or somebody who questioned was seen as resistant. It was clear,' she said, and the hurt was still written on her face, 'that the narrative from those appraisals was something that would be used to get rid of you.'

After four years of being ground down in this way, Claire decided not to apply for her own job, because she thought the odds of getting it were slim. Other people did, and should have saved their time and breath. 'I felt really, really sad,' she said, 'because for the first time ever in my working life, I felt people couldn't wait to see the back of me. I was ready to believe that I was a bit outdated. After such a positive work history in marketing, I couldn't believe that my job would end that way. Because I tend to see the best in people it was really hard for me to grasp that people would behave like that. It was such a nasty way of working, really scheming and really spiteful. It was,' she said, and now her eyes were sad, 'just so alien to anything I'd ever experienced.'

I really wish I could name and shame her former employers. I know, of course, exactly how she felt. Like Claire, I was a bit naïve. My parents brought me up to believe that hard work would be rewarded. They talked about things like honour and truth. At the first 'consultation', with the managing editor and the young woman from HR, I said I wasn't confident that the process would be fair, because the person who had taken over my boss's job had been heard telling people that I was only given a column 'because I was a woman'. The woman from HR assured me that it would be fair, but when I showed a summary of the 'consultation' to a lawyer, that was certainly not how it looked.

You have to be brave or rich to take on an oligarch's lawyers. I am not rich and I am not as brave as that. My union took over the negotiations. There wasn't all that much to negotiate, since our redundancy deal had been cut in half when the oligarch bought the paper, and there was no hope of getting the standard deal back. But at least it meant I didn't have to talk to the management any more. When the managing editor rang, and tried to talk me through the twists and turns of a process that made Kafka look like a model of what businesses like to call 'best practice', his voice made my stomach lurch.

After that last meeting in the editor's office, it took days for the shaking to stop. Even when it did, I couldn't sleep. I have always had trouble waking up in the morning, but almost as soon as I'd fall asleep I would be jolted awake by something that felt like an electric shock. It wasn't just that I'd lost my job and my livelihood. I had also lost my faith in what my father always used to call fair play.

When Gordon Brown lost his job as prime minister, he said he would do one big interview. He chose *The Independent*, and the editor (not the editor who fired me, but the one who was fired before him) picked me to do it. I nearly missed the train from King's Cross. I didn't like thinking about what the editor would say if I told him I'd missed the interview because I'd missed the train. When I left London it was a hot summer's day. As the train passed through the wild east coast of Scotland, the sky got darker and the temperature dropped. By the time I arrived at Kirkcaldy, where Brown had been MP for the last twenty-seven years, the whole world seemed to be made of rain.

I spent the best part of a day with Gordon Brown. He was probably the most interesting person I have ever interviewed. He is complicated. He is fascinating. He is, in his own way, brave. In the car on the way to the football ground of his local football team, Raith Rovers, he told me about his friendship with Nelson Mandela. He told me about the time the British High Commissioner in South Africa opened a parcel in front of an invited audience, thinking it was a medal for Mandela's wife, Graça Machel. When he ripped open the brown paper, purple sequins fell out. It was, in fact, a birthday card made for her by Brown's four-year-old son.

It took me a while to pluck up the courage to ask if he missed being at Downing Street. There was a long pause. 'No,' he said. I wasn't sure that I believed him, but I did admire his stiff upper lip.

When the interview came out, it was mentioned on the ten o'clock news. Someone wrote to the paper saying 'this is what journalism is for'. I didn't know if it was what journalism was for, but I did feel that it was what I was for. I didn't know what I was for any more.

Anger is an energy

Usually, when you leave a newspaper, people go to quite a lot of trouble to organize a 'front page'. This is a mock-up of the front page of your newspaper, with witty headlines and a photo of you as the star. Somebody buys some bottles. Somebody gives a speech. People tell you how great you were at the job and how sorry they will be to see you go. This is not what happens when you have shouted at the editor and he has threatened to get security to march you out.

A reader emailed to tell me that my name had been removed from *The Independent*'s website. Another told me that a colleague's nomination for the Orwell Prize had been mentioned, but not mine. It was the first time I had ever been shortlisted for a major prize. I was the only woman on the shortlist. I found out about it on Twitter.

I had to call the organizers of the prize and tell them to change my biographical note. We decided to say that I was 'now freelance'. It's an interesting word, 'freelance'. In the right mood, it can make you think of galloping over prairies on wild horses, clutching a mane as you gaze at a brilliant sunset in a giant sky. It can make you feel unfettered, unshackled, under no obligation to anyone, anywhere. In the wrong mood, it can make you think of boils.

The word was, apparently, first used by Walter Scott in his novel *Ivanhoe*. I have a complete set of Scott's Waverley novels. They are dark red leather and still smell musty and were my father's and his father's before that. I have to admit that I've never read any of them, but in *Ivanhoe*, at least according to the article I read, Scott used the word 'freelance' of men who offered their skill with a lance to wealthy landowners. They were, in other words, people who killed for cash.

I didn't get the chance to kill anyone, but I did get invited to a party. It was the Arts Council, not *The Independent*, that invited me to the *Independent* Foreign Fiction Prize. I had been going to the prize-giving for years before I even worked at *The Independent* and saw no reason not to go now. Usually, the guests are from the literary world. The editor is better known for his reporting on FTSE 100 companies than on Eastern European literature in translation and it never occurred to me that he would be there. So when I walked into the room, and saw him on the other side of it, I felt my heart jump. He was talking to the managing editor. They both looked as if they had found themselves stranded on an island where the natives spoke a different language and would eat them if they spotted that they couldn't join in.

It was as much of a surprise to me as to them when I marched over and asked them how they were. They both mumbled that they were fine, and I said that I was *very* pleased to hear it. They didn't ask me how I was and I didn't tell them. I didn't tell them about the shaking and the nightmares and how the shadow deputy prime minister had asked me what the paper was doing to its female staff. There was an awkward silence and then a loud noise from the stage and then the speeches started.

All through the speeches, I stood by their side. I loomed above them in my heels. When they tried to inch away from me, I inched my way towards them. It made me feel like one of the daemons in Philip Pullman's books, a creature that looks like a human and follows its master wherever he goes.

The literary editor gave his speech. He thanked *The Independent* for supporting the prize. I started coughing. It was a very loud cough indeed. When somebody else thanked *The Independent*, I started coughing again. I have always been a good girl. At school, I thought it would be the end of the world if a teacher ever told me off. Now no one could tell me off. I was freelance. I was free.

When the speeches finished, I saw a writer I knew. 'Lisa,' I said, 'meet the editor of *The Independent*.' I turned to the editor and his face looked like a cartoon. I'm not exaggerating when I say that I have never seen anyone walk so fast out of a room. He bolted. The editor who had behaved like an emperor actually bolted. A few minutes later, the managing editor did too. I told him that I thought it would be nice to tweet a photograph of him as a final memento of my time at the paper and he literally ran down the stairs and locked himself in the loo. I asked if he would like me to call security and then went back upstairs and told my former colleagues that the managing editor was hiding in the Gents'.

It was probably the most childish thing I have ever done. But it was very, very good fun. I agree with the Sex Pistols. Or to be more accurate, because journalists are meant to try to be accurate, I agree with John Lydon, who used to be Johnny Rotten, and the band he formed when the Sex Pistols crashed. Anger is an energy, he said in 'Rise', a song he wrote for his band Public Image Ltd. He said it more than twenty times. Anger *is* an energy. And if you're going to rise again, you're going to need all the energy you can get.

I interviewed John Lydon once. He didn't seem much like the scrawny, snarling creature I remembered from my adolescence, the one who shocked the nation with his language and his teeth. He said he was still upset about the death of his friend and band-mate Sid Vicious, who died of a drug overdose in a hotel room. He was talking to me about a new album, but he also talked about his childhood in a two-room slum, not far from where I live. He told me that all six members of the family shared one room. The kitchen was shared with rats. I told him that while he was screaming about anarchy in the UK, and upsetting the church, the BBC and anyone who liked the royal family, which is pretty much everyone, I was sulking in my bedroom in suburbia and sighing over Keats. He sighed over Keats too, he said. Books, he said, 'are my one and only joy'. Music, he said, 'is a simulation of something, but language is the greatest thing we possess'.

I never thought I would bond with a former Sex Pistol over a love of Keats. I don't suppose he ever thought that he would be part of a band that changed a culture – and then end up living in California doing ads for butter. This, he thought, was 'hilarious' because butter was 'such a politically incorrect product'. Even former Sex Pistols have to earn a living.

As I fired off emails into the ether, I thought more about some of the people I had interviewed and some of the questions I had asked. All artists, actors, musicians, composers, writers and rock stars are like Scott's mercenaries. They swap their skills for cash. No one pays them to turn up to an office and read their email. I was beginning to realize that I could spend all day every day sitting at a desk writing emails and that it was perfectly possible that none of them would turn into anything that would keep a roof over my head.

When I was first asked to do a weekly 'Big Interview' in the newspaper, I thought it would be quite a challenge to find someone to talk to every week who the editor thought was famous enough to fill the slot. Editors like to feel king of the castle. They don't like being told that their newspaper is not actually top of the pecking order when it comes to celebrities trying to plug their films or shows. This is why I ended up interviewing Jason Donovan, who had been most famous as a teen pin-up in the Australian soap opera *Neighbours* and then as a global pop star, but threw it all away to stuff white powder up his nose.

At his peak, he sold more than thirteen million albums. At the time I met him he was about to star in a West End version of *Priscilla, Queen of the Desert*, a musical which even a character in it calls 'cock on a rock'. For a man who sued a magazine for saying he was gay, this was quite a move. 'Yeah,' he said when I asked him about it, 'things have come full circle. Even my dad said, "How do you feel about doing this part?" I don't think about that. I just get on and do things. I like to work.' It was, he said, 'very simple'. He was 'a survivor'. He had done these things, he said, to pay his bills.

Now, for the first time, I thought of all the actors I had interviewed, and all the times I had asked them why they had taken on a part. I wondered how they had managed to be so polite. The average earnings of an actor in the UK are about £10,000. That's about the same as the average earnings of someone who's self-employed. The actors I interviewed were the successful ones, but even they often struggled to find work. I've never interviewed Michael Caine, but he spoke for many when he said, 'I choose the great roles, and if none of those come, I choose the mediocre ones, and if they don't come, I choose the ones that pay the rent.'

Two weeks before I walked out of that office on Kensington High Street, I interviewed Minnie Driver. It was a freezing day in January, but she was wearing a sleeveless dress. She has been in films like *GoldenEye*, *Sleepers* and *Grosse Pointe Blank*. She was nominated for an Academy Award for her role in *Good Will Hunting* but was then dumped live by Matt Damon on Oprah Winfrey's couch. She put on a red dress, and a brave face, for the Oscars. She didn't win one, but she managed to smile for the cameras. She always manages to smile for the cameras. She is often nominated for awards and sometimes wins them, but she still auditions 'all the time'. She was, she told me, realistic about the options for a woman over forty in an industry dominated by looks. 'I've never known the next film I'm going to do,' she said, 'so it's not much of a surprise for it to be challenging.' It was, she thought, 'quite funny' that people thought you had a choice. 'Mostly,' she said, 'you've just got to bloody work, because you still have a mortgage.'

Unfortunately, the people I was emailing didn't seem to care all that much about mine. I had hoped that some editor somewhere might give me a column or at least some regular work. I worked hard to make my emails sound 'upbeat'. I said that I was 'thinking of taking redundancy' and of 'starting something new'. Some people sent polite replies. Some people didn't reply at all. But even the nicest emails from the nicest editors basically said this: feel free to pitch us ideas and in the unlikely event that we decide to use any of them, we'll pay you a fraction of what you were paid before. It's zero hours now, baby. Zero hours on what will probably turn out to be less than the minimum wage.

I spent a week researching a piece for *The Spectator*. It was about an organization that aimed to get young people from disadvantaged or ethnic minority backgrounds into positions of leadership. They had support from each of the party political leaders. They went on a trip to Downing Street. They had a reception at the Foreign Office and one at the Speaker's house. I interviewed about ten of the young people and was fired up by their energy and drive. It took about ten days to research and write the piece and the fee was £250. After I filed it, the deputy editor told me that the editor had decided not to publish it. The word journalists use for a piece that has been commissioned but not published is 'spiked'. That's also a good word for how it feels to have to track down ten people who will now have to tell their mums not to go out and buy the magazine.

One of the young women I'd interviewed asked if I would mentor her. I didn't feel in much of a state to advise anyone on anything, but thought it would be rude to say no. I helped her apply for a job at *The Guardian*. A few weeks later, she told me she'd got it. I felt like asking her if she would mentor me.

I did another piece for *The Spectator*. It took about a week to research and write and the fee was £250. People kept telling me to accept whatever work I could get, but I didn't know how I was going to have the time to look for work when it seemed to take all my time and energy to earn £50 a day. If I wasn't working, I was sending emails. If I wasn't sending emails I was meeting 'contacts' for coffee or drinks. I tried to look cheerful. I tried to smile. But what I really wanted to say was: 'rescue me!'

My mother bought me a book called *Keeping Your Head After Losing Your Job*. It says: 'if you are unemployed, you are more likely to suffer a reduction in mental health, life satisfaction and objective physical well-being – and that equates to a greater risk of binge drinking, depression, anxiety and suicide'. This didn't surprise me, but it didn't cheer me up. Then it says that 'your negative thoughts can be transformed'. It says that 'this is a transition period; it does not have to be a time of depression, worry or physical deterioration'. It says that you can use 'mindfulness' to 'breathe the sadness away'.

I am not a fan of 'mindfulness'. I have tried. I have really, really tried. I was first taught it in a hut in Cambodia, by a smiley, wizened old monk. The main thing I remember, as I sat cross-legged on a *very* hard cushion, was trying not to think about the pain in my hips. Then there was the chi gong instructor on the holistic holiday in Skyros. Then there was the hairy American at the Thai spa I thought might be a cult. By then I was used to searching for my 'inner smile', but I drew the line at laughing on demand while flexing the muscles in my pelvic floor.

I know you have to practise. That's why I sent away for piles of CDs so I can be 'mindful' without having to find space in my flat for a Buddhist monk. The trouble is, the voices. The boring, droning voices. The trouble is, the grammar. 'Breathing,' says the voice. 'Sitting quietly,' says the voice. It makes me want to yell that you can't use the present participle to give a command.

I know mindfulness is now meant to be the answer to everything. I know HR departments now use it to calm employees down. I know Google loves it and Harvard Business School loves it and banks think it will boost their productivity and their bottom line. I know adults really do go out and buy books with titles like *The Mindfulness Colouring Book*. Perhaps they even buy crayons. All I can say is that breathing in and counting for six and then breathing out and counting for six and feeling the air pass out of your nostrils is not my idea of a good time.

My idea of a good time is a nice chat with someone I like over a nice glass of wine. My idea of a good time is a party. And I was damned if I was going to leave a paper I'd worked on for ten years without a party.

You don't normally have to organize your own leaving party, but it couldn't be helped. I found a pub round the corner from the office. I booked the room. I ordered food. I ordered wine. Normally, people's leaving parties are open to all staff. This one wasn't. I only invited the colleagues I liked. I only invited the bosses I liked. I can't say it was a vast turnout for ten years on a paper, but most people I wanted to be there came.

I didn't expect a 'front page' and I didn't get one, but a kind colleague had organized a whip-round and a card. She had bought me an orchid, a delicate, white orchid. She had also bought me a box of carefully selected wines. It was the journalist's equivalent of bread and roses. A flower for beauty, because we all need beauty, but we also need sustenance and most journalists would happily swap bread for wine.

There was no speech saying what a big loss I would be to the paper, or how much readers would miss my work. There was no speech saying that my departure was a mistake. There was, in fact, no speech, just a few kind words from that kind colleague.

At the end of the evening, there was a lot of food left uneaten. There was even quite a lot of drink left undrunk. I paid the bill. I walked out into Kensington High Street and went to an ATM to get some cash to pay for my bus. The ATM swallowed my card. I was stranded at 2 a.m. on Kensington High Street without cash or a card. In the end, a bus driver let me on the bus anyway. It was this act of kindness that made me cry.

Sex can be like broccoli

It probably isn't a good idea to meet a young Polish man on the train, agree to go for a drink with him and then find that you seem to have invited him back to your flat. This is not what I normally do when I jump on a train at Liverpool Street, but this is what I did one night after going to some networking drinks. I always feel a bit awkward about networking. I don't really like parties that seem to be a kind of shop, a shop where nobody knows who is buying and who is selling and what exactly is being sold. I always feel that you're meant to be slapping people on the back and telling them that you're 'great'. I went round telling people that I had just been fired and was feeling terrible.

I felt a bit less terrible when a Polish man less than half my age told me, on the train at Liverpool Street, that I was beautiful. I knew he was probably just trotting out a line, but still responded in the way I know best: by asking lots of polite questions and then having a discussion about immigration. He suggested that we go for a drink. Two hours later, he was half carrying me into my flat.

A few days later, I was watching *Newsnight* when I heard my buzzer. 'It's Matteus,' said the pale face on the video monitor. 'We met the other night.' I hadn't expected a marriage proposal, but he had said he would call and he hadn't even sent a text. I hate bad manners. I have always hated bad manners. In that moment, I felt as if I had turned from Samantha in *Sex and the City* to Lady Bracknell. 'You,' I said, before slamming down the entry phone, 'are a very rude young man.'

My parents never taught me the etiquette of instant sex with strangers. They didn't need it, and I'd hardly ever needed it before. They met on a hill in Heidelberg when my mother was eighteen and my father was twenty-one. My father had just finished reading classics at Cambridge. My mother was just about to go and read modern languages at Sweden's Cambridge, Lund. My mother didn't speak any English. My father didn't speak any Swedish. It was, they always told us, love at first sight.

For the rest of their three-week German-language course, they wandered through the cobbled streets of the old town, quoted Goethe and talked about Kleist. Under the old bridge by the banks of the Neckar, gazing out to the castle, they kissed. By the time they parted at Cologne station, my father had said the three words that cut to the heart of things in every language, and my mother had said them back.

As soon as he got home, my father wrote to my mother. 'I am thinking', he wrote (in German, but my mother has translated it for me), 'of Beethoven's wonderful song cycle, "An die ferne Geliebte" (to the faraway beloved). Now I understand the inner meaning, the beauty, the tenderness, the melancholy. As you left Cologne, I wanted to say, like Mignon, "There, there, to that place would I go with you, beloved". But the words had to remain unspoken.'

As soon as my mother got his letter, she wrote back. It was, she wrote (in German), 'terrible' to leave him in Cologne. The rails there had 'sung', she told him, the words of a popular song: '*Ich hab mein Herz in Heidelberg verloren.*' I lost my heart in Heidelberg.

Five months after they met, my father sent my mother a telegram. 'Will you marry me?' it said in English. My mother's reply was one word: 'Yes.' They married in June, three years after they met, in the white church next to my mother's grandparents' farm. It was set among wheat fields fringed with cornflowers and marguerites, at the foot of a hill scattered with wild roses. My mother has always loved roses. When he died, forty-seven years later, my father was still bringing her flowers.

This was not a helpful model on the dating front. I needed help as a teenager, and I didn't know where to get it. When I was eleven, I swapped the mixed primary school on the estate where I grew up for a girls' grammar school. I learnt a lot about the Treaty of Versailles and cattle ranching in Argentina. I didn't learn much about boys. My friend Lucy and I felt that our only hope was the twice-yearly barn dance at the local boys' grammar school. We spent months planning our outfits. My brown corduroy pinafore got me a dance with a spotty boy called Nick, but it didn't lead to anything you could call a date.

When we were fourteen, a friend of my brother's invited him to a youth club. My brother said that Lucy and I could go, too. A youth club, we were pretty sure, would have boys. This youth club had a tall dark boy called Andy, and a tall blond boy called Pete and a spiky-haired boy called Ian and a curly-haired boy called Howard. This youth club was also, unfortunately, attached to a Baptist church, but by the time we realized exactly what this meant it was too late. Andy and Pete and Ian and Howard had all given their lives to Jesus. Before long, Lucy and I had, too. Jesus loved us, we learnt, and wanted us to devote ourselves to him. We were not, in other words, allowed to touch the boys.

By the time I told God to fuck off and out of my life, I was twenty-six. I'm sorry about the language – and it's a very long story – but this is literally what I did. I was still a virgin. I had had one boyfriend, for five weeks. When he dumped me, when I was nineteen, my father said, 'It will probably take you years to get over it.' It was a good way of making sure that it did.

It isn't easy to enter the dating arena when you have almost no experience of it, very little confidence and are terrified of sex. When I finally did get going, I felt as if I was slipping around on a frozen pond while Olympic figure skaters whizzed around me, slicing secret codes in the ice. I had no idea how you were meant to show a man that you were interested. I didn't understand why no one ever seemed to ask me out. It was quite a shock to find out, when I was twenty-nine, that some of my male colleagues called me 'the ice maiden'.

When I was thirty-six, I joined a dating agency called Drawing Down the Moon. The name, apparently, came from a Greek myth, where one god falls in love with another god who doesn't fall in love with him. The keen god goes to the Moon Goddess, who makes a clay statue of the other god and weaves a magic spell. Hey presto! A successful love match, if you can call a match successful when it's based on coercion and deceit. I didn't know about the myth, but I was ready to draw down a moon, drink the blood of a virgin, or do what I did do, which was pay a big fee, to get a boyfriend. I hoped to get one of the 'thinking people' the agency said it specialized in, ideally someone tall, handsome and bright. To have a good chance of catching one of these, you had to go into their office, flick through lever-arch files of single men and choose ten lucky candidates to get your photo in the post.

I used a photo that a friend had taken of me on holiday in Goa. When I look at it now, I think of Nora Ephron. Nora Ephron wrote my all-time favourite rom com, *When Harry Met Sally*. We went to see it as a family on Boxing Day just after it came out. When Meg Ryan bit into a sandwich and then pretended to have a screaming orgasm in a New York diner, my father coughed and we all stared firmly at the screen.

'Anything you think is wrong with your body at the age of thirty-five', said Ephron in her book of essays, *I Feel Bad About My Neck*, 'you will be nostalgic for by the age of forty-five.' With the benefit of that span and more, I can say there really wasn't much wrong with how I looked when I was thirty-five. I wouldn't go quite as far as Ephron in saying 'I wish I had worn a bikini for the entire year I was twenty-six', but I do wish I hadn't wasted quite so much time fretting over tiny flaws.

In a good batch of a mail-out to ten men, two or three would get back. I met a man whose breath smelled like a dog. I forced myself to go on a few dates with him, but even the girl at the dating agency said he was 'dull as ditchwater'. I met a man who forgot everything I told him and then told me he'd had ECT. I met a man who slicked his hair back like Michael Douglas in *Wall Street* and took his lapdog on gourmet holidays round the South of France.

I tried. I really tried. But at thirty-six, the dating agency told me, I was past my peak. Men of my age, they said, wanted younger women, women who wouldn't force them into commitment or panic about their eggs. I should, in other words, be grateful for what I could get. It was, I thought, once I had exhausted the file of dog-eared men, an expensive way to make you feel an awful lot worse.

When internet dating took off, it was at least cheaper. One man, with a ponytail and a bad rash all over his face, told me that he bought vibrators for all his women friends and then stuck a tongue in my mouth that made me think of a lizard. Another bought me chocolates and flowers, chased me for weeks and then ran away. He got back in touch, said he had made a bad mistake and did the whole thing all over again. I felt as if I had been dropped into a sweet shop the size of an Amazon warehouse, one where almost everybody wants to take one bite and then move on to something that looks sweeter.

I have been single for my whole adult life. This is not what I planned. This is not what many of us plan, but it happens to quite a few of us anyway. Almost a third of us now live on our own. A third of us never marry either, which, in health terms at least, is a shame. Marriage, according to all the research, is better for your life span and better for your health. And it's an awful lot cheaper to split the bills.

Society still revolves around couples. If you're single, this can make you feel like a freak. Holidays are a challenge. Friends who rush to book you for a midweek drink spend weekends holed up with their family. Christmas can leave you feeling like an urchin waiting to be scooped up.

I know a lot of single women. I'm never sure if this is because there are a lot of us around or if it's because we tend to gravitate towards people like us. There certainly seem to be more educated, successful women who are single than educated, successful men. For people under thirty, this is just a fact, since more young women now graduate than men. I've spent thousands of hours debating the issue with other single friends, usually over a bottle or two of something chilled. Our findings, which have been extensively peer reviewed by other women, over other bottles of wine, are: a) that 'suitable' men of our age who are still single tend to go for younger women, b) that the men who are available tend not to be as intelligent or successful as the women we know who are looking for a partner, and c) that an awful lot of men are terrified of a smart, successful woman. Or maybe they're just terrified of us.

Not long after I lost my job, I went to see a headhunter recommended by a friend. Juliet Taylor is a partner at an executive search firm. She is bright. She is glamorous. She is single. We got on so well that we often meet for a glass of wine and the last thing we usually talk about is work.

'My singleness comes under challenge all the time,' she told me on one of these meetings, over a nice glass of Viognier and a bowl of salty snacks. 'People challenge it unwittingly, through talking about being part of a club I can't be in. Sometimes, people actively question it. In the village I live in, which is full of seventy-something rather conservative people, it's anathema for a woman to be single. No one can understand why I'm not married, and they think there must be something dysfunctional, or I must be a lesbian. I have spent quite a lot of time questioning people's assumptions about why there might be a problem with it.'

She would, she said, much rather be on her own than in a relationship that feels like a compromise. 'I have to feel it in my heart to want to be with somebody, and if that feeling isn't there, thank you very much, we'll be friends or nothing. So I don't cop out and I don't accept a halfway house. Because I'm single-minded, because I'm independent, it's a really big thing for me to give up my space. I'll only give it up for someone if there's something really coming back from that partnership.'

Hear, hear. On the one hand, I would love to meet someone, but where on earth would I put their stuff? I suppose a Californian might say we were 'conflicted'.

My friend Heather has done a lot better on the relationship front than me. In gaps between her relationships, we have been on holiday together, once to Tuscany and three times to Goa. When we stay with each other for weekends we'll say things like 'dinner's ready, darling!', because we sometimes feel like a couple who get on extremely well, but have given up on sex. Heather moved from London to Dorset fifteen years ago. Since she split up with the father of her son, she has been mostly on her own. 'I like my own company,' she told me, when we last huddled round the wood-burning stove in her little thatched cottage, 'and when I'm single and contented with myself I like not having the angst of an unhappy relationship. I like not having to compromise. I like having the freedom to do what I want to do when I want to do it, and not having to share my space.'

She lives in a chocolate-box-pretty village. When I go down there, it feels like something out of *Lark Rise to Candleford*, but there is, it turns out, a tiny worm in this little Garden of Eden. 'I do sometimes feel,' she said, 'that my neighbours look at me with pity. I think they give off a slight sense of "there, but for the grace of God".' She has sometimes found herself at a friend's dinner table, sitting next to an elderly widower, clearly in the hope that sparks will fly. The last one was twenty-three years older than her. 'I was forty-seven!' she said. 'He was seventy. He's an attractive man, but for God's sake!' Another time, she was set up with a friend of a friend. 'He was very taciturn and uptight, the type that wears thick cords and country tweeds. He was a Tory country solicitor. He was so wrong for me in so many ways. I couldn't quite believe that she hadn't seen it.'

Nor, I have to say, can I. Heather sometimes makes me feel like Margaret Thatcher and I've written columns with headlines like 'How Can We Stop This Drift to the Right?' We are, of course, grateful when our friends dredge through their address books and manage to muster a single man. You can almost see the triumph in their faces. You can almost sense them wanting applause. Most of mine exhausted their thin supply a very, very long time ago. I sometimes think they might club together and write a letter to *The Times*. 'We, the undersigned, friends of Christina Patterson, beg the nation to find her a suitable man.' My mother would be the first to sign. She once sent me a card that said: 'Looking for Mr Right?' Inside was the weary answer: 'Look in fiction!'

People in relationships often tell their single friends that they're too fussy, but when you ask them how they got together they don't usually say that it was with a clothes peg on their nose. Most of my friends met their partners when they were young. They liked the look of each other, fell into bed and that was that. They didn't walk around with a clipboard and a questionnaire.

'With hindsight,' said an academic called Mark I met through a friend, 'I was a bit too choosy. I was always looking for somebody who was seventy-five to eighty per cent of what I wanted. Some of them were sixty per cent, and I always felt they weren't quite good enough.' Mark was honest enough to admit that he was 'very demanding' and 'quite difficult to please'. Cynical friends, he said, 'would say the problem is me'.

I have interviewed the poet Benjamin Zephaniah twice. The first time, he was married. The second time he wasn't. 'I was emailing this friend,' he told me, in his office at Brunel University where he teaches, 'and I was saying "my mum keeps going on at me about finding a girlfriend". I told her I can't find anyone who's vegan, kung-fu fighting, da da da da da da, a whole long list of things, and she wrote back and said, "Benjamin, you're ridiculous, how can you want so many things from a woman?"'

Benjamin certainly doesn't seem lonely. The first time I interviewed him, in a café on Balham High Street, he could hardly get through a sentence without being interrupted by a passing pedestrian wanting to slap him on the back. So *did* he, I asked, feel lonely? He smiled. It was a big, sweet, toothy smile. 'No,' he said. 'I really like living alone. There are little moments. Sometimes, when something funny's happened, I think: shit, I want to share this with somebody. I saw something on YouTube the other day, and I thought: there are millions of people laughing at this, but I'm laughing at it on my own.'

But he had recently had a conversation with someone that had made him think. 'He's elderly,' he explained, 'and on his own and ill. Just as we were finishing the conversation, he said, "Oh, by the way, are you married?" I said no and he said, "Have you got a girlfriend?" and I said no. Then I started joking. I said, "I've got all my own space, I can do what I want to do," and he said, "It's not funny. You have to find somebody. Now you're OK. It's all right when you're young and fit but when you're older you need the companionship." This,' said Benjamin, and now he wasn't smiling, 'is going to sound completely contradictory now, but my biggest fear is growing old alone.'

I don't want to grow old alone. I don't think all that many of us do. But why is finding someone to share your life with so unbelievably hard?

My friend Mimi Khalvati has been married three times. She is fiercely intelligent and also wise. Would she, I asked as we shared a pot of tea at her flat, be willing to tell me about her experience of marriage? There was a long pause. Mimi is still beautiful, at seventy. She has perfect cheekbones and big, soulful eyes. She is quiet, she is gentle and she is always incredibly polite. She looked out of the window and drew on her cigarette. 'Fuck 'em!' she almost shrieked, and I almost jumped. 'Oh God! I would like to say it is the greatest area of total abject failure in my life.'

Her first marriage, in Iran when she was nineteen, was, she said, 'a completely idiotic venture'. By twenty-one, she was divorced. Her second marriage, to the father of her children, took place because she couldn't get a work permit. 'I proposed to him in the queue in the Home Office,' she told me. 'I said, "Oh, stuff this, let's go and get married."' The marriage was, she explained, happy for a while, but ended because they both 'changed so dramatically'.

Her third marriage was the worst. 'We spent years and years in this on–off relationship, with my endless moan about him being commitment-phobic. In order to prove his commitment, he went to the registry office and got this form for us to get married and then basically talked non-stop until I couldn't stand it any more and said "all right". I had one dress, so I wore that. We went to the registry office in Hackney. Then the guy said, "Do you, Edward, take Marion?" and we were both looking round saying "Who's Edward and Marion?"'

Edward, it turned out, was her husband's first name, which he never used. Mimi has always been called Mimi, but the name on her birth certificate was Mariam (not Marion). 'So that was a joke,' she said. 'The thing is, we weren't serious. All the energy and thought and heart and commitment and dreams and love that people put into marriages weren't there.'

It always takes me by surprise when I hear stories like Mimi's. For so much of my adult life, I have felt that my friends in relationships were the grown-ups and I was the child. I thought they were the ones who were doing things properly and I was the one who was messing things up. I have felt not just embarrassed about being single, but sometimes also ashamed.

So did she, I asked, feel any sadness about being single? There was another long pause, and another drag on a cigarette. 'Oh yes,' she said and her eyes were wistful. 'How can you not? I don't really believe one was designed to live a solo life. Not really. But,' she added, 'it doesn't tear me apart. There are times when I feel lonely, but I think it's more than anything that thing about a rock. I don't miss the romantic stuff, but I'd love to have more support. But I don't really think that's what men are for, actually. There are some men who are like that, but it's very rare. It's all the sort of charging around stuff I can't stand.'

I know what she means. I've seen a lot of men 'charging around'. Heather has, too. Her last serious relationship was with a man who was handsome and knew it, a man whose ego was so big that feeding it was a full-time job. She is, she says, 'quite contented' now and has got more contented as she has got older. 'But equally,' she says, 'I'm at a life stage where I'm thinking: "Oh God, am I really now going to be single for the rest of my life?"'

Well, am I? If anyone had told me that I'd be single at forty-nine I think I'd have asked them to book me a slot at Dignitas. I want someone to love me. I want someone to go on holiday with, and to snuggle up with at weekends. And I want sex.

On his death bed, the poet John Betjeman said: 'I wish I'd had more sex.' I really hope I don't end up saying the same on mine. Sex is good for you. According to lots of studies, it makes you healthier, happier and may even prolong your life. But these studies make sex sound like broccoli. I'm not all that keen on broccoli. Sex *can* be like broccoli. It can be boring, embarrassing, or an exhausting palaver that leaves you dying for a cup of tea and a book. It can also be very, very, very, very nice.

A few weeks after I walked out of that office on Kensington High Street, I met a man at a conference. We had an interesting conversation about globalization and the fourth industrial revolution, which turned out to be a long-winded way of saying that we had both recently lost our jobs. When he was back in the country a few weeks later, we met for a drink. At the bus stop, he gave me a hug and his shoulder suddenly felt like just the place to put my head. A couple of hours later, we were wrapped in each other's arms.

What happened was lovely. It wasn't explosive, or life-changing, and we both knew that it was unlikely to lead to anything much because we lived 4000 miles apart. But for the few days and nights we spent together, we cuddled and kissed and laughed. He, it turned out, had also had a slightly unwise one-night stand with a Pole. His Pole sounded politer than my Pole. I didn't begrudge him his polite Pole because he's a nice man and he cheered me up.

Motherhood and Michelangelo

After emailing the opinion editor at *The Guardian*, I met her for 'a cup of coffee', which is the euphemism we all use for a meeting to beg for work. I always hoped these meetings would end with an offer of a contract and a column. In fact, they always ran along similar lines: we've had our budgets slashed and we can't offer anything regular, but do feel free to pitch us some ideas. What this often means is that you spend hours ploughing through the papers in order to cobble together some thoughts and then the email isn't answered, or the idea is nicked by someone on the staff.

But the opinion editor at *The Guardian* was kind. A few days after we met, she gave me a call. Would I, she asked, write something for the website about the NHS policy on cutting umbilical cords? The piece, she explained, would be for the part of the *Guardian* website called Comment is Free. They don't exactly expect you to write for free. They pay you £95, which is a fraction of what I got paid for a column before. I said yes, of course.

I had no idea what the NHS policy was on cutting umbilical cords, or if there was any reason it should change. I have never been anywhere near an umbilical cord. I have certainly never produced one. I always thought I would. I thought I would fall in love, get married and then have lovely babies who turned into lovely toddlers and then, perhaps after a brief teenage blip, devoted daughters and sons. I fell at the first hurdle. On the rare occasions I have been in love it has felt more like being in some outer rim of Dante's hell than anything that might lead to a three-bedroom maisonette in Cheam. One minute, you think you have found the answer to everything. The birds are singing, the sun is shining, there are rainbows in your heart. The next, you're staggering around with a bloody stump where you once had a limb. I am, clearly, no expert on how to conduct a successful romance, but I can say with some authority that it's better if the person who shares your bed and then breaks your heart doesn't also share your office.

I wanted a man who loved me, and wanted babies with me, and wanted to be there to watch those babies turn into teachers or football players or poets. I didn't want to harvest a man for his sperm.

For my thirtieth birthday party, I did an invitation with a skull and crossbones. 'Growing Panic at Grosvenor Park,' it said, 'as Christina approaches 30.' I didn't need to spell out what the panic was. It was men. It was babies. It was the whole damn caboodle. It was feeling that everyone else was about to get on a train that I was about to miss. Not long after, I went on a trip to Thailand. There were four of us, plus the guide. One night I slept on my own in a tiny tree house in the jungle. Another night, we all slept in a long house in the hills near Chiang Mai with members of an ancient tribe. But even lying in a tree house, listening to the moans of the frogs and the singing of the cicadas, there were moments when I felt like a maiden aunt. The other people on the trip were all in their early twenties. There was a young Australian girl who kept talking about her boyfriend at home, and two Kenyan Asian boys who were going back to arranged marriages. I felt like begging them to ask their parents if they would arrange a marriage for me.

It now seems a bit mad that I was worrying about this at thirty. So many middle-class women have children so late that they make it feel like the norm. But actually I was right to worry. A woman's fertility starts to decline in her early thirties. At thirty-five, it starts to plummet. At forty, a woman has only a 5 per cent chance of becoming pregnant in any month. And that's if she's actually having sex. If you're a single woman in your thirties, you live with a ticking clock that sometimes feels more like a bomb.

Three of my friends managed to find a man just in time to squeeze the baby in (and out). Another one managed it at forty-three. Two of those men didn't stick around. It was probably best for everyone that they didn't stick around, but I don't think lone parenthood, half-shackled to a narcissist who will always be your little darling's dad, figured all that highly in my friends' childhood dreams.

A couple of weeks after I wrote the column about umbilical cords I had lunch with the journalist Rosie Millard. I emailed her to ask for some advice and she generously invited me to her house. Rosie had a big job at the BBC, but left it when they told her she couldn't also do a column for the *Sunday Times*. Now she seemed to be writing for practically every newspaper I picked up. She seemed, in fact, to be making a big success of freelance life. I hoped she would share the secret, or perhaps just breathe on me so that I'd be infected by her success.

Rosie lives in a big house in Islington. She has written before about her property 'portfolio' – her two London houses, two London flats and flat in Paris – which she has said she and her husband managed to maintain by juggling credit cards. She once created a stir by writing an article about being 'broke', which meant that she sometimes had trouble in a restaurant getting her credit card to clear. I'm jealous. Of course I'm jealous. But someone who has managed to build up a mini property empire on the back of credit cards is clearly an awful lot better at managing their money than me.

Her house in Islington is beautiful. Her kitchen is gigantic. My kitchen is the size of a cupboard. If you swung a cat in it, it would hit its head. The one time I did have a cat in my flat, by the way, it didn't go anywhere near the kitchen. I had borrowed it from neighbours who were on holiday, after weeks of trying to tackle a new influx of mice. The mice, unfortunately, were fans of Nietzsche: what didn't kill them made them stronger. The cat was not a fan of Nietzsche. It spent the week cowering behind the sofa. I was terrified of it, it was terrified of me, and the mice seemed to find it all a big aphrodisiac, had a wild orgy and bred.

Sitting in Rosie's beautiful kitchen, surrounded by photos of her four children, and no signs of any mouse traps, I couldn't decide if I felt more like Jane Eyre or Adrian Mole. Every day in her household, she said, started with the children playing the piano or violin. I didn't want to tell her that every day in my household started with silence and ended with silence and the only voice to break that silence was John Humphrys telling off a politician or someone who sounded a bit like a robot warning me about storms off German Bight. We had a lovely lunch and then, over coffee, she said that when she lost her column at the *Sunday Times*, it was her husband and children who saw her through.

Some people choose not to have children and are happy with the choice they have made. For many of us, not having children doesn't feel much like a choice. About a fifth of women now don't have children. Among women with higher degrees, that figure is more like a third. According to one study, by Satoshi Kanazawa at the LSE, an increase of fifteen IQ points cuts a woman's likelihood of becoming a mother by a quarter. Statistically, it's harder for a highly educated woman to find a partner, and potential father, for her child than for one who isn't. It isn't quite true, as a character said in *Sleepless in Seattle*, that you're 'more likely to get killed by a terrorist than get married' if you're a woman over forty, but it isn't all that far off.

If you don't have children by your late thirties you can start to feel like a freak. Society is arranged around families. Politicians don't even want your vote. If you're not a member of a 'hardworking family', the message seems to be, you must be a wastrel or a weirdo. If you're a woman, you're probably a ball-breaker. Tabloid newspapers will call you a 'career woman' as if it's worryingly masculine for a woman in the twenty-first century to hold down a job. Or you'll be seen as some kind of Anita Brookner heroine, living a pinched life in dowdy clothes in a gloomy basement flat. You must, in other words, live at the margins because you are not a proper woman.

If you are single and childless, you are expected to fit your life and needs around the people who aren't. You will be squeezed into the gaps of your friends' lives. At work, the demands of people with families will come first. 'It's just taken as read,' said a woman I met on a course, 'that if you have children your hours are negotiable in a way that they aren't if you don't. It's almost like a hierarchy of the important things in one's life. I don't know anything else that's considered to be as important as having children.'

Jessica runs a marketing agency. She finds herself constantly having to give way to other people's holiday requests even though she's their boss. 'The whole holiday thing is now a given,' she told me. 'Men do it as much, possibly even more. Women didn't use their children so much because it would have been a disadvantage in the workplace, and now men share more of the parental duties, they're also claiming the holiday entitlement first. Half-term and school holidays are almost built into the calendar. Those without children aren't thought to have any rights.'

Jessica has had her own family pressures. She has a brother with MS and a father with dementia, but this doesn't seem to be the kind of family that counts. 'I could really have done with some flexibility,' she told me. 'I think when you get to a certain age, you realize that the demands of elderly parents or other relatives are as big a deal for you as perhaps a small child. But that isn't recognized. What could you say that could possibly rival children?'

And what, I asked, if you didn't have children, but just wanted to be reminded from time to time that you also had some claim on a life outside work? 'Imagine,' said Jessica, 'if you said, "Well, actually I've bought a canoe and I've decided I want to go canoeing every weekend, so I need to leave early on a Friday, so I'll come in early and leave at four."' Count me in, I said. That should be just fine, though count me out of the canoe. 'It ought to be fine,' she said, 'but I think you'd have to be extremely steely to carry that off. A lot of this stuff is unspoken. And you want to be decent to your colleagues, so it's really hard to say, "Oh, your little Johnny is stuck in the playground; well, that doesn't cut any ice with me."'

I have covered several maternity leaves. For two of these I was paid about an extra tenner a month to do my own job as well as the job of my much better-paid boss. At the end of the maternity leave, nobody said: well, thank you so much for taking on a killing extra workload, why don't you go off travelling for six months and we'll keep you on full pay? In fact, nobody even said thank you. It can make you feel a bit as if you're skulking in the sculleries of someone else's life.

Ask anyone what's most important to them and they will usually say their family. Almost everyone I've interviewed has said it's what has made their life complete. I once heard a film star say that he hadn't been able to look at pictures of starving children since he had children of his own. It does make you wonder what he thinks the rest of us are doing. Giggling at the way their ribs stick out? Do you really need to become a parent to understand that those figures on the TV news aren't just pixels on a screen?

Most of the public figures I have interviewed are artists of one kind or another. Most are men. Artists don't usually get to be world class by doing their fair share of the household chores. Actually, very few men do their fair share of the household chores. According to the Office for National Statistics, women still do 40 per cent more housework, and childcare, than men. The people, in other words, who speak loudest about the importance of family are often not the ones who are doing the work.

*

I have forced myself to smile at a lot of weddings. I have forced myself to smile when friends have told me they are pregnant and when they thrust a little scrap of wriggling flesh in my arms. I love babies. Who doesn't love babies? That soft, soft skin that's like a peach, that luscious flesh, those big, round eyes. They smell so delicious you almost want to eat them. Who wouldn't want one of those to cuddle and kiss and feed and squeeze? Who wouldn't want to see if your little egg or sperm might be the seed that turns into a towering oak of a Shakespeare or a Mandela? Or even just into a vine that makes some *very* nice wine?

Well, my friend Dreda Say Mitchell, for a start. I met Dreda after writing a column in *The Independent* about her award-winning thriller *Running Hot*. It was set partly in Ridley Road market in Dalston, down the road from where I live. Its central character, who's in trouble with the police but wants to be a chef, reminded me of my friend Winston. Dreda sent me an email thanking me for my column and we met up for a drink and have been friends ever since. A few months after I lost my job, she agreed to talk to me for a piece I was writing about women who don't have children. The piece was for the *Sunday Times* magazine. It came out of an email I sent to the editor of the paper, one of the many emails I had sent begging for work. It was the first email that struck something like gold.

'My parents were migrants,' she told me in the cosy sitting room of her house in Walthamstow. 'The whole big thing with migrants is you plant roots. One thing the next generation do is have kids, so the next set of roots keep going.' As the daughter of a Grenadian father who was a factory worker, and a Grenadian mother who worked as a hospital cleaner, Dreda grew up surrounded by big families on an estate in the East End. 'Ours was one of the smaller ones,' she said. 'There were only four of us kids. A lot of them had seven, eight, nine. Having children was just seen as a natural part of life.'

Dreda always thought she'd have several children, but she was the first member of her family to go into further education and when she went to university she had her eyes opened to a whole new world. She 'got the travel bug', trained as a teacher and used her holidays to go travelling. When she met her partner, Tony, they both expected to have children, but one day she saw an ad for 'this fabulous tour to Ethiopia' and realized she didn't want to give up her freedom to travel, or do anything else. 'I had the sense,' she said, 'that being a teacher, and travelling, were not the only things I wanted to do. I always suspected I might want to write. I thought: I can't see some poor kid having the space as well.'

Dreda is one of the most positive people I know. She lives her life as if it's a delicious meal to be gulped down, before handing back her plate and asking for more. So did she, I asked, really have no regrets? Dreda shook her head. 'No, but I do look at my sister, and I see her kids and grandkids, and I see she's got this really personal family that are connected to her. I do look at myself sometimes and think: "Who will be looking after me?"'

Well, quite. My mother broke her ankle two weeks before I lost my job. My brother and I made sure that one of us went to visit her in hospital every day. I can't say I'm looking forward to lying in soiled sheets in a state-run care home with no one to care about my day except a member of staff on minimum wage.

There are countries, of course, where they don't shove you into a care home. In those countries you have children because it's your duty to your parents and because those children will have a duty to look after you. Through Mimi I met Shanta Acharya, a poet who went into investment banking to support her creative writing, publishing several books of wry, witty, sometimes searing poems along the way. Shanta was born in Cuttack, by the Bay of Bengal. As a young university lecturer in India, she wasn't allowed to go out on her own except when she was going to work. 'You always had an escort,' she told me, over tea and cake in her maisonette in Highgate. 'It was, in some ways, a very Jane Austen world.'

As a member of a Brahmin family, who were also academics, she was encouraged to have a career in academia, but she was still expected to have an arranged marriage and children. 'I didn't want to upset my parents too much,' she said, 'but I didn't really fancy that.'

She thought she might meet someone when she came to Britain, to do a DPhil at Oxford, and later at Harvard as a Visiting Scholar. When she left Harvard, and failed to get the academic post she wanted, she joined an American investment bank in London, where she trained as an analyst and portfolio manager. At her next job, at a Swiss bank, her performance proved she was the best fund manager in her peer group. When she left banking to focus on her writing, she continued to win accolades for her work. Her personal life was less successful. 'I kept thinking it would happen,' she said, 'I would meet my life partner, but I didn't.' It has taken a long time for her parents to accept her status as a single, childless woman. 'My mother keeps saying it's OK,' she said, 'and I'm thinking, "Well, I'm calling you. Who's going to call me?"'

When the article about women without children was published, I got an angry email. 'What', said the man who sent it, 'about all us men who have never had children? Do you think we don't feel the same?' I might, he said, find the 'attached spreadsheet' of Census data interesting, showing percentages of people in each age group who were 'not living in a couple, single, never married' and another one about those living 'without dependent children'. When I looked at the spreadsheets, I gasped. He had given them the heading 'The Walking Wounded'.

I didn't need a spreadsheet to know that many men don't have children. My brother doesn't have children. Two of my male cousins don't have children. Nearly all my gay male friends don't have children. Men without children don't get called 'childless'. People don't seem to think they have failed in their primary purpose in the way they sometimes do about childless women. But that doesn't mean that not having children doesn't cause them any pain.

Benjamin Zephaniah was one of nine children, a twin in a family with two sets. 'When I was a kid,' he told me, when I went to interview him for a follow-up piece about men without children, 'I used to say "I'm going to get a woman, right, and I want nine kids, so I'm going to have triplets and then triplets and then triplets".' When his mother 'ran out of the door', fleeing her violent husband, Benjamin followed her. He was eight. He lived alone with her in bedsits until he was sent away to 'an approved school' for being 'a criminal kid'. When he left, at sixteen, his friends were all having babies. 'We didn't even think of condoms,' he said. 'And I just noticed that they were having kids and I wasn't.'

It took him a while to realize that he was the problem. In the end, he had a test, which showed that he produced no sperm at all. During his thirteen-year marriage, to a theatre administrator called Amina, he got tested again. This time it was the mid-1990s, on a TV programme about male infertility with Robert Winston. At the end of the show, he said, Winston promised to do some research, but when he and the producer followed up, he didn't reply. 'It gave us some hope,' he said. 'Then I kind of gave up.'

So was it, I asked, a source of grief? For a moment, Benjamin looked away. 'A little bit,' he said. 'There was a period when I did that thing men do. They look at other men playing with kids in the park and think "I can't do that".' Benjamin is a glass-half-full kind of guy. 'I've got such a good relationship with kids all over the world,' he said. 'People are always saying to me: "if you had your own kid, it would probably take away from your relationship with all these other kids", so I just kind of resigned myself to that.' What he couldn't take, he told me, was the people who kept offering him cures. At a Mind Body Spirit festival, someone even told him that he'd been castrated, in a past life as a slave.

My friend Stefano Nappo has, thank goodness, never been told that he has been castrated. I first met him fifteen years ago, just after I moved into my flat. He and his then boyfriend, Nick, had also just moved in, to an enormous loft apartment on the top floor. One night, they knocked on my door and invited me to join them for a Thai takeaway over *Ally McBeal*. It made me feel as if I was living in an episode of *Friends*.

Stefano is a very successful corporate lawyer. He travels. He goes to the opera. He collects art. It would be easy to think he has a charmed life, and in many ways he does. But Stefano is the son of Italian immigrants. When he was growing up, in Loughborough, 'family was everything'. There would, he told me during one of our Saturday-morning catch-ups in his vast sitting room, be regular dances, christenings and weddings. 'There were always loads of children there,' he said. 'I always assumed that one day I'd have a family. My mother would say, "When are you going to get married and give me grandchildren?"'

Stefano always knew that he 'felt different', but it was only when he was eighteen that he finally acknowledged that he was gay. 'I was lying in my bed, awake at night,' he told me, 'and had a conversation with myself about my options. I said, "Well, you can either kill yourself, because you don't want to be gay, or you can get on with it."'

When he was younger, gay couples rarely had families. During ten years with his last partner, they never even mentioned the possibility of having children. 'I have thought about it over the years,' he said. 'Neither my brother nor sister has children, so if I don't, our little line comes to a grinding halt. I remember feeling wistful about that, but only to a certain level. With my current partner, he's completely anti, so I definitely can't have a child while I'm with him. But if I was with somebody who said, "You know what, I'd really like to talk about having a child," I think I would be very happy to. I'd love to have that sort of opportunity.'

Stefano and I both live in Stoke Newington, which has one of the highest birth rates in the country. Sometimes, when I'm walking on the pavement, I'm forced into the road by a convoy of buggies that seem to think they are tanks. The cafés are full of mothers promising their children that they will get a blueberry smoothie if they finish their organic bok choy. This is motherhood as a Grand Design, one where you, the mother, are Michelangelo and your child is the masterpiece waiting to be cut free from the stone.

When my parents were young, you had a child because everyone had a child. You hoped you would have healthy, well-behaved children, but you didn't expect them to fill an existential void. I thought of this when I read an interview with the deputy prime minister, Nick Clegg. He talked about the moment he held his first child for the first time. 'I thought,' he said, 'so that's what it's all about.' The horrible feeling in my stomach made me think he was probably right.

Maternal deprivation

I am a disappointing child. I wish I wasn't, but I am. In a pub garden in Surrey, my mother made this clear again. My mother was nibbling at a fishcake, because she's a delicate eater and takes tiny bites. I was tucking into a burger and chips, because I'm not and I don't. My mother doesn't actually use the word 'disappointing'. She is a very polite woman and that would not be kind. She just sighs and points out yet again that she's the only person she knows who doesn't have any grandchildren.

My mother adores her children, who are, of course, not children. In terms of my career, or what used to be my career, she has always been my biggest fan. She buys at least two copies of every article I write. She copies them and sends them to her friends. Every time I'm on TV, she both watches and records it. When I was on the *Today* programme once, she phoned as soon as I got out of the studio. I had just been in a fierce discussion about whether actors or poets were better at reading poems. 'I agree,' she said, 'with the other chap.'

My mother has more energy and zest than almost anyone I've met. You would think she has won the pools when she has managed to find a half-price navy skirt. You can imagine what it was like, on the day the first *Star Wars* film came out, to find that she had tracked down lacquered pine kitchen cupboards at Debenhams with 33 per cent off.

She has lived in Sweden, England, Bangkok and Rome. She speaks fluent English, Swedish, Italian and German, good French and basic Thai. She was the best student in her year in her home city of Halmstad and after she met my father she did a four-year degree in two. She brought up three children while working as a teacher, did an Open University degree, had people to stay, sometimes for weeks on end, and served delicious meals several times a day. She drives old ladies, has run various support groups and is known for being a brilliant hostess.

These are all excellent qualities to have in a mother, but when you are a fortysomething single woman who doesn't know most of her neighbours, isn't the lynchpin of any community and has to stay with her seventysomething mother when she's had a big operation, because there's no one else to look after her, it doesn't always make you feel great. When I go to see my mother, I sleep, as I've always slept, in my childhood bed. And because I start to feel like a child, I start behaving like a child. I rifle through her lacquered pine cupboards and sniff out the hidden Kettle Chips.

My mother is not the kind of person to go in for public speaking, but I think she could fill lecture halls with talks on the subject of 'what to do when you don't quite get the children you want'. It isn't that she doesn't like us. We are, at least most of the time, pretty decent, honest and polite. She just didn't realize how much would go wrong with us. She didn't realize how much *could* go wrong with us. Or how much we would end up costing the NHS.

My mother's friends' children are things like doctors and

lawyers. They live in big houses. They have children and husbands or wives. My mother's friends spend Christmas in these big houses with their grandchildren. They don't spend Christmas making polite conversation with their unmarried middle-aged daughter and their unmarried middle-aged son. My mother has supported her children through more ups and downs than she even knew existed. And now, at the age of seventy-eight, treating her youngest child to a burger and chips in a pub garden in Surrey, she tried very hard not to mention the fact that she didn't even have a child with a regular job.

It wasn't my mother who wrote a poem called 'Motherhood', which talks of shutting away the family photos and sweeping everything 'absolutely clear of motherhood', so that there shall, at last, be 'room, time, space, for everything'. That was my friend Mimi, in her book *The Meanest Flower*. I have read an awful lot of poems. I have met an awful lot of poets. Of all the poets I have met and read, Mimi Khalvati is one of the poets I love most.

'I'm sick of the good,' she says in that poem, 'Of drooling over photos / that lie, lie, lie'. The poem is about the anger, grief, pain and sheer bloody effort of motherhood and of how 'everything / everywhere' is a mother's fault. She is not talking about the domestic stuff: the washing, the PE kits, the endless, endless meals. One friend of mine worked out that she had spent about two years of her life doing the washing and wiping the floor. Mimi didn't mind this. She didn't love it, but she didn't mind it. For Mimi, as for my mother, the pain started when her children got ill.

When her daughter Tara was twenty-five, she was diagnosed with a rare genetic disease that usually leads to loss of sight. 'It's not one hundred per cent in every case,' Mimi told me, 'but I think the prognosis was seventy-five per cent likelihood. At first you have a sort of sense of disbelief, really. You have a sense of shock and horror, but also a misplaced sense of optimism that it will be all right.'

She had the same sense of 'misplaced optimism' when, two years later, her son Tom was diagnosed with schizophrenia. 'I had a very strong voice,' she said, 'saying: don't panic, don't worry, it will be all right.' But it soon became clear that there was plenty to panic about.

'I first heard of it,' she told me, over more tea in her sitting room, 'when he was taken into a psychiatric ward in Sussex. He phoned me up and said, "Mum, I'm in hospital." I rushed down there. Your body does one thing. Your body shakes or trembles, you get jelly legs, but then your mind stays like "I've got to deal with this, I've got to cope with it. Think. Stay focused." Your body is out of control, but you get into a sort of cold part of your mind.'

That was twelve years ago. Tom has been in hospital several times since. The longest stay, of five months, was the worst. 'I actually thought he was going to die,' she told me, 'as a result of the medication. He was catatonic. He couldn't eat. He was skin and bones.' It took a year and a half for Mimi to persuade a new young doctor on the ward to do something about the drugs her son was on. 'I presented her with a long list of side effects and said: look at these, these are all Tom's symptoms, including things like inability to swallow.' In the end, they agreed to 'baseline', where they take a patient off all medication, in order to build it up again. 'Well, they took Tom off everything,' she said, 'and within a week, literally only a week, nearly all his symptoms had disappeared.'

This probably saved Tom's life, but it didn't cure his schizo-phrenia. There isn't a cure for schizophrenia. It is, as my mother knows all too well, a case of messing around with medication, a case, in fact, of trial and error. Mimi has written poems about her son's illness. In the first poem of a sequence called 'Sundays', she writes about Sundays with her son, eating sour cherry rice and meatballs after a walk in the park. Tom is listening to the radio 'to stall / hallucinations' and drown out the voices in his head. Afterwards, he plays the piano. 'Between his fingers', she writes, 'things grow, little demons, / fountains, crocuses. Spring is announced and enters, / one long green glove unfingering the other, / icicles melt and rivers run, bluetits / hop and trill.'

In the music there *is* a kind of spring, but here, too, are demons. It's like those old medieval maps showing the edge of the world. Here be Dragons. Dragons, unfortunately, that often can't be slayed.

Tom is handsome and gentle and very loving to his mother. He is also a brilliant musician. He is, of course, the one who has paid the heaviest price for his illness. He's the one who has gone to A & E with panic attacks and who has to live with the daily terror of what his illness might bring. In the next poem in the sequence, Mimi writes about how, on another Sunday visit to her flat, he 'can't even swallow his own saliva' without hearing 'the voices' or 'seeing / babies streaming towards his mouth'. I don't know how many of us would be able to eat if we saw babies 'streaming' towards our mouths. Mimi has written a few poems about his illness. 'It's a political decision,' she told me, 'because I think mental illness should be more visible and understood.'

There are times when Mimi has no idea how Tom is because

he sometimes won't see her for months on end. It was during one of these periods that Mimi had 'a very, very overpowering feeling that something was drastically wrong'. She went round to his flat, and there was no answer. 'I knew, somehow knew,' she said, 'that he was in there. In the end, I borrowed a ladder from a neighbour. I climbed up the ladder to this first-floor window, climbed in through the window and Tom was in the most terrible state. I called an ambulance immediately. He was taken away and hospitalized.'

You'd have thought all this would be enough for a mother to bear, but some of Tom's therapists have suggested that his illness is Mimi's fault. 'All sorts of things were suggested,' said Mimi, with a weary smile. 'Sexual abuse, just for starters. Plus, all the other sins that mothers commit. I'm over-protective or controlling, or too loving, too close, too dominant, too passive. I think we live in a mother-blaming culture. As mothers, we know very well that we're always to blame for everything. If something's gone wrong, it's our fault.'

When Katherine had her son, she knew straight away that something wasn't right. 'I'd been in labour for four days,' she told me, over grilled trout in a members' club in Soho, 'and all sorts of things had gone wrong. He was screaming and the midwife said, "I'll take him off you, we'll be able to settle him." I was like, I don't actually care if you throw him out of the window.'

I nodded politely, and tried to hide my shock. 'I had,' she said, 'no bond.' The midwife came back after forty-five minutes. 'They couldn't shut him up. I thought: "I've got this baby that nobody can deal with. How am I going to do it?"'

I met Katherine on Twitter. She used to read my column in *The Independent*, and we became 'Twitter friends' and finally met for lunch. One of the things she tweets about is the challenge of dealing with her autistic son. There is autism in my family. Autism is, in fact, part of daily life for about three million people in this country, but many families affected by it find it hard to discuss.

'Right from when he was born,' she said, 'I knew that when you hold them, they're meant to mimic your facial expressions. It's one of the first things they can do and he didn't. He wouldn't look at me.' Katherine was composed as she talked, but in her eyes I could see the memory flooding back. 'I had this baby that would never, ever stop shrieking. Literally, before he woke up, he would be shrieking. When he was a toddler, I lost all my friends, even friends I'd had for a long time, because he just hit their children.'

It didn't help that the healthcare professionals thought there wasn't much wrong. 'I was really overweight then,' said Katherine, who is now so slim and gorgeous that I felt a stab of envy when I watched the waiter eye her up, 'because I'd eaten to try and cope, and so they just had this picture of me as this fat woman who couldn't look after her son. They'd give me,' she added, and the contempt was clear in her voice, 'all these books on positive parenting.' Oh yes, that old standby for mothers, 'positive parenting'. It makes me think of the book I once found on my mother's bedside table. It was called *Maternal Deprivation*. She read it for the A level in sociology she did on Tuesday nights, but only after cooking the dinner, of course.

It was when Katherine's son went to school that he was finally diagnosed with severe autism. 'He didn't quite fit any of the models,' she says. 'He's very bright and in some areas he excels, but his social skills and impulse control and sensory problems are more like a child who can't talk.' Katherine learnt the hard way that her son can't use his imagination. 'He can't put himself in the future, or in someone else's shoes. So he's like a toddler. If there's something happening he doesn't like, it's going to go on for ever, and that's why he just destroys everything.'

It sounded, I wanted to tell her, like hell, but you can't really tell someone else that their life sounds to you like a scene from Hieronymus Bosch. So what, I asked, was the average day? Katherine made that face you make when you've been pretending everything is fine, but it isn't. 'Well,' she said, 'by the time he was ten or eleven he'd kind of withdrawn into himself a bit more, which was a relief. He'd wake up and go to the loo and he'd get his iPad and sit in bed with that. At some point, you'd have to go in and get him ready for school. Sometimes, we'd have to sit on him to get the clothes on him. Who was the one with the rock? Sisyphus? It was the fact that we'd been doing this since he was two, and we'd never be able to stop doing it. Every single day. Having the same arguments with him, and having to explain why he had to wear socks, why he had to wear shoes. He was always unhappy and then he would lash out. He would punch and kick us. He would kick my shins and headbutt me, sometimes just in this blind rage.'

I was on my way back from a holiday when I got a call from my friend Louise Murray. I have known Louise since I was twenty-three. We met when we were both doing a 'diploma in printing and publishing for graduates' at the London College of Printing, in a tower block at the Elephant and Castle. It wasn't the dreaming spire I fantasized about when I watched *Brideshead Revisited*, but whenever we go past it, my mother says, 'There's your alma mater!' In that tower block we were taught by retired printers who had practised their trade in the days of hot metal and didn't have all that much time for English literature graduates who dreamt of discovering the new Sylvia Plath. I was instantly drawn to the fiercely bright Scot with shiny pink Doc Martens and spiky red hair. She had dangly earrings that looked like daggers, which matched, I thought, her razor-sharp tongue.

We both went on to get jobs in publishing and met in cafés and bars in Camden to swap tales of office life. We once travelled round southern Spain together and rounded off our trip with a couple of nights in Torremolinos. It was, to be honest, a bit of a relief after the mountain villages where the people had seemed rather dour. In Torremolinos we finally got a friendly smile from the waiter, and the paella we had been constantly told was on tomorrow, but never tonight.

When Louise fell in love with an academic called Stephen, I knew it was time to panic. The two other women in our little group of friends from the Elephant tower block had also found partners, and I was the only singleton left. Two years later, Louise got pregnant. When I saw her cradling a scrap of pink flesh in a hospital bed, I felt as if she had managed to get to the other side of a chasm I might never reach. When her son Sam was three, she took a sabbatical from her job and went to live with Stephen in Japan. She was quite pleased to leave behind the long hours in the office. She loved Japan and she liked being a full-time mum. Then she discovered that she was pregnant with twins.

'I had spent the whole first year of my son's life thinking he was going to die,' she told me, in a hotel bar in Edinburgh. 'I couldn't believe I'd brought something so precious into the world and I thought there was going to be a cot death. I didn't relax until he was a year old and the risk of cot death had faded. By the time I got pregnant again, I was pretty relaxed about it all, but when I found out what could go wrong with twins, I thought: I've really got to get a grip here because I could be miserable for the next nine months. I thought: let's not read too much about it and get on with things, which I did.'

Because of the risk, Louise decided to go to stay with her parents near Glasgow for the last few months of the pregnancy. She was on a Scottish island with her parents when the contractions started, fifteen weeks before the babies were due. When a doctor saw her, he called an air ambulance. 'It was a beautiful journey,' she told me. 'There was an amazing view of the Scottish islands. When we got to Glasgow airport, we landed in a ring of fire engines and police cars and in my arrogance I thought: ah, they've done that just for me. In fact, one of the engines had failed on the plane and the police came and took the pilot away. The midwife burst into tears and said she was never flying again. And I was thinking: hang on, I'm in labour here, early, I'm supposed to be the centre of attention, but I was also thinking: this is going to make a great story.'

There was an ambulance on the runway, waiting to take her to the hospital. 'I still thought it was all going to be all right. I thought it was Braxton Hicks,' she said, 'pretend contractions.

By the time I got to the hospital I thought: this is really hurting quite a lot.' She was taken to a delivery room and given an epidural. 'When the first one came out, I said, "Is it alive?" And they said, "It's too soon to tell." And then they said, "The good news is it's a girl, and girls are more likely to survive."'

Both babies were girls, and both were put in incubators straight after the birth. After a week in hospital, Louise went back to her parents' home. Every four hours in the night, she was told to get up to express milk. 'Basically, you're producing a teaspoon,' she said, 'because milk doesn't come until twenty-eight weeks. I spent most of my days at the hospital.' And what, I asked, did she think was going to happen? 'I thought,' she said, 'they were going to die.'

'I felt that I was falling into an abyss, actually. The psychologist comes along on day two or three and leaves a note on the incubator saying you might like to talk, and I thought I would, but I never did. I'm glad I didn't. I talked to friends instead.' I have never seen Louise cry, but now I saw that there were tears trickling down her cheeks. 'Sorry,' she said. 'I felt very buoyed by the affection I was getting. In particular I remember you, actually. You were so upset.'

I certainly was upset. I remember clutching the phone in a multistorey car park at Gatwick and thinking: my friend's babies are probably going to die. It was only in that hotel bar in Edinburgh, thirteen years later, that I got the full story of what happened next.

She was in a park with Sam when the hospital called. 'I got to the ward,' she said, 'and they always close the ward when babies die and the woman at the door said, "Sorry, the ward's closed," and I was trying to say, "I know. That's me. It's my baby." They let me in, put me in a room on my own and the head consultant and the nurse came in, and said, "I'm sorry, Flora's dead."'

By now, we were both crying. But one of the many reasons I love Louise is that she's so honest. 'For all the shock of grief,' she said, 'all kinds of things went through my head, like the doctor put his arm around me and I thought: he's going to know how fat and heavy I am. And another thing I felt was extensive vindication, actually. Here we all are trying to pretend life is rosy and actually it isn't. And also relief. I've only got one left to worry about. I was thinking all these things.'

They had a small funeral for Flora a few days later, just Louise, Stephen, her sisters and her parents. Louise read two of the poems from the anthology I had sent her. One of the poems I had marked out for her was Raymond Carver's 'Late Fragment'. A very short poem for a very short life. The title of the book was *Staying Alive*. In the circumstances, it wasn't ideal. But the thing is, one of her twins did stay alive. Beatrice was in hospital for five months. She was on a monitor to make sure she didn't stop breathing. Louise was trained to resuscitate her if her breathing stopped. She rented the cheapest house she could find and had Beatrice sleeping, with oxygen tanks, in her room. By the time she bought a house, within relatively easy travelling distance of the hospital, she could breathe well enough without the tanks.

'There was a possibility,' said Louise, 'that she'd be absolutely fine. Some kids are.' But it soon became clear that Beatrice was not. I have met Beatrice many times, but I have never been entirely clear what she can and can't do. 'She can't do anything,' said Louise. 'She's thirteen now, but she's like a two-month-old baby. She's profoundly brain damaged. She has six per cent of the vision you or I have and she's completely deaf. She can't stand up, she can't sit up, she can't really hold her head up. She is,' she said, so matter-of-factly that I had to fight the tears again, 'about as disabled as you get.'

Louise went from being a happy and successful publisher in London, on an exciting sabbatical in Japan, to being the full-time carer, in a tiny village in Scotland, for a child who can't even lift her head. Stephen is still in Japan during term-time, so Louise spends most of her life as a single mum. When she was in London, she had the busiest social life of anyone I knew. Now her life is one of nappies and oxygen tanks and emergency trips to the hospital. Does she, I asked, feel like a prisoner? There was a very long pause. 'I did,' she said. 'But for the first few years of Beatrice's life, it was very, very hard work looking after her and I didn't really have time to think.'

For most of my adult life, I haven't been to school reunions. I didn't want to be the one who didn't have a partner, didn't have children, the one, in fact, who didn't seem to have grown up. For years, I watched the lives of my school friends from afar. I didn't know how they had managed to get the husband, the house, the family and the career when I couldn't even seem to find a nice bloke for a weekend in Brighton. I thought they had perfect lives, or as perfect as lives ever get.

When I finally went to a school reunion a few years ago, I found out that one has a daughter with anorexia. One has a daughter with severe anxiety. One has a child who left school with almost no qualifications and seems to be stuck in low-wage dead-end work.

Another friend called about a column I had written about gangs. His son had got caught up in one, he said, and ended up in jail. When people first hold a baby in their arms, they don't have dreams of visiting them in jail.

I don't know how my friends have coped with these situations. I have never really understood how Mimi and Louise have coped with theirs, or how they have done it with such grace. But now I have sat down with them and listened to their stories and later I will tell you some of the things I have learnt.

When I talk to them, I can see the love. I can certainly see the love. But love, as my mother will tell you, can come at quite a price.

Depression with a smile

I have the genes to crack up. An awful lot of us do. About 10 per cent of us, according to mental health charity Mind, will have some form of mental illness in our lives, but in my family the odds seem to be higher. My father's side of the family has more than its fair share of brilliant minds that can flip into depression. At a dinner party, my father could transfix the table with his dry wit. But just one weather forecast could set the tone for the weekend. 'Well, that's it, then,' he would mutter, if the weather man said rain. And then there would certainly be clouds.

I'm a mix of my mother's vivaciousness and my father's tendency to gloom. When I was a small child, they called me 'the sunshine girl'. I was plump and smiley and laughed all the time. By the time I was thirteen or fourteen, that sunny smile had been swapped for something more like a scowl. It was partly adolescence. Of course it was partly adolescence. But that adolescence seemed to go on for a very long time.

When I discovered Thomas Hardy, I thought I had found my soulmate. It wasn't Tess of the D'Urbervilles who hooked me in, poor Tess who dug turnips, was tricked by a libertine and was marched off to be hanged before she could be reunited with her Angel Clare. No, it was Jude the Obscure. Here was someone who understood me! Someone who wanted to study among dreaming spires, someone who believed in the life of the mind. Someone, in fact, who tried hard to fulfil his dreams, but felt that his lonely struggle was doomed. 'Somebody might have come along that way who would have asked him his trouble,' says Hardy at a moment of particularly intense misery for Jude. 'But nobody did come, because nobody does.' Like I say, not the sunshine girl any more.

When my sister was fourteen, she went to stay with a Norwegian family. She and the younger daughter stayed with the girls' grandmother in a tiny island off the western coast. My sister wrote a letter to my parents saying that she was 'terribly homesick'. When she got back, she hardly spoke. At night, we heard heavy steps up and down the landing and the sound of doors being slammed. Three weeks after she got back, she disappeared. She was, my mother said, in a 'unit'. It took a while for my brother Tom and me to understand that it was the adolescent unit of a mental hospital.

When Caroline came out, I hardly recognized her. She still had matchstick arms and legs, but now she had a swollen tummy as if she was just a couple of months away from giving birth. Her face was covered in spots, her hands shook and she was hunched over like an old woman. When she went out in the sun, her skin turned red. She walked as if she was on the edge of a cliff she might fall off. It was, my mother said, the pills that made her skin go red, the pills that made her hands shake, the pills that made her fat. The pills, my mother said, were making her better, but she didn't seem better to me.

For my sister, everything was a struggle. While my brother

and I got straight As in almost everything, she battled to scrape a pass. Tom and I went to the local grammar schools. She went to the local secondary modern and was put in the bottom stream. When she was seventeen, she was given a special prize by her school for 'outstanding effort' in German. I was twelve and thought it wasn't effort that mattered. I thought what mattered was what you achieved.

I was seventeen when Caroline's illness finally had a name. Schizophrenia seemed like a long word for the shadow that hung over us all. Schizophrenia, with a dash of depression. I have had times in my life when I have felt so desperate that I have wanted, as Keats did, to 'Fade far away, dissolve, and quite forget' the 'weariness, the fever, and the fret', but I don't think despair is the same as depression. When I lost my job, I was full of grief and rage, but I'm not sure I would say I was depressed.

My cousin Robin knows all about depression. He's the only one of my cousins who lives in London and he's not just my cousin, but my friend. He sings in the BBC Symphony Chorus and has taught me most of what I know about classical music. I still don't know all that much, but I do know what I like and I honestly couldn't imagine life without Handel and Bach. If you have heard Joyce DiDonato singing the libretto from Handel's *Rinaldo*, you'll know what I mean. When she sang '*Lascia ch'io pianga*', in her pure, electric voice, at a recent concert at the Barbican, it was like a thunderbolt from heaven, or hell. Allow me to weep, sings Almirena in the opera. Yes, allow me to weep. Sometimes we have reasons to weep.

Robin had his first breakdown when he was seventeen. 'It

was the pressure of approaching A level exams,' he told me, when I invited him over for a Sunday roast in exchange for a grilling. I am, by the way, quite good at Sunday roast. You just unwrap the polythene from a chicken or a piece of lamb and stick it in the oven. It's quite hard to burn. Even for me, whose cooking attempts often set off the smoke alarm, it's really quite hard to get wrong.

'I'd been very successful at secondary school,' Robin told me, 'but I was asked to write an essay on something I hadn't been doing essays on and I suddenly found I couldn't do it. I found I could not express myself. My essays had been getting longer and longer and less and less productive. In the end, I walked out of a couple of A level exams.' Not long after, he was diagnosed with depression. 'The GP told me I was a smiling depressive,' he said, with a smile. 'I was still smiling although depressed and very anxious.'

When Robin said this, I remembered the time I had burst into tears in a kind of group therapy session on a 'holistic holiday', because I had been ill and could not get well. 'Did you know that when you cry,' someone told me, 'you smile?' I was so shocked that I looked in the mirror the next time I cried. He was right that the corners of my mouth turned up, but it looked, I thought, more like the painted-on smile of a clown.

Robin was put on antidepressants, which eventually made things even worse. 'It was one particular drug,' he said, 'which is now not used, that pushed me over the edge several times, into mania. I lost track of time. I did strange things. I had all sorts of ideas and connections about how things would work. I became very animated. I filled out my UCCA form in a weird way, with lots of strange writing. One day I cut down a lot of plants in the garden, thinking that extreme pruning would make them grow better.'

This, he explained, is why he has never wanted to get drunk. I had wondered, over the years, why he would often stick to one glass of wine, while I would be knocking back my third. 'Once,' he said, 'I was watching a programme about Rosicrucians. It was all very mystical and it pushed me into a second bout of mania.' A couple of years later, when he had, in spite of his struggles, made it to Oxford, he was put back on a much smaller dose of the same drug. 'I remember someone came to visit me in my room,' he said, 'and I organized my books into a kind of skewed pile, a sort of spiral. I'd do some very strange things and get all sorts of strange ideas about what things meant.'

In the end, Robin had to leave Oxford. They kept his place open for him, but he decided he wouldn't be able to cope if he went back. And then he told me something I never knew. 'I took a lot of paracetamol that night. I think my parents had visitors. I had my stomach pumped. I was in for a couple of nights, on a drip. In a strange way,' he said, and this time the smile was wry, 'it seemed to take the pressure off.'

I thought of Uncle Maurice and of Auntie Bell, who is probably the person in our extended family who looks most like me. We are made, in so many ways, of the same stuff. Her hands, like mine, go blue even when it isn't all that cold. Our tiny hands are frozen. Well, perhaps they're not tiny, but they are certainly frozen. And now I thought her heart must have been nearly frozen, too.

'When I phoned my mother from my fortieth birthday party,' said Robin, 'she told me that the worst time in their lives was when I was at home and ill. Weeping for months, with no sense of direction, unable to commit to any plans. I think they fought very hard so I wouldn't be admitted to hospital. I think it was partly because they were aware how difficult it had been for Caroline and your parents.'

My mother does not like to talk about that time, but I know, because she has shown me her diaries, that the second time my sister was put in a mental hospital, my mother watched her change before her eyes. In the end, Caroline refused to believe that my mother was her mother. My mother, her mother, fought like a tigress to get her out.

It's hard to imagine what it must have been like for Maxine's mother when she found her eleven-year-old daughter trying to drown herself in a stream. 'It was,' said Maxine, 'the first time I tried to kill myself. I kept trying to lie in this stream and keep my head under water and of course I couldn't, and then I remembered Virginia Woolf and tried to use stones.' She was eleven and she 'remembered Virginia Woolf'? 'I read everything,' said Maxine, 'it was one of the ways I survived.'

I met Maxine through a friend. She was happy to talk to me about her depression, but she didn't want to use her real name. There is still a stigma. There's no use pretending that there isn't still a stigma, and what she told me made me feel sick.

'When I was three and a half,' she said, 'my mother took me to play school for the first time. I walked in and they all ran away from me. None of them would speak to me, and they were all pointing and laughing. And there was a black-haired girl who suddenly said, "You're a nigger and niggers have to go to custody."'

Even now, in this café in Soho, the word is like a grenade. 'Weirdly, the word I latched on to,' said Maxine, 'was custody because I liked custard, so I asked her what it meant. And she said, "Custody is prison and there are witches in prison." I suddenly had a very strong vision of a witch stirring a cauldron of custard in a cell and that I would have to be in there. I don't think I ever asked her what nigger meant.'

Maxine is the daughter of a light-skinned Jamaican mother and a white English father. She grew up in a small village in the New Forest. That first conversation at nursery school set the tone for the rest of her childhood. At lunchtime, the children all sat on a carpet to eat their packed lunches. 'I was very anxious that I had the same food as the other children,' she said, 'because that was the only time in the day they would touch me, because there wasn't quite enough space. I realized that the only way I would be tolerated, literally allowed to sit on the same carpet where occasionally our knees would touch, was if I was perfect.'

It wasn't, it turned out, just the children who were racist. 'The teachers that weren't racist,' she explained, 'would comfort me by saying "you aren't a nigger, because you're not one of those women in Africa with a pot on their head". But some teachers would call me a nigger and other stuff as well. It was so much to do with cleanliness and dirt and that being brown meant you were dirty. They would make me sit at a desk on my own. I would go home and wonder what a wog was.'

This was not in the 1950s. It was in the 1970s and 1980s. No wonder Maxine was depressed and anxious throughout her teens. When she finally escaped to university, and then heard that the person who had encouraged her to apply had committed suicide, she had a breakdown. 'I felt quite outside my body,' she said, 'but mainly I just couldn't function and this was always a sign for me. I couldn't really read. It's like being used to having a car with a big engine and one time you go to overtake somebody on the motorway and you put your foot down and there's nothing there and the car's just freewheeling.'

Depression slows you down. Everyone I know who has suffered from depression has said that their depression has slowed them down. There are times when it's hard enough to function in the world even when your brain is in full gear. When it isn't, it's like being sent to climb a mountain without climbing shoes, a pickaxe or even a proper coat. It's a cold, dark, terrifying place.

Robin has had just one bout of serious depression since that overdose at the age of twenty-one. Maxine has had a few more. But they have both continued to hold down good jobs. Maxine works at a senior level for a charity. Robin works in IT for a bank. Most of the time, they are fine. They have both been in such screaming mental pain that they have wanted to die, but most of the time they are fine. They have both learnt that when you feel you're in a cold, dark place, that isn't usually where you stay.

I first met Frieda Hughes at the Ledbury poetry festival. I was meant to be introducing her reading, but nearly missed it because I had got stuck in traffic after picking up a new car. I had recently taken over as director of the Poetry Society, and decided that perhaps now I could afford to swap my father's old Nissan Micra for something that didn't look as if it had been caught in a hail of bullets. I took out a loan, bought a *What Car?* magazine and tracked down a second-hand silver Mazda MX-5. My father drove me to the garage to pick it up. It was only when I was sweating in a ten-mile traffic jam that I realized I couldn't work out how to open the windows. By the time I got to Ledbury five hours later, I felt like a boiled ham.

Frieda, who is tall and stately and beautiful, was reading from her second collection of poems, *Stonepicker*. Her first, *Wooroloo*, had been published two years before. She's a painter as well as a poet and her poems, like her paintings, are full of bleak landscapes, animals and rocks. She writes about love and greed and pain and sorrow. Her voice is strong and clear. And she writes about death. In the last poem in *Stonepicker*, she has a conversation with Death. 'You took him too soon,' she says to Death, as she sits by her father's coffin. 'You could have left him longer.' In answer, Death gloats. 'I let him ripen on his tree / Like a heavy fruit,' he boasts. He could, he says, have waited 'until his stalk broke', but his victory was 'To take him at the peak of his / Perfection.'

Death – and the poem – is talking about Ted Hughes. He died in 1998, just before the publication of his masterpiece, *Birthday Letters*, which talks about his first meeting with Sylvia Plath. In 1963, Sylvia Plath laid out bread and milk on a table in her children's bedroom, sealed the door of the kitchen and then placed her head on a folded cloth in the oven, switched on the taps and waited to die. When she did this, she unleashed a myth and a legacy. The myth was of a fragile creature crushed by a monstrous man. The legacy was an obsession with Plath and her death that seems to have made her the queen of suicide and depression.

The real legacy of Sylvia Plath is her poetry, which will last for as long as poetry is read. Anyone who thinks it's all about misery and rage and 'skin / Bright as a Nazi lampshade' or 'The boot in the face, the brute / Brute heart of a brute like you' has obviously chosen to ignore the love that 'set you going like a fat gold watch', the baby 'Like a sprat in a pickle jug', the tulips 'opening like the mouth of some great African cat'. Plath's poems do speak of rage and grief. But they also speak of love, joy, babies, poppies and potatoes.

Plath's other legacy, with Ted Hughes – who was, by the way, at least on the occasions I met him, an unusually kind and gentle man – is that baby 'Like a sprat', Frieda Hughes. It was Frieda, aged nearly three, and her one-year-old brother Nicholas, who were left in that flat with the milk and bread as their mother took her last few breaths. Frieda grew up in the shadow of her mother's death, and of a myth that turned her parents into public property.

'I tried in my own ways to accommodate what had happened around me,' she told me, 'because the interesting thing is, it sort of wasn't done to me in that I wasn't physically damaged. It was all psychological and almost as though what I felt was a by-product of everybody else's pain.' We were drinking coffee, and eating home-made cake, in the huge kitchen of her house in Wales. Staring out at us across the room were two white-faced scops owls, not in a cage. In a vast aviary outside, there were more owls. In the kitchen, there was a vivarium containing a royal python and a box of dead chicks. When Frieda Hughes says she loves the natural world, she isn't joking.

I've met Frieda a few times since that poetry reading in Ledbury. She invited me to the launch of her book of poems and paintings, *Alternative Values*, and afterwards agreed to talk to me about her experience of living in the shadow of depression, suicide and grief. By now, she pretty much has a PhD in grief. She has, in fact, trained as a bereavement counsellor. But what strikes you when you meet her is her almost electric energy and her passion for life.

Frieda hardly ever talks about her parents, so I felt honoured when she said I could come to her house in Wales and that she would talk openly to me. 'When I first came here,' she said, 'somebody dropped some potting mixture off and said, "You're the daughter of that dead poet, aren't you?" I just said, "Oh, put the potting mix over there."' Frieda has had plenty of practice in batting away unwanted questions. Some of her friends didn't find out who her parents were until years after Frieda had been their friend. 'A long time ago,' she told me, 'there was some conversation I was having with somebody and she said "so and so is studying Ted Hughes", and I finally thought: if I don't say something now, it's going to be embarrassing later.'

You can see why Frieda ended up spending seven years living in the Australian bush. It started, she told me, with a visit to her uncle in Melbourne and a friend in Perth. 'I looked down from the aeroplane window,' she said, 'and for the first time in my whole life I felt like I was coming home.' She moved there in 1991 and only came back to London when her father was diagnosed with cancer. It was just a few years before, when she was thirty-four, that she had finally acknowledged that she had to write poems. Writing poetry is hard. I have been too scared even to try. And when you're the daughter of two of the finest poets of the twentieth century? That, you'd really have to call balls.

'I started saying to myself,' said Frieda, 'that if I want to really be "me", then the real "me" is the daughter of Plath and Hughes, so I have to accept that. Once I'd stopped rejecting it, then it became a lot easier. It's like saying I've got three legs. If I just accept the fact that I've got a third leg, I'll stop falling over it.'

At the end of *Alternative Values*, she writes for the first time about the memory loss that hit her when her mother died. In the first poem, 'Departure', she remembers her grandmother's visit to the family home in Devon, and her attempt to get Sylvia and her children to leave. 'Unable', she writes, 'to put either parent back / Into the holes from which / They tore one another, / It was as if I went to sleep while still walking.' In the next poem, 'Separation', she asks: 'Did I watch my mother's face / As she left us bread and milk before / She shut us in and Sellotaped our door?' She can never know the answer. 'I had', she says, 'already let myself slip through the gap / Between the floorboards of my consciousness.'

In the next poem, 'Waking Nameless', she remembers waking 'in the back of a strange car / In the middle of the night', but 'left without history / Or any memory of daylight, / Wiped clean like a beach'. In the front seats were Ted Hughes and his sister, Olwyn. Frieda was on the back seat with Nicholas. She didn't know who the grown-ups were. I felt a wave of goose flesh when she told me this. Did she, I asked, really not recognize her father? 'I knew I had parents,' she said, 'but I could not remember what they looked like. I never got that memory back. So I thought: what I'm going to do is, I'm going to sit and wait for something to happen. I waited,' she said, and now I was fighting tears, 'to be collected by my parents. But they never came.'

For years, she thought she was adopted. It was only when she was fourteen, and read the poet and critic Al Alvarez's famous piece about Plath, which mentioned both Nicholas and Frieda, that she finally accepted that she was indeed the daughter of Plath and Hughes. She had been told that her mother had died of pneumonia, but found out, through a classmate when she was eleven, just before Alvarez's piece was first published, that she had committed suicide. Hughes later asked Frieda if she was angry with her mother. He knew that anger is often a big part of what people feel when someone takes their own life and rips a hole in the universe of the people they leave behind. No, said Frieda. She didn't. She said her mother's pain must have been unbearable for her to want to die.

'But by then,' she said, and for a moment she looked out of the window, 'it was too late to undo those feelings that I didn't belong. I used to stand on the sidelines. The interesting thing is, that sensation informed my whole life. One of the things I got from that as a child was being very conscious and very watchful and thinking: I don't know anything, I need more information, but what can I do with what I do know and what I have got?'

Frieda smiled. She has a dazzling smile. 'I thought,' she said, 'how can I make things better? But also "make" is a very important word. I'll make almost anything, if the components will sit still long enough. Creating something positive and new out of raw materials – even if those materials are simply experiences – is my challenge. I was thrown on to my own resources. It was literally sink or swim, in the psychological and emotional sense. But it also meant that I was sort of permanently unsupported, because there was no sense of feeling of genuinely belonging anywhere, or to anyone.'

No wonder Frieda Hughes wanted to create a world of her own. No wonder she drew pictures of that world and later felt she could not live if she could not paint. And the poems came, even though she knew that with the poems would come pain. She didn't read her parents' poems until she was in her thirties, but still the poems came. 'Poems,' she said, 'had leaked and I'd shoved them in a box and stuffed them away. They were in boxes all over the house, but I hadn't admitted that I would write poetry, because I had made the decision not to, and it was a very conscious decision, that I would not follow my parents. And the idea of getting my head kicked in by the critics was just too painful to contemplate.'

She tried not to write, but she couldn't not write. In the end, she showed her poems to her father, who thought some of them were very good indeed. (When she told him that his poems were on her school syllabus, he offered to help her, but she thought his own interpretation of his poems could well lead her to fail her exams.) Her father was right. Her poems *are* powerful. They are not Sylvia Plath, but there was only one Sylvia Plath. 'The thing was,' said Frieda, 'if I'm lying on my death bed, who would I have pleased by not living how I need to live, in order to have a happy, or reasonable, or successful, or productive, or even a completely non-successful, but, you know, quite muddling-along-in-an-OK-fashion life? It's up to us how we get from A to B to C to D. I might never light up the sky. None of us might. It doesn't matter. What matters is: did you do the best you could with the tools you had at hand?'

The body speaks

When Frieda Hughes was thirty-four, her body packed up. 'I got this noise in my head,' she told me, 'it was like a "ping" and something breaking and after that "ping" I couldn't move my limbs. It was as though somebody had snapped the string that made everything work. After that, it was like being a cripple. I thought I was dying.'

Frieda's day was cut to four hours, in twenty-minute stretches. 'The lights went out,' she said. 'When I was conscious, I couldn't read.' At the time, she was writing children's books, but she couldn't even read back what she wrote. 'I looked at the letters on the page,' she told me, 'and they didn't make sense. I had thirty-six blood tests. They tested me for everything. They had given me a psychiatric test. They'd done brain scans. Then they came up with the magic bullet. They said, "You've got chronic fatigue." I said, "Great, give me a pill!" And the doctor said, "You really don't get it, do you? There is no cure."'

Something similar happened to me when I was twenty-five. It wasn't as dramatic, but it was quite dramatic enough for me. I had just got back from a holiday when I felt a funny pain in my wrist. A few days later, I had a pain in my ankle. I wondered how I could have sprained it without falling over, but I laughed it off as I limped around. Within a few days, the pain had spread to both ankles and both knees. Within a week, I couldn't walk more than a few yards without wanting to scream.

They did tests. They did loads of tests, but they didn't find anything wrong. I took painkillers. They didn't work. I had steroid injections. They didn't work. I saw a naturopath, which didn't work, had acupuncture, which didn't work, took medication they give people with arthritis, which also didn't work. I had walking sticks, which didn't help much. I would use them to hop down the alleyway from the bus stop to the office. I had to get a minicab to the bus stop in the morning. I couldn't go out for a sandwich. A colleague would bring one back and I would eat it after everyone else had had their lunch. In the evening, kind Brian from sales would drop me off on his way home.

I was working at Faber & Faber. It had been my dream to work at the place where T. S. Eliot had worked, the place that published him, and Seamus Heaney and Ted Hughes and Ezra Pound. It had not been my dream to be stuck at a desk I couldn't leave, find myself almost crawling to the loo and fighting to save my tears till I got home.

I had left Faber and was still racked with pain when a receptionist told me over the phone that blood tests I'd had a year earlier had been found. I had, she told me, got lupus. By this stage, I knew a bit about lupus. I knew it was an autoimmune disease where the body attacks its own tissue. I knew it could give you a rash on your face that made you look like a wolf. I remembered from my Latin A level that lupus was the Latin word for wolf. I knew it could attack your organs: your kidneys, your heart, your brain. And I knew that there wasn't a cure.

More than twenty years on, I can tell you that I don't look much like a wolf. My organs, as far as I know, are fine. I did hear recently that people who drink more than about a thimble of wine a week are being sent off to have tests on their liver, but I have so far managed not to have a test on mine. I can walk. I can talk. Well, most of the time I can walk. I had two years when I couldn't really walk, or at least not without serious pain. And that first time I had the crippling pain in my knees and legs was by far the longest, but it wasn't the last.

So I shouldn't have been surprised. I really shouldn't have been surprised when I went for a run a few months after I lost my job and found I had a pain in my left foot. I wasn't sure how I could have hurt it without falling over, or tripping up. I'm never sure how I could have hurt it without falling over, or tripping up. After a few days, I went to the minor injuries unit at my local hospital. I had an X-ray and they found nothing. By now, the pain was in both knees. It took me a while to realize that the pain in my foot had started just after I'd had a phone call saying that I'd failed to get a second interview for a part-time role I wanted a lot.

When I'm upset, it's my body that cracks up. I wish it didn't, but it does. Freud would have loved me. He'd have looked at my medical history, slapped his thigh and yelled that he was right. The body, he would say, speaks when we can't.

For me, it started with spots. Spots are funny. In books, films and TV programmes, spots are funny, but spots aren't all that funny when you're the one who has them and you feel so ugly you just want to hide.

Mine started with a sprinkling of tiny bumps on my face when I was thirteen. My forehead, I realized one day when I was washing my face, felt like an avocado. My parents were proud of our new avocado bathroom suite, but I didn't feel proud of my new avocado face. Soon my cheeks and chin were peppered with tiny pink dots. I did everything *Jackie* magazine told me to do: cleansed and toned twice a day and plastered the dots in Clearasil, several shades darker than my skin. From the age of fourteen, I was on antibiotics all the time. They didn't clear up the spots, but I thought if I came off them, they'd get worse.

The spots were bad enough, but what happened on my face when I was twenty-three was more like an Old Testament plague. Now my face was covered in deep red lumps. They throbbed for days, and then turned into giant pustules. I couldn't look in a mirror without feeling sick.

My mother paid for me to see a dermatologist, who prescribed a drug called Roaccutane. He said my acne would get better, but first it might get worse. It certainly did get worse. Soon, I had red throbbing lumps in places I didn't know you could get spots. I had them on my eyebrows, on the skin between the eyes and the hairline, and behind my ears. I had them on my chest, like a rash that was spreading down my body, and on my back. When I looked in a mirror, I couldn't see my eyes, or nose, or mouth. All I could see was spots. I looked in mirrors all the time, and also in car wing mirrors, saucepan lids and spoons. Every time I looked, I hoped that what I would see wasn't as bad as I thought it was. When I saw the face staring back at me, it was.

At a hospital for skin diseases, the consultant invited a group of students in to stare. He prescribed a treatment called PUVA.

This meant I had to go to hospital every day, and be blasted with a special kind of ultraviolet light in a metal box like an upright coffin. After a few weeks, the light had burnt off most of the spots, and several layers of skin. It didn't burn off the scars.

I wish I could say that that was the end of it, but up until my mid-thirties, I nearly always had spots on my chin. I was pretty good at covering them up, but I never wanted to be seen without make-up, or in bright light. There were times when my skin seemed relatively calm. At other times, it would explode in angry, weeping, pulsing lumps. My skin would explode, in fact, in what seemed to be a kind of rage.

Over the years, I tried every drug the dermatologists could find. I tried a cream they use on lepers. I did weird diets, where you have to give up everything you like. I saw a homeopathic doctor, who gave me little white pills, which brought me out in boils the size of coins. I saw a Chinese herbalist, who made me boil up vats of twigs and herbs and I tried not to retch as I forced the liquid down. I had a facial with a woman who used a metal cylinder covered in spikes. I saw a woman who did something called 'body work' and told me to imagine myself with clear skin. I did imagine myself with clear skin. The spots carried on coming anyway.

I bought books with titles like *The Acne Cure* and *Super Skin*. I had a book called *Acne: Advice on Clearing Your Skin*. 'Acne', it said, in the first line of the first chapter, 'is a skin disease that we still need to research.' It is, in other words, a disease that doesn't have a cure. Some skin conditions don't. 'Why did I marry so young?' said the novelist John Updike, who had psoriasis from the age of six. 'Because, having once found a comely female who forgave me my skin, I dared not risk losing her and trying to find another.' He wrote this in a book called *Self-Consciousness*, in an essay called 'At War with My Skin'.

Skin is the membrane that contains our flesh, our blood, our hearts, our brains. It also contains our hopes, our dreams and our disappointments. Skin is what separates us from the world. No wonder it can feel like a battleground. It can feel like a secret battleground, in a war that fills you with shame. Sarah, from my yoga class, knows all about that war. 'I've had skin problems since I was four,' she told me. 'It started with eczema and flaky, painful skin behind my ears. I've seen dermatologists over the years and there doesn't really seem to be anything they can do, apart from prescribe steroid cream. I really don't know what the cause is, and I really don't know what the answer is. It's something I have to live with.'

When she said this, I actually felt grateful for my skin. My acne did go in the end, but some skin conditions don't. 'It's like having permanent toothache,' she said. 'A dull ache. It's always there. It can be quite debilitating and depressing, because you just think "why can't I be normal?" It's disruptive, it's tiring, it keeps you awake at night.' It has, she told me, affected her love life. Most of us aren't confident that the best way to build desire is to rip off your clothes and reveal a nasty pink rash. She has no doubt that what happens on her skin is often related to what happens in her life. 'It doesn't flare up immediately,' she said, 'but even when you think you're fine, if you've had a really severe emotional setback, it takes its toll somewhere.'

It can be a vicious circle. You're upset, or stressed, or reeling from a loss and your skin explodes in big red lumps. And then you have to chair a public event with a face covered in big red lumps. Show me someone who can do that with the calm of the Buddhist monk who tried to teach me mindfulness and I'll show you someone who's on Valium.

My friend Claire and I were working together when we first bonded over our battles with our lumps and bumps. Hers started, she told me, the summer she was fourteen. Before she broke up for the summer holiday, she had 'a few teenage spots'. When she went back to school at the end of it, people came up to her and said, "Oh my God, what happened to your face?" The boys in her class called her Pizza Face and Gangrene. People started treating her differently. 'I think they thought I wasn't very bright,' she said. 'It's as if somehow by being ugly you failed on every single level.'

Like me, Claire was on semi-permanent antibiotics. Like me, she plastered her face with fierce creams. One day, when she ran out of antibiotics, she walked ten miles from her village to the GP surgery in the nearest town. Another time, when the surgery was closed, she banged on the door until someone opened it up. 'I put neat Dettol on my face,' she said, 'which gave me these terrible brown marks. I sat in the sun until I got sunburnt. I thought at least if my face is red because it's sunburnt you wouldn't be able to see the spots so much.'

She left parties before the lights came on. 'I always felt,' she explained, 'I had to be seen in the dark. I thought nobody would ever want to go out with me. I would really hate it if anyone said they wanted to meet in a place where I knew the lighting was harsh. I would spend the whole time looking at my feet, not meeting their eye.' I nodded as I poured us each another glass of wine and told her that I'd sometimes bolted at the end of a date, just to avoid the strip light of a Tube. 'Right up until my early thirties,' she said, 'I was constantly worrying about my face.'

When Claire realized that the acne wasn't just going to go away, she was put on antidepressants. She spent most of her adolescence on antidepressants. This is quite common. A fifth of acne sufferers, according to a recent study, have thought about suicide. 'I wonder sometimes,' she said, 'if that sense of being out of control has been one of the reasons I'm so anxious. I felt quite helpless. I panic a bit when I get that feeling now.'

Well, you do panic when you feel helpless. And it's not all that weird to panic if your face looks like something from a medical textbook. Or if you can't walk. I could practically have sent a child to Eton on what I wasted on treatments for my acne and the pain in my legs. The nutritionists. The homeopaths. The hypnotherapy. The cranial osteopathy. The physiotherapy. The psychotherapy. The weird machines I was wired up to that were meant to measure energy patterns. The reiki. The acupuncture at Waterloo. The acupuncture in Soho. The Chinese herbalists. The shiatsu. The cognitive analytic therapy. The neurologist. The pain specialist. I wouldn't have done any of this, of course, if the drugs the doctors had given me had worked. But they didn't. The Verve were right. The drugs often don't work. I will tell you later what did.

Anna was twenty-two when she first had trouble walking. She was having difficulty breathing after a run, went into hospital with chest pain, and was told she had a 'massive virus'. When she left hospital two weeks later, her legs kept giving way. It was a few weeks after that, on an outpatients visit at her local hospital, that she found out what it was. 'My mum was outside in the corridor,' she told me, 'and I was behind the curtain. The neurologist was on the other side. I was pulling up my jeans and he said, "You've got MS."'

I know Anna through a friend and also through bits of my work. I've sometimes noticed that she looks a bit uncomfortable if she's standing up for a long time. At one party, I saw her laughing it off with a fellow guest and saying she had a bad back. It was only recently that she told me that her back is fine, but she doesn't want people to know she has MS. Whenever I've met her, she has always seemed cheerful, so I wanted to find out how she manages to handle such a serious disease with such good humour and grace.

Anna was in her last year at university when she was diagnosed. She loved clubbing and was 'dancing all the time'. Suddenly, she couldn't dance. She couldn't run. She could barely walk. She was due to sit her finals, but had to put them off for a year. 'Nobody had warned me about the tiredness,' she told me over a bowl of spaghetti near her office. 'I couldn't really study for more than an hour at a time and was used to putting in an eighteen-hour day.'

She lost a year and missed graduating with her friends. But they were still a big part of what got her through. 'There was a group of lads,' she said, 'who basically had a party house. They were immensely kind and looked out for me. They let me live with them, rent-free, for months. It's really interesting where kindness emerges, often from the least likely people. I can think of a couple of cards that some really laddish lads on my course sent me. They were a bit rude, but there was so much sentiment in there as well. They came round with a load of weed for me!'

Not everyone hit the right note. 'Some of the letters I got,' she said, 'were shocking in their self-absorption. Some older people wrote long letters about confronting mortality. Luckily, I could laugh at it. I could also laugh at the level of egotism.' Anna laughed and put on a droning-academic voice: '"This is my pre-occupation, now that I'm coming to the end of my career. I'm now going to share my thoughts on mortality, to you, who are twenty-two, and have just been diagnosed." That,' she added cheerfully, 'was quite bad.'

It took her about eighteen months to make a reasonable recovery. If she got a temperature, or was too hot, her walking suffered, but she was largely fine until she was thirty-eight and pregnant with her third child. 'I got a stomach bug,' she said, 'and it absolutely floored me. In A & E, my body just completely gave out.' She was in hospital for a week and then moved to a 'step-down unit' for rehabilitation. 'There are literally people dying around you,' she said. 'I was about a third of the age of the others. People would think I was the nurse. When one woman died, someone actually started singing "Roll Out the Barrel" as she was wheeled out.'

It was, she said, not just depressing, but also strangely un-nerving. 'They take away every bit of you when you're in there,' she said. 'It feels very systematic. First of all, they remove your clothes and put you in a hospital gown. Then they take your jewellery, and then your hair doesn't look like it normally does, and bit by bit it's very depersonalizing.' At one point, she found herself suspended, naked, seven feet in the air. 'Someone was bathing me,' she said, almost wincing at the memory. 'I was on one of those raised seats, eight months pregnant and they just left me hanging there while they were chatting to people. The door was wide open. I'm in there thinking: OK, most people have no vision whatsoever, but still.'

Most of us would not be thrilled to be hanging naked seven feet in the air. Anna found a practical way to cope with it. 'If the hospital and the medical system strip you of every sign of yourself,' she said, 'which bit do you retain and which bit do you actually just hand over? You do need to find your inner core, that private self that you only share with your friends and family.'

Anna is now forty-five. She hasn't been back in hospital, but she does still sometimes have problems with her walking. 'My leg gives way,' she said. 'I often have pins and needles down my left arm, and pins and needles across my lip and face.' When she has to get up early, the symptoms are worse. 'Airports are an issue,' she said, 'because you often have to wake up very early. We joke I have an airport walk!'

Anna tells colleagues she has back pain. 'Most things can be explained with back pain,' she told me. 'But you can look really drunk. One day, on the way back to the office after a nine a.m. meeting on a really hot day, a couple of cab drivers wouldn't pick me up. My friend got really upset on my behalf and I was like, it's fine, it happens.'

The thing I noticed most as we had lunch was that Anna laughed a lot. 'I suppose we make jokes about it,' she said. 'It's a source of humour in the family. It's a distancing mechanism, sometimes.' And didn't she, I asked, ever think that what had happened to her was unfair? Anna looked surprised. 'No. It's one of those things. If that starts, it's going to be really difficult to come back from.'

I wish that's how I'd felt when I was told I had lupus when I was twenty-six. I wish it's how I'd felt when the dermatologist called his students in to stare. It wasn't. What I felt was: cursed. After my years at the Baptist youth club, I was still an evangelical Christian and everybody kept telling me that Jesus wanted to heal me. At meeting after meeting, I would hobble up to whoever was offering prayer. The people praying would tell me that whatever I asked in Jesus's name, he would do. I didn't think it was unreasonable to ask if he would mind making me look a bit less like a leper, and possibly just reducing the pain in my knees so it wasn't pure agony to walk. Jesus seemed to be very good at curing other people's headaches and colds. What, I wondered, as I dragged myself home in tears, happened to 'take up your bed and walk'?

When the body goes wrong, the answer is not God. Well, it may be for some people – there are many studies on the power of the placebo – but it certainly wasn't for me. It wasn't the answer to lupus, or acne, or migraines, or stomach pain, or insomnia. It wasn't the answer to shadows on scans or lumps.

I have been carved, and radiated, and drugged and recon-structed. What I can tell you from all of this is that sometimes medicine works and sometimes it doesn't. Sometimes, the body will not be told.

In her book *Illness as Metaphor*, Susan Sontag says that we should be very careful about looking at illness in emotional terms. In theory, I think she's right. All I know is that when I'm unhappy, I get ill. I also know that every time I've been ill, I have got better.

A change in grammar

It wasn't a big surprise when my uncle Maurice died, but that didn't stop me feeling sad. He was a gentle Geordie, the son of a miner and one of the sweetest men I have ever met. At his sons' school rugby matches, standing on the sidelines, he would often start cheering for the other side. He was on the side of the underdog. He was always on the side of the underdog. He was the only person who dared to tease my fierce Scottish grandmother, the mother-in-law even my mother feared. He called her 'the Duchess' and she loved it. Whatever he said, people loved it. Wherever he went, he brought smiles.

He was ninety-three. He had dementia. He had recently moved into a home. All the women there were in love with him. He just kept telling them how much he loved his wife. His was a gentle death at the end of a long, good life. This is often not what death is like.

I had only been running the Poetry Society for a few months when I answered the phone and heard my father's voice. I knew straight away that something was wrong. My father believed you shouldn't use work time, or work phones, for personal things. When he needed to call my mother about something when he was working at the Cabinet Office, he would go out of the office in his lunch break and use a pay phone in the street.

My sister, he said, had collapsed while she was washing up at 'the bookshop', the mental health café and bookshop she went to almost every day. The ambulance had taken forty minutes to get there. The paramedics had done their best.

I lay down on the floor of my office. My head was wedged against the filing cabinet, but I didn't think I could move it. I heard a wail, and realized it was coming out of me.

A few hours later, I met my friend Tina. We drank Chilean Chardonnay and had a bowl of chips. Anyone watching us might have thought we were on a nice girls' night out, but I had no idea what you were meant to do when the person you had shared half your life with had been rushed to hospital and 'not survived'.

We don't talk about death. No one prepares you for it, and no one tells you what to do when the person you loved suddenly isn't there. No one even prepares you for the change in grammar. You love them – and then, in a micro-second, you can't love them any more. You loved them. You loved a person, who has been a big part of your life, and now what is there to love? A memory? A ghost? Or just some atoms, floating in the air?

In Papua New Guinea, when someone dies, the women from the surrounding villages gather in the house of the person who has died and wail non-stop for days. Aboriginals keen and then smoke out the dead person's home. Jews tear their clothes as a sign of their grief. The Irish watch over the body, and friends and family will come to the house to eat and laugh and cry until the person who died is laid to rest. Most of us in Britain don't do any of this. We sweep our feelings under the carpet and carry on.

A few weeks after my sister died, I went to have a facial. A friend had given me a voucher because she could see I was exhausted with the effort of just trying to behave as if everything was fine, when it wasn't. It didn't help that I was also being taken to tribunal by my stalker. He was someone I had been kind to, because I knew he had schizophrenia and my sister had taught me all about an illness you wouldn't wish on a rabid dog. My kindness had backfired and he had sent me letters, poems and pictures begging me to marry him. He had even once sent me a bottle of the perfume I wear all the time. He must have sniffed all the testers in Boots until he found the right one. When he applied for a job at the Poetry Society and I didn't shortlist him, I got a letter telling me that I was being taken to an employment tribunal for discriminating against someone with a disability. At first I thought it was a joke, but I soon discovered that it was not.

When I was lying on that beautician's couch, she asked me to take a deep breath. When I did, she said, 'Well done.' I almost laughed, because when you keep going, even though your heart is breaking, nobody says well done. But actually somebody should say it all the time because you are still, somehow, managing to breathe.

I was in my second year at *The Independent* when I got a call at work to say that the poet Michael Donaghy had died. I left the office and walked round the block, but nothing in my head could make the words real. I had known Michael since I first started working at the Southbank Centre, twelve years before. He had done mesmerizing readings and led workshops on poetry and dance. In my years at the Poetry Society, I had got to know him better. Michael was brilliant. He was charming. He was handsome. He was sparkling. He was sweet. He was irresistible. He was dead.

There was a memorial service at the Union Chapel. Even that huge hall was full. We tried not to cry, because we knew that his wife, Maddy, wanted it to be a celebration. Some of us gazed at the crowds queuing up to squeeze in and muttered that we'd only need a broom cupboard for ours.

Ten years after Michael's death, Maddy Paxman published a memoir about her grief called *The Great Below*. 'I was hanging out the washing in the back garden,' she writes in the first chapter, 'when he yelled down in panic through the open window that he couldn't move his left arm and leg. My first reaction was "What NOW?"'

She had, she writes, got tired of his hypochondria, and the parade of psychosomatic symptoms his body produced, which after one argument included 'an egg-shaped lump on his back'. She finished hanging up the washing before she followed the ambulance to hospital. She was still hoping to make it to her book group that night. A few hours later, she walked into the resuscitation unit and saw Michael 'stretched out naked on a gurney like an experimental animal, with tubes inserted into every orifice'. Four days later, she had to make the decision to turn off the machine that was keeping him alive.

She held his toes as he died. His heart carried on beating as she watched him turn blue. With a nurse, she washed his body. She cut his toenails and put him in a clean hospital gown. As the light faded outside, she sang the song she sang to him when they were first in love, 'To Althea, from Prison'. Words from Richard

Lovelace, set to an Irish melody, a song, she says, 'about how the spirit can be free even when the body is in chains'.

Maddy's memoir is an extremely moving account of his death and the years that followed. It is also brutally honest, so honest that it lost her some friends. She is honest about the irritation she so often felt with Michael. She is honest about the fact that everyone who knew him seemed to think he was a saint. She is honest about their relationship. Poets, she writes, are 'the most self-absorbed of all artists'. Having worked with poets for years, I think she may be right, though the ones I'm proud to call my close friends aren't. And she is honest about the fact that at the time of Michael's death, they were 'far apart, in the way only a warring couple can be'. This is not what somebody usually says when the person they love has died.

'So much fiction and film around death is just rubbish, really,' she told me. We were sitting at the kitchen table in the house she used to share with Michael and their son. 'I think stunned silence is probably how most people respond, rather than a big outpouring. It's too big a thing to start feeling the grief immediately.' On his last day, she said, she had a sense of 'absolute clarity', but that soon gave way to 'the more usual sense of chaotic muddle'.

She's unusually clear about the complicated feelings that can hit you when someone dies. 'We'd had a really bad year,' she told me. 'He'd been pretty under the weather and grumpy and anxious and demanding.' They had been together for twenty-one years, but had only got married the year before. She had hoped that marriage would rekindle the romance of the early years. 'Getting married was very romantic,' she said, 'but being married . . .' She put her mug down and sighed. 'I didn't like it much, to be honest.'

One of the things she felt when Michael died was a 'feeling of relief' that she didn't have to look after him any more. And one of the things that hit her, as the weeks and months passed, was how deep, in spite of all the irritations, their love had been. 'I think the book was really a sort of journey for me,' she told me, 'from that feeling of having been set free from quite a burden, in some ways, to actually realizing how much we loved each other, and how much I missed that.'

Maddy met Michael when she was twenty-five and he was twenty-nine. 'I never really was an adult for any length of time without a partner,' she said. 'We had completely separate social worlds, so it was a real shock to me how incredibly dependent on him I was. Some of this is to do with how you are regarded. Society regards you, particularly as a woman on your own, as a bit odd and lacking in something. I felt like "who's out there to know what's going on with me?" It's simple things like: you go to Sainsbury's and they're not selling the cheese you like any more and you want to tell somebody, but you can't ring up a friend and say they haven't got the cheese any more! I remember when I was ill at some point and saying something to a friend and he said, "Well, that's what being single is."'

Yes, I wanted to say. That's what being single is. In all my years of illness as an adult, I have nearly always been on my own. After a big operation a few years ago, I had to go and stay with my seventy-five-year-old mum. I have never been in a supermarket and thought: I must tell someone about that cheese. But then I have never put up with the compromises of a long-term relationship. If you don't put in the hours, I suppose, you don't get the Lemsips, or the chats about cheese.

'What I missed from Michael,' Maddy said with a sad smile, 'was that emotional shield that I hadn't really been aware of until it wasn't there. Someone who loved you. And he was an incredibly accepting person, too. I never forget ringing him up and telling him I'd crashed the car and he said, "Are you all right?", while I'd be saying, "What do you mean, you've crashed the car?"'

For all her sometimes shocking honesty, the love is clear. 'Grief,' she said, and now she was looking wistful, 'is a whole other landscape. You start trying to limit it to emotions we're already familiar with. Yes, you feel anger, yes, you feel bargaining or whatever, you think "if only I'd done that". Sometimes you feel acceptance, but it all happens in a kind of tumble. It's not a smooth progression at all. It makes you feel like you're going mad.'

I met Angela at my friend Maura's. She is tiny and delicate-looking and made me think of a china doll. I knew that she had been widowed and asked if I could talk to her about her experience of grief because I liked her air of quizzical calm.

Angela was forty when her husband got ill. 'He developed this cough and had flu symptoms,' she told me when we met for coffee at the Southbank Centre. 'He was a very thin man, but his waist was getting bigger and we thought it was middle-aged spread. It turned out his spleen was enormous. The GP referred him to the hospital and he was told he had lymphoma. The word was, if you're going to get cancer, this was a good one to get.'

Like Maddy, she had been with her husband, John, for twenty-one years. They met at university, just before finals. 'There was a party,' she said. 'John came and started dropping in. He had the most beautiful voice.' Angela is generally matter-of-fact. She tends towards understatement, which is why I felt even more upset when tears sprang into her eyes. 'I'm all right,' she said, 'when I'm not tired. Anyway, tears are normal. I would hear him,' she continued, 'in the next-door room. I thought he was coming to see my flatmate. It turns out he was coming to see me! We just sort of went bananas for each other. We fell in love and that was it.'

After university, she went back to live with her family. Her father was a school caretaker. Her mother was the school cleaner. There were six children and, she said, 'absolutely no money at all'. Having grown up in a school, she didn't want to be a teacher, and got the first job she could get. Later, when she had her first son, and when her husband was studying for his bar exams, she felt she had no choice but to go into teaching. She didn't particularly enjoy it, but her focus was on her family.

Their eldest son was thirteen when John was diagnosed. Their youngest was ten. They both tried to keep things as normal for the boys as they could. They also tried every treatment they could find. 'I embarked on boiling herbs,' she said. 'I had this wonderful friend, Maria, who was also on the wheel of cancer, who never gave up. She was sort of sending me things. You can get this, you can do that.'

At one point, they thought he was getting better. 'We were going to go to Paris on Eurostar. We were making it the story we wanted it to be, which was that he had got better. Before we went, we went to the hospital for some blood tests. The blood tests had been awful, and all of a sudden, that was it, it all kind of went into a great whirl. We went into a little room and they said, "We can't do any more for John."'

For the last month, Angela looked after him at home. 'Part of you accepts it,' she said, 'part of you thinks "right, he's going to die at home", because he hated hospital. By then, there was nothing worse. I still can't see a wrapped-up sandwich if I'm in the right mood without feeling dreadful.' John had, she said, never talked about dying. 'Out of the blue, he said to me, "I want to be buried at St Hugh's," and – this is the funny thing about operating on different levels – I said, "Well, I don't think you can just be buried where you want. You have to sign up. Like schools! You've got to be in the catchment area!" So we started going to the church.'

He died just before their twentieth wedding anniversary. 'I can remember a palliative care doctor saying to me, "It's so much harder for you, because you never thought he was going to die." And I thought: "I don't believe he's dead now! How am I going to grasp that someone is going to die? Can you tell me what it means?" And of course we were marvellous patients, we were wonderful because, my God, I had my make-up on every day.

'Immediately after he died,' she said, 'and for a long time since, I have thought about the gap between hope and despair and how you're such a good person when you're being strong. "My goodness, aren't they marvellous, you know, they just carry on." Everyone loves that story. I notice that when it became a bad story, people fell away. We want life to be about overcoming. We want it to be about how we make our own stories. We fucking don't make our own stories.' She almost slammed down her coffee cup and I felt like slamming down mine. 'I'm so annoyed,' she said, 'when I hear people say that.'

*

My mother's friends Mike and Morag have had every reason to despair. Two months before my sister died, a police car turned up at their house. 'We were coming down to get our breakfast, still in our pyjamas,' Morag told me, 'and Mike said, "Who on earth is that police car for?"'

Mike sighed, and it was one of the longest sighs I've ever heard. 'You can't quite take it in,' he said. 'They're not talking to me, are they? They can't be talking to me. It's as if you want to get rid of them, but you can't. So really you're absolutely stunned.' They were even more stunned when they took in what the policeman had said. Their son Anthony had been on his way back from a party with a friend when the car veered off the road and into a tree. The friend, who had been driving, was severely injured. By the time the emergency services turned up, Anthony was dead.

I have known Morag and Mike since I was about twelve. My mother met Morag at a sociology evening class, invited them both round for dinner and they have all been friends ever since. Morag and Mike are cheerful, good company and they are incredibly kind. And they laugh a lot. This couple, who lost their eldest son in terrible circumstances, still laugh a lot. And the thing is, he wasn't the first son they have lost.

I wasn't sure if my mother would approve when I asked them if they would talk to me about their loss. Everyone thinks my mother is very open, but she is actually very private and she assumes other people prefer to be private, too. But Morag and Mike agreed to talk to me, perhaps because they are so kind.

They had, Morag told me, met a couple on holiday, with a daughter the same age as theirs. When they got back to England, she invited them to a picnic near the swimming pool on the local common. 'Unfortunately,' said Morag, 'this woman forgot the armbands of her little girl.' Mike took the armbands off their three-year-old son, Patrick, and gave them to the girl. He then took Patrick off to play on the swings. Somehow, Patrick disappeared. 'We all went to look at the cars,' said Morag, 'because he loved looking at cars. We never even thought of the pool. Of course he was at the stage when he loved jumping in. And of course he didn't have his water wings. He was pulled out and they couldn't do anything.'

I knew that Patrick had drowned, but I never knew about the water wings. I had never thought about how a simple act of kindness could wipe out a life. 'When these things happen,' said Mike, who is very English and speaks about personal things in a slightly clipped tone, 'the actual awfulness of it doesn't give you time to grieve. There is,' he said, in such a low voice that I had to strain to hear it, 'always that guilt thing.'

So what, I asked, were the worst times? 'Well,' said Mike, 'just the immediate aftermath was terrible, really.' There was such a long pause I thought he might not speak again. And did he, I asked, ever feel so desperate that he didn't know how he would carry on? Mike took a sip of the tea my mother had brought us. We were in the sitting room in the house that has been my family home all my life. 'I never felt that, really,' he said. 'I tried to be positive. I thought "if you don't get hold of this, it will destroy everything". You've got two alternatives, really. You let the thing wipe you out or you try to face up to it.'

Morag and Mike did not let it 'destroy everything'. They did everything they could to get on with their lives. They had to keep going for their daughter, Emma. And then, nine months to the day after Patrick died, Morag had Anthony. 'It was a miracle,' said Morag. 'Our friends called him the miracle baby.'

Her face softened at the memory of the 'miracle baby' she adored. 'As he grew up,' she said, 'people used to say "don't you worry that something might happen?" I never did. I thought,' she said, and it made me want to wrap her in my arms, 'it can't happen to me twice.'

When Morag and Mike turned up at my mother's house, they were each holding a brown envelope. Inside it were notes they had typed in preparation for the interview. It's the only time in my life when my interviewees have done more preparation than me. 'Mike was quite worried about coming to talk,' said Morag. 'You'll see, he probably dealt with this quite differently. I haven't read his and he hasn't read mine.'

Both lists talk about the things that got them through. I had told them that I was writing about 'the art of not falling apart' and Mike's first paragraph, which he read aloud, made me gasp. 'There is no such thing as "art" when it comes to surviving the death of a loved one,' he read, 'only struggling along a craggy path without a guide.

'Grief,' he continued, 'in my experience, comes in many forms. For example, the death of one's parents, however sad, is a grief that one can come to terms with normally in a reasonable time, with resignation, as part of the order of things.

'When you lose a young child, the world collapses around you. A dreadful darkness pervades everything. The feeling of guilt and horror of the actual circumstances fill every minute of the day, almost taking over the actual grieving. Sleep is purgatory, because you will wake to this different world where everything is dark and hopeless.'

I looked at this couple I've known so long and like so much. When I think of them, I always think of their laughter. I think of their laughter and Morag's hugs. I know my mother does, too. 'I can remember sitting in this room,' said Morag, 'when Mum lost Caroline and I felt it was a terrific bond between us, because we both shared that. I knew what she was feeling.'

And did she, I asked, still miss Anthony? For a moment, Morag's smile disappeared. 'Every day,' she said. 'Every day. I often just feel he's there. Strange, isn't it?' and now there were tears rolling down her cheeks. 'I've learnt to live with it now.'

I can't think of anything worse than losing a child. Losing the partner you love long before their time must come a pretty close second. But at Uncle Maurice's funeral, there was laughter as well as tears. The vicar told the congregation that he was the only person he had ever sacked for doing a good deed. My uncle had always 'kept an eye' on the vicar's chickens while he was away, but when the vicar heard that, well into his eighties, Maurice was climbing over the wall and spending hours every day anxiously counting them, he knew it was time for him to stop. My cousin Michael said that the last time he went to visit his father, his face lit up. 'Ah, Jackie Milburn!' my uncle said to his eldest son. From a lifelong Newcastle FC fan, there could be no higher praise.

After the service, at the local church, there was a buffet lunch at Auntie Bell's. She now lives in a bungalow at the other end of the village from the house Uncle Maurice had built, the house we used to stay in every Whitsun half-term. The house had its own big field. The boys all played football in the field. Once, my uncle kept some sheep in it. The sheep escaped early one morning, and Maurice chased them round the village in his pyjamas.

I walked back from the church with Maurice's niece, Diana. Because my knees were still bad, I was hobbling in the special old-lady shoes I'd had to buy to wear when I wasn't wearing trainers. Diana told me she was sorry to hear about my job. 'I used to love your column in *The Independent*,' she said. I should have just smiled, because people said this all the time. Instead, I burst into tears. I felt even worse that at the funeral of my beloved uncle, some of my tears were for me.

Stuck

It had just started to rain. I'd been hanging around in cafés for six and a half hours, but it was still two hours before I was due to be picked up. The last two I'd spent in the library, flicking through newspapers and magazines. The man sitting next to me was asleep. The man sitting opposite me was rocking and humming. The man on the other side was holding a newspaper the wrong way up. All I wanted was to crawl into my bed, which was just a ten-minute walk down the road. The trouble was that for the next ten days my bed belonged to someone else.

I wandered across the road and into a church. When I saw the candles flickering in that dark place, I felt a sob rising like a spasm running through me. I thought if I didn't clamp my jaws together, then the noise that came out of me would echo round the church. A man came in with his children and lit some candles. I hoped he wouldn't ask me if I was OK. I didn't know how I'd explain that after months of sending emails that often weren't answered, and doing bits and pieces of freelance work at a fraction of my former rate, I was so tired I could hardly keep awake. And that I couldn't just go and lie down in my bed because my bed now seemed to be better at earning money than me.

It was a friend who told me about Airbnb. She could see that

I was exhausted and said that perhaps I could rent out my flat and take a break. I put it on the website and booked two weeks at a writing retreat in Spain. While I was there, I got a request for the week when I was due back. I asked my mother if I could stay with her for a week, and then said yes.

When you rent out your flat to strangers, they assume that you're staying with your boyfriend, or that you just happen to have another flat down the road. They don't assume that you are camping out in cafés, sleeping in friends' spare rooms or travelling down to your childhood home to sleep in your childhood bed. But for a while it seemed easier to rent out my home than to keep trying to tout around my brain.

After months of effort, I felt stuck. I had been trying so hard to get some projects off the ground, but they kept getting knocked off course. I had managed to persuade a think tank to work with me on a big research project, but then the director of the think tank had been fired. I had been promised a retainer to do some work with a healthcare company, but then they looked at their budgets and changed their mind. I had been asked to apply for a couple of non-executive roles, and then failed even to get interviews. I was working nearly all the time, but after all my efforts, I was barely scraping a living as a jobbing hack.

For a while, in my thirties, I felt stuck in a job. I once told my boss that I was 'bored out of my fucking mind'. I now want to shake that girl who got a regular pay cheque for doing something perfectly pleasant and tell her to grow up. But you can't tell anyone how to feel. If you feel stuck, you feel stuck. And there aren't all that many species on this planet that are at their best when they feel trapped.

*

My friend Jonathan had been 'swimming around for a role' when he was headhunted for a job as a lawyer for an international company. 'I knew it would be a roller coaster,' he told me as I gazed at the works of art in his beautiful sitting room, 'and I thought: I'm ready for that, I'm up for it.' There was no London office, so he knew he would have to work from home. Which, by the way, isn't quite as much fun as you think it will be unless you've always dreamt of being a Trappist monk.

'The working from home was fine for a while,' said Jonathan, 'and then it got busier. There was a lot of shit to shovel, basically, that just got more and more intense, so I started to give things up. I didn't entertain as much, I didn't see my friends as much.' It was Jonathan's first job as a consultant and he wanted it to go well. Soon, he was working every night till the early hours. 'It was dark and I was isolated up in my study,' he said. 'I really felt as though that was my world, that box.'

By working every waking hour, he managed to sort out a multimillion refinancing deal in many different countries, but the deal came at quite a cost. 'I felt like a shadow,' he said, 'and in some senses I was. The CEO was a bully. I didn't trust him. I felt like a little appendage hanging off this machine. You get pulled along by a little ball on a string. And then I started to feel as if I was being frozen out.'

I have known Jonathan for fifteen years. He lives near me, so we usually bump into each other quite a lot. During this time, he seemed different. His voice was a whisper and he had a hunted look in his eyes. Was he, I asked, depressed? Jonathan grimaced. 'I wasn't sleeping and I think that's a symptom of depression.

It was difficult to get out of bed. I tried to do some mindfulness and stuff like that, but it wasn't really effective.' I gave a sympathetic nod. You know what I think about mindfulness. Brilliant if you love counting, but count me out.

Soon, he told me, he was battling not just with the pressures of legal difficulties in many countries pouring into his inbox, but with a sense of shock. 'The figures were massaged to present a façade,' he said, 'and there just seemed to be more and more distance between the surface presentation and the true picture. There were people in positions of power who were behaving in ways I couldn't believe. Not illegally, but in terms of decency. I thought: "I'm working with these people and they're horrible!"'

After one particular meeting, something in him snapped. A friend put him in touch with a psychiatrist who specialized in stress. The doctor signed him off and persuaded him to go on a mild antidepressant. When Jonathan sent in the letter from the doctor, the HR person asked him to do handover notes. 'I said, "I could,"' he told me, '"but I'm not going to." I didn't say that, actually, but I wanted to so much!' The glint was back in his eye. I was so pleased to see that the glint was back in his eye. 'I had actually structured everything as I went along,' he said, 'so it's not like I left a great big pile of crap. The crap was in little boxes, for each country, this little piece of poo, that little piece of poo, so it was all neatly arranged like little pebbles, little mineral samples, like some geeky archaeologist, but it was still all smelling away, so at least it was there for somebody to deal with.'

That's the Jonathan I know and love. I was so relieved when he escaped, but he's a very bright guy and he's not exactly strapped for cash. Why, I asked, had he felt he had to stick with this god-awful job? Jonathan sighed and the expression on his face was pained. 'It's a good question,' he said. 'I just felt that there was no way out. I really did. I was trapped. It felt very dark. I felt that there was nothing I could do.'

Jonathan was lucky. He's a lawyer and lawyers, damn their eyes, know how to get good pay-offs. He got himself a *very* nice deal, with a gagging clause, which is why I can't give his real name. He had the best part of a year off, seeing friends and catching up with the culture he felt he'd missed. He's now doing another contract, earning more in a day than I sometimes do in a month. But for most of us, resigning from a job we hate feels more like leaping off a cliff into a pool of sharks.

Rolien van Heerden works at a company that specializes in communications training. I did a couple of days' work for them and thought she was one of the calmest people I'd met. She's so cheerful you'd think her professional life had been a gentle glide on a still lake in soft, early-evening sun. Over coffee in her office overlooking Hyde Park, she put me right.

'I came over to England from South Africa with two hundred pounds,' she said. 'My father had died, and I just wanted to get away and start to pay off my student debt, which I knew would be easier in sterling than in South African rand. I had no money and I stayed in a house with six other people and one bathroom. It was terribly cold. I was miserable. I was just going to put my head down and work my butt off for however long I needed to, to stay at a better place.'

Through someone she had known in South Africa, she got a job in a training company. At first, it all looked pretty good.

'We were a big team,' she said, 'we made a ton of money and then the recession knocked us all over and it just kind of spiralled out of control. It went downhill from there. People left, one after the other, but I had to stay because the company had sponsored me for a work permit. If I left, I'd have had to go home.'

When someone in Nigeria signed documents on Rolien's behalf, she didn't know what to do. It was her first proper job and no one had told her what you *should* do when your employers appear to be crooks. 'It was shortcuts,' she said, 'small things that added up to the bigger scheme of things. It would be something like providing visa support letters for people to come from abroad to enter the country when they were only going to be with us for a couple of days. Initially, I just thought "oh, that's the way we do things", until I started figuring it out. You gradually realize that this is not how other people operate.'

She felt trapped. She *was* trapped. 'Unfortunately,' she said, 'the only other person who worked with me in the end was the company owner's sister. She kept a close eye on pretty much everything I did. There was always someone looking over your shoulder, clocking your time. I just literally felt like a slave.' You could see as a white South African she wasn't using the word lightly. 'Insignificant,' she added. 'I felt insignificant.' The word seemed to take on a weight of its own.

Rolien worked out how long she had to stay, and literally ticked the days off. You can, she told me, only apply for 'indefinite leave to remain' after five years, but her first two, on a working holiday visa, didn't count. It took King Solomon seven years to build a temple to replace the tent the Israelites had to worship in before. Rolien had to get through seven years, too. When I was the age she started that job, I jacked in a permanent post to take up a six-month contract because I thought six months sounded like a really long time.

Luckily, she had studied drama. The lecturers at her university had told her she wasn't good enough, but she had phoned her mum, who told her to thank them for their opinion, and tell them that she would be doing drama anyway. She now carries those skills wherever she goes. 'It was important,' she said, 'that I had to show that I was not unhappy. Carry yourself in a certain way. Look the part, fake it till you make it. It's also to protect yourself. Don't show your weakness. Especially with bullies.'

She had nearly reached the end of her seven years when she walked out. 'I just knew,' she said, 'that I couldn't do it any more. Resigning was probably the scariest thing I've ever done. I can still recall that sensation in the pit of my stomach. I could have been kicked out of the country.'

That night, when she got home, there was a package waiting on the doorstep. 'It was,' said Rolien, and now her smile made me smile, 'the documents stating that I have jumped through all the hoops successfully. "Here's your indefinite leave to remain and welcome to the country."'

I never understood how bright, independent women could get stuck in abusive relationships. I didn't understand why they didn't just walk away. Then I met a very bright woman who did both. I had been asked to run a communications workshop at a business. I made such a mess of it, and was in such a state afterwards, that one of the organizers took me out for a drink. I'll call her Laura. You'll soon see why she can't give her real name. We got on so well that we agreed to meet again. This time she told me some of her story.

'I met my husband,' she told me, 'when I was twenty-four. He had a great sense of humour. He was a personal trainer, an ex-soldier. We were good in the early days and then my career really took off.' Laura was offered a big job in Belgium, and her husband, who I'll call Jon, went with her. 'From there on,' she said, 'he never actually found his groove. He didn't learn the language very well. I got headhunted several times and my salary got bigger, but he was just doing bits and pieces. Very gradually, I was ending up earning the money, but then doing all of the home-making. So that built up a little bit of resentment.'

A little bit? I'd have been spitting. But things, she said, soon got worse. 'Even though he wasn't pulling his weight in the home, he had a very dominant personality. He kind of called the shots, in terms of how things should be in the home. He took over the cooking. Logically, I should have been pleased, but I was gradually made to realize I wasn't a good cook. Which,' she added, in a tone that still sounded wounded, 'isn't true!'

Meanwhile, Jon was pushing her to get bigger and better jobs, because he was getting used to the money. 'He had a large collection of designer watches,' she explained, 'and he was mad about cars. By the age of thirty, he had his Porsche. Our holidays got more and more expensive. I just sort of let him take over. I lost control over finances, over the way our money was spent.'

If you met Laura, you'd find this as hard to believe as me. She has that glossy sheen of competence you sometimes find in the business world. She has done tough jobs in male-dominated worlds. 'It was almost as if I had two personas,' she said. 'At work, I was this super-confident professional woman. At home, it got to the point where I was no longer confident in any area. I couldn't choose the things I wanted in the home. He had to have his say in everything. It got to the point where – it sounds really stupid – I didn't even have the confidence to fill my own car up with petrol.'

I looked at Laura, who is very attractive, and has the air of someone who is used to being admired, and had to force myself not to gasp. 'If I ever stood my ground on something . . .' she said, and her voice tailed off. 'He had a very short temper. He often used to do this game where he'd show me that he could actually kill me quite quickly. He used to do this move where he tied my hands, not with a rope or anything, and did this movement at the back of my neck.'

I tried hard not to look as shocked as I felt. Did she, I asked, ever feel that he might actually hurt her? Laura sighed. 'Yes, because his eyes changed. They changed to pure ice.'

I bought us both another drink. What she told me later was much worse.

I have never had to work for a crook. I have never been stuck in a marriage with someone who shows me how they could kill me as their eyes turn to ice. I have had, in all kinds of ways, an easy life.

But pain isn't scientific. It isn't carefully calibrated to its cause. Some people take an overdose when they fail an exam. Other people seem to take it in their stride when they lose an arm or an eye.

In that dark church in Stoke Newington, I tried not to cry.

I knew that I should feel lucky to have a flat to let out, and some redundancy money in the bank. That was not how I felt. What I felt, most of all, was shame. Every time I sent an email that wasn't replied to, or heard myself described as 'former' or 'ex', I felt my cheeks burn.

When the man and his children left, I lay down on a pew. After a while, I shut my eyes, but I jumped up when I heard a woman's voice. 'I'm about to lock up,' she said. 'Could you please leave?' I nodded and grabbed my bag. I hoped the vicar's wife – if she was the vicar's wife – didn't watch Sky News. I hoped, in fact, that if she switched it on that night, and saw me chatting about the next day's front pages, she wouldn't recognize me as the person she had found trying to sleep on a pew.

Octopus pot

It's a shock to see a heart in a jar. I saw one in a medical museum when I was doing some research for an essay I'd been commissioned to write about skin. The veins looked like something you could use to plumb a sink.

It was the Greek philosopher Galen who first did some serious studies on the heart. He did it by cutting up monkeys and pigs. He thought that moods were due to balances of bile, that the soul was made up of three parts, and the 'spiritual' bit was found in the heart. For almost 1500 years, medical students learnt that the circulatory system was a kind of dual carriageway, but in 1628 William Harvey proved Galen wrong. He tied the veins and arteries of snakes and fish, which must have been quite fiddly, and worked out that it was veins that allowed the blood to flow to the chambers of the heart.

When you see a heart in a jar, you don't think this is something that could easily break. You don't think, as Anna Karenina did, when she talked about her broken heart, that that slab of meat could ever be like 'the pieces of a broken vase'.

At a private view in Piccadilly, I glimpsed the man who, four years ago, broke mine. After he told me that I should stop crying because I was 'not an eight-year-old child, but a middle-aged woman', I preferred to think of him as dead. I thought I'd never see him again. I thought he was 6000 miles away. In the time since I'd last seen him, I had had the shadows and the operations. In the time since then, I had seen my star on the newspaper rise and then, dramatically, fall. In the time since then, I had learnt that there are so many things other than a failed romance that can break your heart.

The great works of literature often seem to tell us that the most important thing in life is romantic love. They are packed with examples of what happens when it's lost. Anna Karenina leapt in front of a train. Romeo drank poison when he thought Juliet was dead. Dido stabbed herself with Aeneas's sword when he left her to set sail. Young Werther shot himself because the girl he loved was married to someone else. Ophelia was so fed up with Hamlet – and who wouldn't be? – that she threw herself in a river and drowned.

When the writer Diana Athill's fiancé stopped writing to her, the pain of the silence was like 'a finger crushed in a door, or a tooth under a drill'. After two years of silence, he asked to be released from their engagement. Her soul, she says in her memoir *Instead of a Letter*, 'shrivelled to the size of a pea'. She felt that her unhappiness was 'not a misfortune, but a taint', one that 'substitutes for blood some thin, acrid fluid with a disagreeable smell'. I first read the book when I was twenty-five and thought it was a tragic portrait of a middle-aged spinster who had been forced to find solace in books. When I read it again, for an interview for *The Independent*, it sent shivers down my spine.

When I talked to Diana Athill, at her care home in Highgate, she was ninety-three. I found myself telling her that I, too, had been dumped by my first love when I was nineteen. (But I didn't say 'dumped'. Like a Victorian governess, I said 'jilted'.) I told her that, for many years afterwards, I, too, kept my heart locked up. I told her that I, too, thought I would marry and have children, but have not.

Diana Athill gave a regal nod. It isn't just her prose that's cool. She did, in fact, eventually find happiness in a relationship, with the Jamaican playwright Barry Reckford, but she never fell in love with him, and when she found out he was having an affair, she invited his mistress to move in. 'Where spouses are concerned,' she said crisply, 'it seems to me that kindness and consideration should be the key words – not loyalty – and sexual infidelity does not necessarily wipe them out.'

Well, maybe. But most people I know have not been quite as relaxed as Diana Athill when they have found out that their partner is having an affair.

It sounds like a French farce to find your girlfriend in bed with your best friend, but my friend Andrew really did. 'She was very much my first and biggest love,' he told me. 'We were together for a few years. It felt very good and how a relationship should be.' And then, one day, he went round to see his friend. 'It was the sort of place where everyone kept their doors open,' he said. 'I walked into the house and found the two of them in bed together in the back room.'

Andrew has a quiet voice, and as he told me this, I had to strain to hear. The memory of the humiliation was written all over his face. 'I've probably blotted the precise details out of my mind, but I remember being very upset and running off home in tears. She moved out and I wrote long, agonizing letters to her, saying how much I loved her. The next two or three years were hell. I found it very difficult,' he said a bit stiffly, 'to come to terms with it.'

My friend Patsy is much more cheerful about her husband's infidelities, but she certainly wasn't at the time. I met her when we were both working in a bookshop. I was twenty-two. She was forty-two. She has been a close friend ever since. 'I was a virgin when I got married,' she told me, when we met for whitebait and chips at the Wolesley. 'The nearest I had got to sex before that was when my dad caught my first boyfriend, Daniel, in his house, in my bedroom, and chased him out. And then we broke up after that.' When she was nineteen, a builder called Jason jumped out of his van and started 'stalking' her. A few months later, she married him. 'I was waiting for my father to ask, "Are you sure about this? It's not too late to change your mind." I was waiting for that speech, so I could say no, I'm not sure. But he didn't ask and I went through with the whole thing. It was as if I was in a fog or a dream, or just stupid. I think,' she said and she laughed her infectious laugh, 'I was just stupid.'

The marriage lasted a couple of years and then she left him, moved into a basement flat with a friend, and worked in a publishing company just across the road from Francis Bacon's studio. 'The first Laura Ashley shop had just opened,' she said. 'We'd go to the Mary Quant shop in the King's Road. I was reading a lot of Herman Hesse. It was all Swinging London. But I wasn't really part of that.'

When she moved back to her parents' house for a while, in 1968, she bumped into her teenage sweetheart, Daniel. 'He drove me off down to Windsor,' she told me. 'It was the hottest day ever recorded. I was wearing a mini dress and I stuck to the seat. We just kept driving. We got to Windsor, and his favourite pub.' She smiled at the memory. Patsy has big, blue eyes and one of the most open faces I have ever seen. To me, she still looks like the woman I met, and was in awe of, when I was twenty-two. 'It was really amazing,' she said, 'like being given a present you didn't know was coming. It was like my birthday. And that was it!'

She got married in a white hat, white suit and pink high heels. 'On the way to the registry office, we met a friend of Daniel's and he said, "Are you coming for a drink, guys?" We thought we looked really amazing, but he thought we were just walking down the road! We said no, we're going to get married round the corner. I started crying when I said the words. It was all very emotional.'

Things were good, she told me, for a while, and then she walked into a room at a party and found Daniel kissing a neighbour. 'I just went home and didn't say anything,' she said. 'I couldn't do anything about it, but you can't deny things that happen in the heart. There's just this little closing thing that you don't even realize.'

Patsy is generous, sometimes to a fault. So I wasn't surprised when she told me that she just tried to put it out of her mind. 'We had a lovely few years,' she said, 'and then I think what happened was the drink.' Daniel would just disappear. Sometimes, he was with other women, sometimes just drinking with 'the boys'. By this time, she had her daughter, Jane. 'I thought about escaping, but I've got two cats, I've got a baby, you can't just go anywhere. Sometimes when he didn't come home from a Sunday morning at the pub I would end up putting his lunch in the bin. I remember once throwing the pushchair out of the front door and then seeing these lovely people who lived in the lodge opposite. "Oh hello!"' Across the table from me, Patsy did a genteel wave. '"Hello, Margery!"' We both laughed. '"And",' she continued in the tone she clearly sometimes used with Daniel, '"take that fucking pram with you!"'

She lost a baby. I never knew this. She gave birth to a baby at seven months, but it was, she was told, 'not survivable'. After that, she had an early miscarriage. Daniel had a skiing holiday booked and went without her. When he came back, he asked Patsy to pick him up. 'He got in the car and leant over to kiss me,' she said, 'and he was like a complete stranger. He'd broken something really serious. So I suppose it went down and down from there. It wasn't really till he got in the car and I thought: who is this person? He isn't wicked,' she sighed, 'just silly.'

Melanie is not as generous about her husband's infidelity. She is forty-eight. She had been with him half her life. I met her at a friend's hen party, and then again at that friend's fiftieth birthday. She told me that her marriage had ended and we arranged to go for a drink.

'I found out on iPad,' she said, 'iMessages. It's the most common way. What a dick. It was a work-based affair, as it always is. It was a colleague he was working with very, very intensely. She's ten years younger than him. A minute before, I'd have said he wasn't the sort of person to do that. That's how clever he was. In that moment,' she said, and she tried to keep her voice even, 'my whole world came collapsing down.'

As any sane woman would, she scrolled back through the

messages and felt sick. They were already in couples therapy, but not, she realized, the kind of therapy where you talk about what's really going on. Melanie decided to wait till the next session to tell her husband what she knew. 'He came straight from one of these team meetings with this woman,' she said. 'He was tripping down the road in his smart clothes, all these younger-men clothes that I'd helped him buy. Looking back, it was laughable. I said, "You're having an affair." He said, "No, I'm not." I saw him look me in the eye as if he was just saying he'd had a cheese sandwich for lunch. Of course, I didn't say, "Well, I've been watching what's happening on iMessage," but I saw just how good he was.'

Two weeks later, he told her that he'd had three previous affairs. 'I felt I was just stumbling from one parallel universe to another,' she said. She took another gulp of her wine and her face went red. 'Just when I was getting used to events, I was bumped into a universe where everything was completely different.'

It was eighteen months since all this happened, but the pain, it was clear, was still raw. 'It was,' said Melanie, 'just the most horrendous time. I'm starting to shake a bit when I think about it. Out of the blue, I lost three quarters of a stone. I felt sick the whole time. I don't have much weight to lose. I oscillated between days when I was consumed with anger and days when I was consumed with sadness. I would either be in bed sobbing, or I'd be stomping around, the angriest person in the world.'

I know that feeling. I certainly know that feeling, though not from the same cause. 'Even today,' she said, 'I've thought about him being with other women probably four or five times. When I talk about it now, I feel sick.' And were they still having sex, I

141

asked in as delicate a tone as I could muster, while he was having these affairs? Melanie made a noise that sounded like a snort. 'Yes,' she said. 'In fact, he was even more turned on than he normally was. Sometimes I was thinking: oh, what's going on here? I was a bit surprised.'

Melanie, like many women, was the one who had taken on most of the domestic burden. She was the one who sacrificed her career. 'I went,' she said, 'from living my life as a single person in London to a married mother in a little village in Oxfordshire. It was like going back to the 1950s. You wouldn't believe how difficult it can be to look after babies and small children. There is nobody validating you. Your child does not say thanks, Mum, for changing my nappy. When we started out, our careers were about here.' She raised her hands and put them roughly level. 'Within two or three years of producing children,' she said, and her left hand swooped up in a steep curve, while the other one stayed where it was, 'you're here.'

'I changed my passwords to "brutal" because it felt like my life was brutal.' Now she was crying. Her whole body was shaking with her sobs. 'When people have affairs, they do go bonkers. To have an affair and leave your husband or wife, you have to have an absolute obsession to drive you through that. That,' she said, wiping away tears, 'is what I saw in him.'

I don't know how many of my friends have had affairs. People tend not to talk about these things, even with their closest friends. I have friends of both sexes who have been rocked by the discovery that their partner has strayed. It isn't always the sex that hurts most. It's the lying. No one wants to think that they have been curled up with someone who has been sneaking off to curl up with someone else.

The research about affairs isn't clear, because – well, because people lie. But some studies seem to show that about half of married men and women will have at least one affair. Figures among co-habiting unmarried couples appear to be even higher. Among my friends, there's probably only a handful I know have had affairs. I have quite a few friends. Either they're unusually faithful or some of them are keeping things very quiet.

Some of my friends have had emotionally charged friendships with people they have met, which have probably stopped short of sex. I have had them too, and they are sweet. There have been times in my life when I've been invited out for lunches, drinks and dinners by quite a few married men. I don't think many of them expected an affair. If they did, they didn't get it. I have never wanted to be squeezed into the gaps of someone else's life. But I did feel that they were playing with a possibility, one that gave them, and perhaps their marriage, an extra edge. Sometimes I resented it. When you're single and the other person isn't, this feels unequal. I don't want to be the chilli in any couple's carne.

I have watched a few friends' relationships break down and it can be like watching a war. Most of my women friends have ended up with the children most of the time. One male friend fought like a tiger to get half and half. I wrote him a character reference, to be read out in court. He has done his children proud.

But until I met Laura, at that business where I messed up the workshop, I had never heard of a custody battle like this.

'When we met,' she told me, 'we agreed we wouldn't have children, but that changed for me. I had the biological clock ticking, and I wanted a child. He agreed reluctantly, because I think he realized he'd probably lose me. So we had our baby. I remember praying that it was going to be a boy because there would be more chance of him bonding.' The baby *was* a boy. I'll call him Aidan. 'I actually chose not to breastfeed,' she said, 'so Jon could take part in the nightly routine. He didn't, actually. He put earplugs in. I thought having a baby might bring us closer together, but it didn't.'

Since she was the breadwinner, and was being treated by her husband as a cash cow, Laura took the minimum maternity leave of four months. 'I wanted to go part-time,' she said, 'but my ex was pointing out all the outgoings, and it wasn't possible. So I'd be getting up at five, spending breakfast time with Aidan. I found a really good nanny round the corner. I did all the picking up and everything. I was still the primary carer, really. But my company was being restructured again and I was getting pushed by my husband into taking the transfer. I'm basically,' she said with a weary smile, 'getting told what to do.'

Under pressure from her husband, she took the transfer, and then another one. She was working nearly all the time and he wasn't working at all. 'He was,' she explained, 'living the ex-patriate lifestyle. Aidan was school age. Jon was just swanning about. Even though I was earning this big money, there was no money left over at the end of the month.'

One Christmas, when her mother and his parents were staying over, it all blew up. 'Jon had already bought himself a watch and booked himself a skiing holiday,' Laura told me. 'I was beginning to worry about money and I said, well, you're not getting any Christmas presents from me. On Christmas morning, we were all up, Aidan was opening his presents, and his father was in bed. He couldn't,' she said, and now her voice was flat, 'be bothered to get up.'

On New Year's Eve, they were all watching a film on TV and Jon strode in and changed the channel. 'I said something like, "Don't be an idiot, what are you doing?", thinking of our guests. He just completely lost it,' she said, 'completely. I thought: right, OK. I have tried so hard. I've put myself into jobs and locations that I wouldn't have chosen. We have a beautiful home, a beautiful son. If we can't be happy now, when will we be?'

For several weeks, they talked about whether it was possible to make it work. When Laura came back from a weekend in London, Jon handed her an envelope with a date for an interim court hearing. 'He was on legal aid,' she said, 'but he'd found a really good lawyer. In my panic, I found a shitty one. It was, basically, a war on when each paper could be stamped and dated. Luckily for me, my lawyers were just around the corner from the court and were able to get their divorce papers stamped before Jon could get his. That meant the divorce and financial hearing would be in the UK. But the child custody paper was a separate document. The family law side closed early that day, so we missed it by a matter of nanoseconds. That meant that his papers, the child stuff, were dated earlier than mine. So,' she said, in a tone of such resignation that it almost made my heart stop, 'it was a car crash.'

Jon wouldn't let her access her own papers, to prepare for the hearing. 'He locked the office in our house,' she said, 'and I actually had to call the police, because I felt quite threatened. So we turned up at the court. My lawyer turned up late. She was ill-prepared. My ex came across as the caring primary carer. They put me down as some frazzled career woman who kept changing jobs and expecting her family to follow her, but actually it was the other way round.'

When she left the court room, she phoned her mother. 'It was at that point,' she said, 'that I realized what was happening to me, and I collapsed. Some lovely people took me to the local doctors.' She broke off. Laura has such an air of calm that I almost panicked when she broke off. 'Sorry,' she said, trying to blink away her tears, 'it's quite emotional now. I was so keen to keep up my strength for my son, because I had to go back to him, have dinner with him, read him a story. I spent all afternoon in this room, just bawling my eyes out. There were some animal screams. I was actually having a breakdown. This lovely woman kept stroking my head and letting me get it out of my system, so when I went back home I was able to show up well to my son. But from there on, the nervous energy was all-consuming. I was losing weight. By June, I must have lost a couple of stone. People,' she said, and the tears were still rolling down her face, 'didn't recognize me any more.'

Laura lost custody of her son. Jon's parents coached him on how to be a 'fun dad' and it seemed to do the trick, at least in court. She has been through seven court hearings. She pays whacking fees in spousal maintenance as well as maintenance for her son. 'At one point,' she said, 'I had sixty thousand pounds of debt. I was earning this big salary, with nothing to show for it. I couldn't afford to get on the train to work. I was eating cereal for tea.'

And does she, I asked, feel any stigma for being the woman

who lost her son? Laura put her hand to her forehead. 'Oh my God. The initial reaction of people going "there must be something wrong with you, why didn't you fight for him, why didn't you camp out on the lawn?"' She shrugged. 'They just come out with it.'

For a while, I didn't know what to say. Did she, I said in the end, feel her heart was broken by this? Laura looked down and then back at me. 'Yeah. I would go over and have these fun weekends with Aidan, and I'd say goodbye and just felt like I'd lost a limb. It was,' she said, 'like he'd died.'

There are so many ways to break a heart. There are too many ways to break a heart. I have made those animal noises, when I was lying on a hospital couch and had just been told that the kind of cancer I had was the type that meant I was more likely to die. I had lost my breast. I had lost a chunk of my stomach, to replace the gap where there had been a breast. I couldn't stand upright and at night I felt as if I was being stretched on a rack. And now the doctor was telling me, in effect, that it might all be in vain because the cells that were trying to kill me might well win.

I waited for the doctor to leave the room and then the animal noises came out. I thought they were terrible noises, but I couldn't stop them coming out. One nurse removed the stitches and another nurse stroked my hair. I will never, ever forget that nurse who stroked my hair.

Six weeks before, I had been dumped by the man I saw at that private view. I thought at the time that my heart was breaking, but I didn't know then that a broken heart can keep on breaking and keep on beating, too.

There's a medical condition called 'broken heart syndrome', where the heart muscle becomes suddenly weakened or stunned. The left ventricle or chamber changes shape and makes the heart beat at an irregular pace. The syndrome was discovered by Japanese doctors in 1991. It's also found in antelopes, Arabian oryx and pronghorn sheep. The medical name for it is Takotsubo cardiomyopathy because the shape of the ventricle reminded the doctors of a special Japanese pot used to catch octopuses.

There are two main things to learn from this research:

1) You can die of a broken heart, but you probably won't.
2) Your broken heart might well turn out to be useful for something else.

Part II

Gathering

'I love those who can smile in trouble, who can
gather strength from distress'

Leonardo da Vinci

A sentimental journey

I believe in parties. If you have parties to mark the fact that people have died, I think you should certainly make an effort to mark the fact that you were born and are still alive.

I didn't think I would face my fiftieth birthday without a partner, a family, a regular income or a job. But there you are. It's no reason not to have a party.

I have a party in December almost every year. I usually give the impression it's an early Christmas party, but most of my friends know it's my birthday on 8 December. If they turn up with cards and presents – well, I'm not going to turn them away. I like parties because I like chatting, and laughing, and eating, and drinking. I like introducing people I like to each other. It's a good way of doing several of my favourite things at once.

I am, as you know, not keen on cooking. That's why most of the cookery books on that shelf in my study still look brand new. I did once go on a cookery course in Ireland for a piece I was writing for the *Independent* magazine. When I got back, I spent the whole of a Saturday afternoon sweating over a fish stew. I invited my friend Winston, who's a trained chef, to try it. He took a mouthful and frowned. Most of the white fish had fallen apart, but the octopus was still springy and raw. 'It's not a *total* disaster,' he said, but I just wanted to pour the whole pot over his head. Life, as Shirley Conran once said, is too short to stuff a mushroom and it's certainly too short to spend your precious Saturday afternoons producing something that will make your home stink for weeks of boiled fish.

I met Winston sixteen years ago at a rice and peas stall at the Elephant and Castle. We went out for a while and have been friends ever since. Winston's a brilliant cook. Stick him in a kitchen with a near-empty fridge and a couple of tins and he will still somehow create a feast. Winston has done the food for almost every party I've had since we met. He did the food for my fortieth birthday party, which was the year I first had cancer. He also paid for me to have a DJ. At one point, he got the DJ to drop a mic from the mezzanine and sang a song he had written for me, before presenting me with a giant cake slathered with cream.

Winston now lives in Yorkshire, but he still sometimes helps me with my parties. He got the Megabus down the night before this party, seared some beef and set the smoke alarm off at 1 a.m. My friend Lorna planned the rest of the menu and emailed through scans of Ottolenghi recipes. I hadn't heard of half the ingredients, but then I have (honestly) googled how to boil an egg.

Lorna turned up at lunchtime, with home-made sloe gin. All afternoon, we toiled away, bruising aubergine, blanching pine nuts and taking nips of bright pink gin. She didn't just command my tiny kitchen. She also, later, lent me her boyfriend, to let people in, take their coats and offer them drinks.

One by one they came, these people who have made me laugh, or rushed to buy me a drink or cook me a meal, or visit me in hospital, or offer me a sofa bed, or search their heads and hearts to find words to console when life has been tough. If they could get babysitters, and had partners who could come, then, like the animals in the ark, they came two by two. And every time I saw a new face arriving, I felt a flutter of joy. These people make me proud. These people are my gang.

Three months after I lost my job, I went to a wedding. It was a big, smart wedding full of successful people and I had to control my face every time someone asked me 'what do you do?' I saw a man I hadn't seen for years. He was the finance manager of the Poetry Society when I was its director. Now he was married with a family, a large house and a business that was clearly going well. Yes, I said, I still live in the same flat. No, I said, I haven't met anyone. No, I'm not at *The Independent* any more. I am, I said while trying to smile, freelance. And then I changed the subject because I didn't want to spoil the mood.

For my friends who were getting married, I did smile. I smiled because they are lovely people who deserved to find love. I smiled because Stuart, my friend Ros's new husband, had found the love of his life in his fifties and was marrying at fifty-eight, for the first time. I smiled because how could you see all this and not want to crack open the champagne?

When I was running the Poetry Society, we couldn't afford champagne. But whenever we got good news about a funding application, I'd nip out for cava and Kettle Chips. I believe in bubbles. I believe in crisps. On one staff away day, when we were doing a SWOT analysis, I asked my colleagues to suggest some weaknesses and one yelled out, 'Kettle Chips.' We all laughed, but I wanted to say that she was wrong. Kettle Chips are not a 'weakness'. They're a strength. There are, I have learnt, very few situations that can't be improved with some bubbles and some crisps.

When I started the job, I introduced a fortnightly poetry reading group. If it was sunny, we'd have it with margaritas on the roof. If it was cold or wet, we'd have it in the Poetry Café, which was also a bar. I was the licence holder for that bar. To become a licence holder, I had to do a course in Bethnal Green with pub landlords from all over the East End. In the morning, we had the teaching. In the afternoon, we had the exam. The adjudicator was a woman with a tiny dog. She wandered round the room and peered over at our answers as the dog trotted by her side. It was, thank goodness, multiple choice. In order to pass, you had to get the first ten questions right. 'I think,' she whispered kindly, 'you should have another little look at number four.'

On Friday nights at the Poetry Society, we would mark the end of the week by nipping down to the Poetry Café for a drink. We called it the 5.45. Sometimes, we had music. The finance manager was in two bands. Sometimes, we just talked and laughed and drank wine or beer and ate crisps. 'I've never had a boss,' wrote one of my colleagues on my leaving card, 'who has come back from a day off sick and confessed she'd had a hangover the day before.' That, by the way, was after the Faber summer party, which is one of the big literary parties of the year. The next day I really wasn't well. I phoned my deputy to tell her that I couldn't go in, and was touched when people kept phoning with suggestions for hangover remedies. I tried to tell them how grateful I was, but it was quite hard to speak with my face pressed against the mat on the bathroom floor.

I've actually only had a handful of hangovers in my life. I have hardly ever been drunk. When I went to the lupus clinic after the pain in my knees came back, the rheumatologist asked me if I smoked. I said no. She asked me if I drank. 'Oh yes,' I said. 'I love it!' She wrote a letter to my GP which said 'Ms Patterson is a heavy social drinker'. I felt a bit embarrassed, but I suppose that's exactly what I am. I don't drink for consolation, or Dutch courage. I rarely drink on my own. I drink because there's something about being with someone I like that makes me want to raise a glass.

I always thought wine was invented by the Romans. It's one of the many reasons I'm pleased to have been born in Rome. Apparently it wasn't. Apparently some of the earliest wine was made 7000 years ago in Iran. It makes it all the more unfair that you can't actually drink it in Iran. In Iran, you can be publicly lashed, or even executed, for drinking wine. In Iran, it's a 'crime of God' to drink wine. I think it's a 'crime of God', or of a government pretending to be a kind of God, that you can't.

I fell in love with Iran. I loved the pottery from 9000 years ago, carved with scorpions, snakes and fish. I loved the Sumerian tablet from 6000 years ago, covered with one of the oldest alphabets in the world. I loved the parks and gardens full of cypress trees and roses, where teenagers pretend to study as they swap shy smiles. I loved the ruins of the palace at Persepolis, which was burnt to the ground by Alexander the Great, and the carved stone showing Scythians in pointy hats. I loved Isfahan, and its square that's three times the size of St Mark's Square in Venice, smaller only than Tiananmen Square in Beijing. And I loved Shiraz. At the tomb of Hafez, Persia's greatest poet, I watched men and women weep as they recited his poems and I had to wipe away a few tears, too. But I didn't like being in Shiraz and not being able to have a glass of Shiraz.

I love Shiraz. I love Rioja. I love Marlborough Sauvignon and Viognier and Vermentino and Gavi and Chablis and Chilean Chardonnay and Pinot Noir. I love sipping delicious wine with a delicious meal. But most of all, I love sipping wine with crisps. I know it's not very sophisticated, but I really, really love crisps. I eat so many crisps that one boyfriend used to call me Crispina.

At a push, I'll grab a bag of Walkers, ready salted or salt and vinegar. They're not in the premier league, but they fit the job description of a crisp because they're salty and they're crisp. Then I discovered Kettle Chips. Potatoes grown in rough earth by a jolly red-faced farmer and sliced up in his rustic kitchen by his jolly red-faced wife. Then chucked in a copper kettle full of bubbling oil until they are – well, crisp. Of course I know that's not how they're really made, but I don't want to think about big, ugly factories when I'm biting on a deep-fried sliver of potato any more than I want to think about a slaughter house when I'm eating a bacon bap. Kettle Chips. Tyrrell's crisps. 'Handcooked English crisps', according to the packet. Whatever else is happening in the world, I think we can all now agree that we are thoroughly spoilt for crisps.

How do I love them? Let me count the ways. I love the colour of them, golden like a holiday, of sand and sea and sun. I love the shape of them: the soft curves, the curls, the sudden slopes. Crisps, for me, are like snowflakes. No two are the same. If

William Blake saw a world in a grain of sand, why can't you see it in a crisp? I love the sudden shock of salt when you've felt that itch on your tongue. I love the snap and crackle and crunch. Crisps make me think of celebration. They make me think of parties and wine and fun.

To 'celebrate', according to the Oxford Dictionary, is to 'honour with rites and rejoicings'. I think there's a lot to be said for 'rites and rejoicings'. Birthdays in our family, for example, always started with the sound of singing. There would be a knock on your bedroom door, the opening notes of 'Happy Birthday' and the whole family would troop in. My mother would carry the tray with the presents. My father would carry the tray with the coffee and candles. You'd open your cards and presents as you drank your coffee and ripped the purple wrapper off a Fry's Turkish Delight. I always wondered why every birthday of my childhood started with the sweet taste of pink jelly. A few years ago I asked my mother if it had a special meaning. For a moment, she looked baffled. 'I think,' she said in the end, 'that Dad just liked Turkish Delight.'

Swedes love their rituals. At formal Swedish dinners, you're not meant to take a sip of your drink unless you catch someone's eye and make a toast. They also love singing songs. When my mother and I went to Sweden a few years ago, we went to see my uncle and aunt. My aunt invited some elderly neighbours round for dinner. There were seven of us round that table, including my eldest cousin. On the table were sheets of paper covered with words in Swedish I didn't understand. I sent a panicked signal to my mother, but she just smiled. As soon as she sat down, Auntie Lisbeth picked up her sheet of paper and indicated that we should pick ours up, too. Between courses, it was clear, we would sing Swedish folk songs. I'm not sure that I'd recommend singing songs you don't know in a language you don't speak with your uncle, aunt and their elderly neighbours when you're forty-five. But I knew that my aunt wanted to celebrate the fact that her sister was there, so I sang along anyway.

I think you should celebrate birthdays and anniversaries and leaving jobs. I think you should celebrate new books and new babies and new romances and new starts. I think you should celebrate the end of the working day and the start of the week-end. I think you should celebrate – and the scientific evidence backs this up – because thinking about good things makes you feel better.

A few years ago I was eating pizza in an Italian piazza when I got a call from the deputy editor of the paper. He said that the editor wanted me to come back from holiday and write the lead piece on the wedding of Prince William to Kate Middleton. I was tempted to say that the wedding had been planned for quite a while and so, by the way, had my holiday. But if the editor of a newspaper asks you to do something, he isn't really asking a question. So I went to an internet café, and booked a Ryanair flight home.

I've got mixed feelings about the royal family. Of course it's ridiculous to have an aristocracy, and baronets, and dukes and duchesses and princes and princesses and queens. It's ridiculous that a country can be ruled, or theoretically ruled, by whatever scrap of flesh and brain pops out of someone's womb. But the 'ruling monarch' of this country doesn't really rule the country.

And I'd rather have lovely, dutiful Elizabeth theoretically in charge than a Mugabe or Putin. I'm not mad about Charles. He seems a bit of a fusspot. But William seems nice enough and Harry seems like fun. And boy, have those boys been through the mill.

I was nervous as I wandered round the crowds and as I stood in Trafalgar Square and watched the wedding on a giant screen. I was even more nervous when I went back to the office and tried to fill the space on the page as the clock ticked. I'm not a news journalist. I hadn't done this kind of reporting before, and certainly not for the front-page story on one of the biggest events of the year. But I was pleased to do it, because what I saw that day, behind all the fuss, was that a young man who learnt about death when he was far too young, and who had had to walk behind a coffin in front of the eyes of the world, had swapped his sadness for joy. Who could begrudge a giant party for that?

On my fiftieth birthday, when I'd finished clearing up from the night before, I opened my presents. One friend had bought me a history of opera. When I was a child, I hated opera. The wails coming out of my father's 'wireless' as he gardened made me think of a cat that was having its organs taken out, one by one. I wasn't surprised to hear a few years ago that police in Sweden had broken down the door of a woman they thought was being viciously attacked, but who was just practising her scales. Perhaps we all turn into our parents, because as an adult, I have learnt to love opera. I've interviewed several opera singers and every time has felt like a massive treat. Bryn Terfel, for example, has a speaking voice like a mixture of whisky and the darkest, most expensive chocolate you can buy. Sitting three feet away from me in a tiny 'interview room' at the Royal Opera House, he was so magnetic that he had me fumbling with my tape recorder as I felt my cheeks flush. I wasn't surprised, when I saw his Flying Dutchman, that his voice on stage was like the voice of God.

My friend Arifa Akbar gave me a book called *The Modern Art Cookbook*. It has paintings by Matisse and Picasso and Van Gogh and Duncan Grant. It has a poem about oysters by Seamus Heaney. It has an extract from Joyce's *The Dubliners*, about peas. There's Frida Kahlo's recipe for red snapper and Cézanne's for baked tomatoes. I'm not likely to follow the recipes, but oh, what a feast of food and writing and art!

My friend Paul Brandford gave me a book called *The Vanity of Small Differences* by Grayson Perry. It's about taste and art and class and how we live now. There were two inscriptions at the beginning, one by Grayson Perry and one by his alter-ego, Claire. I was so excited to have a book signed by Grayson Perry, and only a little bit disappointed to find out that both inscriptions had been written by Paul.

It wasn't clear at first who had given me the two leather-bound volumes of Laurence Sterne's *A Sentimental Journey*. Ever since reading *The Life and Opinions of Tristram Shandy*, as part of my MA on 'The Novel', I've been a big fan of Sterne. I've stayed in the house he used to live in, in a village in Yorkshire, Shandy Hall. When Michael Winterbottom made a film of *Tristram Shandy*, I was invited to the world premiere in the village hall. The film was called *Cock and Bull*. There was a real bull outside the village hall and a competition to guess its weight. There was also one to guess the name of a big ceramic cock. I wrote a feature about the film, and the drinks in the pub afterwards, and the villagers, and the cock and the bull. It was one of my first features for *The Independent*'s arts pages, and I still think it was probably the one that was the most fun to do.

A Sentimental Journey was written and published by Sterne in 1768, as he was facing death. It's often seen as an epilogue to *Tristram Shandy* and describes his travels through Italy and France. It's a 'sentimental' journey, because it's a journey with feelings, an early example of travel writing that allows the writer to bring him or herself into whatever it is they see. It's partly because of Laurence Sterne that journalists like me could bring personal feelings into, for example, travel pieces about trips to Iran.

The leather-bound volumes were, it turned out, from my friend and former *Independent* colleague Chris Schuler. When I opened them, I gasped. The books were printed just ten years after Sterne died and were nearly 250 years old.

'I pity the man', says the narrator of *A Sentimental Journey*, Yorick, 'who can travel from Dan to Beersheba, and cry, 'Tis all barren – and so it is; and so is all the world to him who will not cultivate the fruits it offers.'

Well, I'll drink to that. How can you not want to 'cultivate' all the 'fruits' the world offers? How can you not want to drink in the beauty of the world, and its art, and its landscapes, and its wine? I'll drink to thoughtful, kind, generous friends. And I'll drink to the fact that the bastards didn't actually kill you, even if they sometimes seem to have tried.

Coffee and cake

My mother took me out for tea at the Savoy. We've been there for tea a few times over the years, but if you can't go to the Savoy for your fiftieth birthday, I don't know when you can.

Actually, I don't just go to the Savoy on special occasions. My friend Tina and I used to call it our 'local', even though I live in Stoke Newington and she lives in Tooting Bec. At the time, she had a rich husband and would have a champagne cocktail. I didn't, and would have a glass of house white. The thing about the Savoy is the surroundings. Where else can you sit in luxury for a fiver? The thing about the Savoy is the free snacks. At first you feel as if the person who serves you is going to phone your bank manager before you're allowed to sit down. But once you're safely settled, they're all charm. Would madam like another drink? Well, yes, now you mention it, madam would. Would madam like some more nibbles? Madam would always, always like some more nibbles. And so you can sit there all evening, gorge on hand-cooked crisps and salted nuts and olives, and gaze at the rich people. It's always fascinating to watch rich people. They seem to have a sheen, as if they have been dipped in something shiny, but there's something about the corner of their mouths that make you think that it might be quite an effort for them to smile.

Most people having a drink or tea at the Savoy aren't actually all that rich. That's what I love about posh hotels. They're democratic. Anyone can have a taste of that luxury for the price of a glass of wine or a cup of tea. Sure, it's usually quite a pricey glass of wine or cup of tea, but have you *seen* the prices at Starbucks? You clutch a paper bucket if you want to, but I'll stick with bone china and glass.

I have only ever stayed in posh hotels for what's loosely called work. When I was first asked to write for the travel desk at *The Independent*, I had fantasies of sleeping on planks and getting lost in the Serengeti, as Martha Gellhorn said she did in *Travels with Myself and Another*. I wasn't expecting to be sent off to spas. When I was told that the editor liked travel pieces to be about luxury, because it was all about 'aspiration', I was shocked. But if that's what the editor wants, that's what the editor gets, so I soon learnt to overcome my embarrassment about sleeping (alone) in beds the size of rooms, beds sometimes covered in giant hearts made out of rose petals or towels folded into swans. Partly because I didn't have a partner or a family, I spent many of my holidays on press trips for the travel pages, and sometimes for other publications, too. There is a small price to be paid. You do have to make a lot of small talk to a lot of hotel managers and you don't usually get to choose how you spend your time. But oh, the gains! I think on my death bed I will be grateful for the extraordinary, thrilling privilege of trips to Cambodia, and China, and Zambia, and Thailand, and Syria, and Prague and Iran.

One trip was to South Africa. Like every visitor to that country, I was upset by the contrasts between the townships and the comfort and luxury of so many white South Africans' lives.

On the last day, I went to Robben Island to see the cell where Nelson Mandela had spent so much of his life. Afterwards, our little group had tea at the Mount Nelson. Tea at the Mount Nelson is even more lavish than tea at the Savoy. As I piled my plate with dainty little sandwiches, and delicate sponges dusted with sugar, I remembered what Samuel, our guide, had told us. He's one of South Africa's four million 'coloureds'. He grew up knowing that there were places he would never be allowed to go to. But then Mandela made his long walk to freedom and then many of his fellow citizens did, too. When Samuel got his job as a tour guide, he saved up and took his mother for tea at the Mount Nelson. 'Son,' she told him, wiping away tears, 'I never thought I'd see the day.'

My mother took me for tea at the Savoy because we both love treats, and we both love cakes. In Sweden, when you serve a cup of coffee, you usually serve it with a little cake. My mother has a special way with cakes. She always has a good supply in her larder and when she pauses for her cup of morning coffee, she will lay out a small tray with her cup and a few little cakes. She will then sit down with her newspaper and take a sip of her coffee. After a few minutes, she will take a tiny nibble of her cake. She will read a few more paragraphs before she takes another sip of her coffee and carry on like this for about half an hour. If she has finished the coffee before the cake is finished, she will leave what's left of the cake. Yes, she really will leave what's left of the cake. Not if I'm there, obviously. If I'm there, I'll wolf down my cake in a few swift mouthfuls and then wolf down what's left of hers.

Whenever my mother and I meet, we always have coffee and

cake. When I see her in Guildford, we have coffee and cake. When we meet in London, we have coffee and cake. Even tea and cake feels as if something's slightly wrong. Once, we met for lunch at the café bit of the Wolseley and shocked the waiter by ordering coffee and cake just before our lunch. Don't get me wrong. My mother's not greedy. After a few mouthfuls of anything, she will clutch her stomach and announce she's full. I'm the greedy one. At home I don't always eat all that much, but when I'm with other people I just want to grab it all – the food, the company, the conversation – and gulp it down.

In the years since my father died, my mother and I have been on quite a few holidays and weekends away. In Bruges, we loved the canals, and the little bridges, and the bright colours of the Flemish art. But, most of all, we loved the fact that when you ordered a cup of coffee, you got a couple of tiny cakes.

In Stockholm, we had *vaterbrod*, which we used to eat at the *sommarstugan* or 'summer cottage' we went to every summer, and *pepperkakor*, the ginger biscuits you have to break into three pieces to get a wish. We had waffles at Drottningholm, and pastries at the outdoor museum called Skansen. We went to the opera house, and saw the opera of Queen Christina. I didn't understand much of the Swedish, or much of the plot, but every time a character sang 'Christina', my mother clutched my arm.

In Vienna, where I took her for a weekend for a travel piece, we had *truffeltorte* at the Gerstner café. We had *maroniblüte* at Freud's favourite café, Café Landtmann. We had *sachertorte* at the Hotel Sacher. We stayed at the Hotel Sacher. We were both quite excited to be staying in a hotel that had given its name to a cake.

*

My father didn't share my mother's passion for cakes, but he certainly liked his food. He would sit down at the kitchen table, after a long day in the office and a long commute home, pile a giant mouthful of whatever my mother had cooked on to his fork, put it in his mouth and sigh. It was a sigh of contentment. Now he could eat the lovely food in front of him and perhaps go out to the garden. My father had high-level jobs in the civil service, but when he was at home he relaxed. It's me and my mother who toil away pretty much all the time.

My father loved his garden. He would kneel on a little leather pad and listen to Radio 3 on his 'wireless' as he snipped and trimmed and hacked. He loved the sight of green shoots bursting up through earth, and of tiny buds opening into flowers. When I bought my first flat, an ex-local authority place on an early Victorian street that was basically a big council estate, he helped me with my patch of garden. My flat used to be the attic. The garden was so far away it felt like an allotment and I was often too lazy to go down and water the flowers. But my father put up a trellis and made me a patio. He planted clematis and ceanothus and marguerites. He made me a little sanctuary in a grimy patch of South London, because he loved flowers and because he loved me.

My father was with me when I went to see the flat I live in now. 'I don't think,' he said, 'that you could do better,' and on what I was earning he was probably right. I don't have my own garden, but there is a shared garden. Like the garden of the cottage in Sweden, it has silver birches. When my parents bought the house in Guildford my mother still lives in, my father planted five silver birches in the front garden. They were, he said, to remind my mother of Sweden. One tree for every member of the family.

Every summer, we would get up early to drive to Tilbury and then get a ferry to Gothenburg in a journey that took two days. My brother, sister and I would be wedged between packets of cornflakes and cans of baked beans. Food was, said my mother, far too expensive in Sweden, so she would do a big shop and cram as much in the car as she could. On the ferry to Gothenburg, we would eat the cheese sandwiches she had prepared as we gazed at blond families piling their plates high with meatballs, or salmon, and chips. Once, a man saw us staring at his three blond children drinking cans of Coke. He offered to buy us each one. My father thought that would be extravagant, but he said he could buy us one to share. So we sat there, each with a straw poking out of the single hole, like piglets sucking at a teat.

At the cottage in Sweden, when we had visits from relatives, we were allowed to drink *läsk*, little bottles of fizzy drink that tasted of orange or apple or pear. Throughout my childhood, fizzy drinks were a treat. On Saturday nights, when we were watching TV, my mother would walk in with a bowl of peanuts and a bottle of R. Whites Lemonade, as if it was caviar and Château Lafite. We would have to wait a week for the next fizzy drink and the next episode of *Starsky and Hutch* or *War and Peace*. What I was taught as a child, which I seem to have forgotten, was that things you want don't always happen straight away.

We'd travel back from Sweden sitting on flat packs of Ikea furniture. I went to the first ever Ikea, in Småland, when I was still a baby, on the way to visit Auntie Lisbeth and Uncle Hans.

As a toddler, I'd play hide and seek while my mother gazed at tables and armchairs and sofas she couldn't squeeze into the car. We'd have meatballs. All year, we'd look forward to those meatballs. Apart from a hotdog by the beach, it was the only meal we had out. Those childhood trips to Ikea left me with a love of meatballs, a love of furniture, and a love of Scandinavian design.

When I want to cheer myself up, I often go to Ikea. It used to mean a trip to Croydon or Neasden, and the crawl in traffic managed to kill off an awful lot of the pleasure. Now I can just nip up to Tottenham in about quarter of an hour. I know a lot of people don't find Ikea all that relaxing. One friend of mine had such a screaming row with her husband in the car park that the people around them ended up calling the police. When you see a diagram of an item of furniture in pieces and another diagram of it assembled, with no steps in between, or when you get to the last leg of a table and find that final screw missing, you do feel like calling 999 and yelling for a man in a uniform to come and sort it out. But most of the time I find Ikea like a soothing bath. First, I have coffee and cake. Later, I have meatballs and chips. In the time between snacks, I look at sofas, and armchairs, and desks, and incredibly cheap candles or boxes, which I then have to buy, and find myself almost tempted to hum a Swedish folk song.

My desk is from Ikea. My big sofa is from Ikea. Lots of my furniture isn't. There is, for example, the bergere suite, with cane back and sides, which I saw in a street in Camden, snapped up and had covered and repaired. And there's the pre-Civil War chest. I saw it when I went to the literary festival at Hay-on-Wye just after I'd bought my first flat. I knew it would be ridiculous to buy it. It was £430 and I didn't even have money for a bed. That night, I dreamt about the chest and the following day I went back and bought it anyway. I had to sleep on a mattress on the floor for ages, and get a clothes rail instead of a wardrobe, but I honestly think my life would be poorer without that chest.

When I'm at home, trying to meet a deadline, or sending emails that may or may not be answered, I spend a lot of my time wandering to and from the kettle. Almost every time I pass that chest, I think: what a lovely chest! Almost every time I see my bergere suite, I think how much I like the mix of gentle curves in mahogany with cane. And almost every time I see the gnarled old dairy table in my hallway, I want to run my fingers over its beautiful grooves.

When my friend told me about Airbnb, I looked at other people's listings for their homes and saw they nearly all had Nespresso machines. So I bought one. I bought pretty much the cheapest one, but the coffee it makes is *delicious*. I make it in those little Italian glass cups with the metal handles, so you can see the *crema* at the top. One of the best moments of my working day is when I take my first sip of my first coffee. Every day I love that first sip. And I love the sight of the flowers – the tulips, or daffodils, or roses – that I nearly always have on my desk.

Every day, even on a bad day, there are small pleasures scattered throughout the day, small pleasures that you could, if you wanted, make yourself notice and count up.

When I see my mother, we always talk about the news. We talk about our own news, of course. She tells me about her book groups, and her coffee parties, and her lectures at the University of the Third Age. She tells me what her friends are up to, and who she has seen, and who she hasn't seen, and the places she has been to, and the gardens or houses she has visited. My mother has a constant pile of books to read for her book groups. She has a constant pile of papers to catch up on. My mother is interested in everything. She regards a cancelled coffee morning as a gift from God, because it gives her more time to catch up with all the things she wants to do and see and read. She doesn't want to go to bed at night because she doesn't want to miss anything. This is probably why I feel the same.

But when I say we talk about the news, I mean the real news. My mother follows the news so much you would think she was on standby to edit *Newsnight*. She reads the whole paper every day. She used to read *The Independent*, of course, but when I left, she switched to *The Times*. She has TVs and radios in every room of the house and catches up with the news almost every hour. It's almost as if she's trying to catch them out. Well, Mr Edwards, at six o'clock you said this, and now you seem to have changed your tune. I would like to hear my mother argue with John Humphrys. I don't think he'd get away with half as much.

At my fiftieth birthday tea at the Savoy, we talked about what I'd been up to, of course. My mother gave me a card, which had a photograph of me on Sky News. She said in the card that she thought *The Independent*'s management were 'fools'. My mother has a lot of respect for authority. If a doctor tells her to do something, she'll do it. So when my mother calls your former bosses 'fools', you wouldn't want to be one of them, and cross her path.

I told my mother about my party, and the food, and the

friends, and the presents. I told her about the book I was reviewing, and the pieces I was working on for the *Sunday Times*
magazine. I told her about the conference I'd just spoken at and
the workshops I'd run at a university. I told her about the parties
I'd been to, and the interesting people I'd met. And as I told her
these things, I realized that I hadn't thought that things were
getting better, but they were.

A kind of sustaining grace

Paula Rego has been described as 'the best painter of women's experience alive'. Her paintings are full of women who cry, and rage, and fight, and struggle. When I interviewed her for *The Independent*, just before I left, she said that in a painting, you can 'punish the people you don't like, who have been naughty to you'. At the time, it didn't occur to me that you might want to 'punish' anyone.

I was pleased, a few weeks after my fiftieth birthday, when an editor from the *Sunday Times* magazine told me that they were going to run an interview with her, and that she had asked for the interview to be done by me. Her studio in North London still looked, from the outside, like the kind of place you might find the rotting remains of a corpse. Once you go inside, you find skeletons, naked bodies, monkeys, rats and skulls. You find, in fact, life-sized versions of the figures that live in her head.

Paula Rego told me that she had met her husband at a party, and he had asked her to 'take off your knickers', and she did. She told me that she had had nine abortions because she thought using contraception might ruin his sexual pleasure. She told me that when she was a child, her mother used to rub her 'down there'. All of this was surprising, but for me the most surprising thing was that this woman, who was still quite frail after having breast cancer, and who had serious arthritis and a medical condition called diverticulitis, was still, at nearly eighty, coming to her studio six days a week.

She has been shortlisted for the Turner Prize, made a Dame of the British Empire and had a museum in Portugal specially built for her work, but she told me that her art was 'always disappointing'. Her paintings sometimes sell for half a million pounds, but when she finished one, she just felt cross. 'I never,' she said, and she looked really sad when she said it, 'do it properly.'

Most artists I've interviewed would say the same. When I asked Howard Hodgkin if he could look on his work with pride, he told me about the time he had been around an exhibition with the painter Patrick Caulfield. It was a retrospective of Caulfield's work. 'He just kept saying,' said Hodgkin, and tears slid down his cheeks as he remembered it, '"not enough, not enough".'

It was Beckett, in his novella *Worstward Ho*, who told us to 'fail better'. There's now a lot of research to show that failure is central to success. The American basketball player Michael Jordan, for example, has said: 'I've missed more than 9000 shots in my career. I've lost almost 300 games. Twenty-six times, I've been trusted to take the game winning shot and missed. I've failed over and over and over again in my life. And that is why I succeed.' James Dyson came up with 5127 prototypes before he developed the vacuum cleaner that made his name. The psychologist Carol Dweck talks about the importance of failure in her book *Mindset: The New Psychology of Success*. Most artists and writers I know would rather eat their own liver than go near a book like this, but they know this anyway. It's because they have learnt from their failures that their work rises above the rest.

Art may console us, but it doesn't necessarily console the people who make it. I love Philip Larkin, but his letters show that he wasn't Pollyanna. Seamus Heaney quotes Larkin's poem 'The Trees' in an essay he wrote about Howard Hodgkin's work. 'The trees are coming into leaf', the poem begins, 'Like something almost being said'. It isn't, the poem says, that the trees don't die. They die too. But every year, while they're alive, they get new leaves. It's the last two lines of the poem that always make my heart stop:

> Last year is dead, they seem to say,
> Begin afresh, afresh, afresh.

Among the paintings Hodgkin showed me was one that seemed to have the same theme as the poem. It's called *And the Skies Are Not Cloudy All Day*. One of the many good things about art is that it reminds us that they are not.

I used to read poetry and fiction all the time. For my last few years at *The Independent* I was so busy catching up with current affairs and researching my next interview that I never seemed to have time to read books for pleasure. A couple of months after I left, I bumped into the literary editor of the *Sunday Times*. I used to review for him before I started working at *The Independent*. 'Right,' he said, when I told him what had happened. 'You're going to review for us now.'

Book reviews don't make you rich – unless you're a very fast reader, which I'm not. The reward is what happens on the page. When I had my fling with the man I met at that conference, I was reading a novel by the American novelist Elizabeth Strout. He wasn't very pleased that we didn't get to eat until after midnight because I was still sweating over my review. I wasn't either. I've been reviewing books for nearly twenty-five years and I still find it hard. But I am so grateful to have read those books.

Strout's novel *The Burgess Boys* is set in a small town in Maine, but the way she writes reminds us that there's nothing small about the human heart. The story that unfolds – of clashing cultures, clashing siblings, good intentions and quiet disappointments – felt so truthful that it sometimes made me gasp. She brings the same sympathetic gaze to every character, and every life. 'I think', says one of her characters, 'there is no perfect way to live a life.'

I read Siri Hustvedt's *The Blazing World* when I was sleeping in my study. I had rented out my bedroom to a friend of a friend for a month, and was sleeping on a narrow couch and using a filing cabinet to store my clothes. *The Blazing World* is a brilliant, blistering novel about what it takes to be an artist. Which, the novel makes clear, is an awful lot.

I read Miriam Toews's *All My Puny Sorrows* when I was staying with my mother, after I'd rented out my flat. The novel is about a woman whose sister has begged her to help her die. It's about screaming at strangers in car parks because you don't know what to do with your anger, and then getting drunk and having a one-night stand with your mother's mechanic. It is, to echo the opening of *Lady Chatterley's Lover*, which the central character quotes in her final letter to her sister, about how 'no matter how many skies have fallen', you've 'got to live'.

*

We all have friends who turn up in our lives at a pivotal moment, friends who shift something in the air around us, so that the landscape looks different. For me, one of those friends is Maura Dooley. She literally set my life on a different path.

We met when I was twenty-six. I had just been through a very rough eighteen months. I was in serious pain. I couldn't walk without wanting to cry. I had been told I had lupus, but all the treatments I had tried had failed. I still believed in God, but I hated him. I had told him to 'fuck off' and out of my life. I had lost my job, my health, my faith and now my Christian community. I tried to smile and look as if everything was fine as I dragged myself around, but I felt like the little mermaid, walking on knives.

I had, at least, found a good GP. The first time I saw her, I was in for nearly an hour. She asked me if I felt like Job. GPs don't usually ask you if you feel like Job. I told her that I did. If I hadn't yet had the plagues and the locusts, I had certainly had the boils. The GP referred me to a psychotherapist. At first I found therapy weird and embarrassing, but after a few months the twisting pains in my knees started to feel less sharp. I knew I would have to find a way to earn a living, even if I was still in pain. I saw an ad for a proofreader for *Loot*, a magazine selling second-hand cars. I also saw an ad asking for someone to work at the Southbank Centre, doing 'literary PR'. Luckily, I had the interview at the Southbank Centre first.

Maura started the literature programme at the Southbank Centre, and revived the Poetry International festival started there in 1963 by the theatre director Patrick Garland and Ted Hughes.

Maura is a poet and she looks like a poet. I don't mean she looks like Byron or Keats, but she has wild curls and big brown eyes, and when I saw her at the interview I couldn't help thinking: this is what a poet should look like. Maura has read more poetry than anyone I've met. She's brilliant and she's erudite, but she's also warm and funny. When she phoned me to let me know that I'd got the job, I felt like someone who had been trying to stay afloat in an icy sea but had been spotted by a passing boat and lifted to dry land.

The job was a part-time freelance role for two days a week. I could drive to work, in the seventeen-year-old Ford Fiesta my mother had lent me, park in the underground car park and get the lift right up to the office. At first it was difficult to get around, but as the months passed, I was able to move more. When Maura's deputy left, I applied for her job and got it. Now I was actually organizing and presenting literary events and not just promoting them. Through Maura, in fact, I got one of the things Freud thought was necessary for a successful, happy life: work you believe in and love. I had the opportunity to meet some of the greatest writers and poets of the twentieth century. I met almost every living writer I had heard of. I had dinner with Martin Amis, and Doris Lessing, and Salman Rushdie and Derek Walcott and Octavio Paz. I got to read poetry and literature I would never have read before. And when Maura left, and was no longer my boss, I gained a friendship that has so far lasted for quarter of a century.

Maura's poems are like her. They are subtle and tender and intelligent and complex, but they are also often witty and surprisingly down to earth. In her poems, you get a glimpse of a life in a handbag, a handkerchief or a snow storm. In her poem 'Up on the Roof', for example, she writes about a conversation on a roof while gazing at the stars.

> I cannot name the dust of starlight, the pinheaded planets,
> but I can join the dots to make a farming tool,
> the belt of a god: all any of us needs is work,
> mystery, a little time alone up on the roof.

I couldn't put it better. I couldn't, in fact, put it a fraction as well. We all need work. We all need a sense of what we don't know and we all need time to gaze at the stars. For a poet, a writer, or an artist, 'work' is what you produce. It may or may not be how you earn your living – very few poets actually earn a living from writing poems – but it is certainly the fruit of your labour. And it *is* labour. As Siri Hustvedt made clear in *The Blazing World*, creating anything you could call art takes massive effort. Picasso's scrawled lines on a napkin may have looked easy, but that's because no one had seen the decades of practice that brought those lines alive.

'I can't remember not writing,' Maura told me. 'I loved rhyme as a child. I think most children do. It was pleasure more than refuge. I wasn't an angst-ridden teenager in my room.' We were in the sitting room of the house in South London where I have spent so many happy evenings with her, her partner David and their two very lovely daughters. It's common to talk about a 'book-lined room', but theirs is a book-lined house. I have never seen so many books in one home – and I've got a fair few in mine.

Maura won a poetry competition when she was ten and first

started getting her poems published as a teenager. Since then, she has edited several poetry anthologies and published six poetry collections, two of them shortlisted for the T. S. Eliot Prize, poetry's version of the Booker. In all our years of friendship, I have never actually talked to Maura in detail about her work, and decided the time had come. So was there, I asked, a moment when she thought 'I am a poet'?

Maura glanced down at the pulsating red bar on my phone and laughed. 'No,' she said, 'I've never thought that. I remember some years back, my mother bought me a set of perfume and a mirror called "Poet" and she was so thrilled to find it. In the US, I've noticed there's a beer called "Poet". There's also a paint shade called "Poet". It's a sort of wafty notion, a Farrow & Ball shade.'

I'm a fan of Farrow & Ball. A few years ago I got my kitchen cupboards painted in Farrow & Ball's 'Lamp Room Grey'. But poetry is not Farrow & Ball. I've interviewed some of the world's leading poets and very few of them talk about being poets. They talk about writing poems. Art is about making something, not being something. If you want to make something well, you have to practise it a lot. Like all good writers and artists, Maura spent years learning her craft. And writing a poem is, for her and pretty much all the other poets I've interviewed, still hard work.

It often starts, she explained, 'with a bit of an idea, or a sensation going on up here,' and she patted her head, 'in your brain. In my case, on the right-hand side of it. Something begins to fizz a bit, and then you start to write things down. That,' she said with a rueful smile, 'is the easy bit. Then all the drafting begins, the endless drafting. There's the getting of it down and

once you've done that there's quite a long process, endless agonizing over commas and line breaks and full stops and whether
or not you're saying the same thing twice. I'm not saying it's like
doing a crossword puzzle, but it's the same kind of concentrated
looking to find what will work and fit.'

Some poems, she said, take years to finish. Most take several
months. Many people who read a poem have no idea how long it
might have taken to write. 'The thing about poetry,' she said,
'because it's short, if you do pick up an anthology, you're buf-
feted with all these emotions and perceptions that writers over
centuries have found. It is absolutely extraordinary that in a
sonnet – fourteen lines – you can experience such a different
outlook on the world. You can experience so many shoes in
which to stand.'

So how, I asked her, does the task of writing poetry relate to
her life? Maura took a sip of her tea as she thought. 'Well, it's
not passing the time! To be a writer is supposed to be a vocation
– and rather like saying "yes, I am a poet", there's something
slightly absurd, it seems to me, in claiming that it is my vocation.
But I do think that writing poetry is part of my purpose in life.
It's what I want to be doing.'

And what about this question of being 'difficult'? Quite a few
people seem to think contemporary poetry is hard to understand,
just because it doesn't always rhyme or scan. 'Poetry,' said Maura,
'more than any other art form, suffers from being accused of
being difficult. Part of that difficulty lies in the fact that, in order
to unlock some poems, you need, as a reader, to come to them
and work at it a bit. I want my work to be readily understood at
a reading, but to then reward the reader with much more subse-

quently. That's why they take so long to write because there's the endless weaving in of what you hope will be a sustaining kind of grace.'

I first met Paul Brandford at Shandy Hall, the place where Laurence Sterne wrote *Tristram Shandy*. He's a friend of Patrick Wildgust, the visionary curator of Shandy Hall and the man who organized that world premiere of *Cock and Bull* in the village hall. Paul told me that he was an artist, and that his work was 'very good'. I attacked him for his arrogance. We have been friends ever since. Every few months, we meet to go round an exhibition and then, of course, have a drink. Paul teaches workshops and gives tours at the Royal Academy. He has given me private tours of David Hockney, and the Summer Exhibition and Anish Kapoor. He always makes me look at an artist's work with fresh eyes.

Paul grew up in Welwyn Garden City. His father worked for the company that made Polyfilla and his mother worked in a factory packaging drugs. His parents weren't keen on books and art, he told me as we sipped red wine in paper cups in his Hackney studio. He decided to do an arts foundation course because he 'didn't want to do the academic stuff' and was sent a list of galleries to visit before he started. It was a trip to the National Gallery that changed his life. 'Manet, Corot, Degas, that nineteenth-century stuff,' he said, 'where the language of paint was breaking away from the illusionism. Just walking around there for the very first time, I thought "fucking hell, this is what can be done". In a way, that's all I've been doing since, just finding out what can be done.'

His parents weren't thrilled with his career choice. 'I think,' he said with the cheeky grin that always cheers me up, 'my dad probably wanted me to be some sort of sportsman. Being an artist was probably the reverse of that. Not manly enough. I do love sport. As you know, I'm an Arsenal fan.' I nodded wearily. Show me a man who isn't. 'But art,' he said, 'is a tough business. You take many rejections. Most people aren't interested. You have to have some sort of belief that drags you through the hard times. It's not an easy choice.'

That's one of the reasons I have come to admire Paul so much. In art, it's nearly all rejection. You do it because you have to do it, not because you're expecting rounds of applause. Mind you, Paul has won prizes. He's had pictures in the Summer Exhibition and major exhibitions of his work. By the time he asked me to write a piece for his website, I agreed with his assessment of his work. He *is* a 'very good' artist. He paints fierce, subtle, haunting portraits of politicians, dictators and people in authority, paintings full of energy and rage. In the face of Tony Blair, for example, you can just about see the eyes, but what you really see is paint and shadow and a terrible blankness. In *Dying for a Piss*, you see soldiers urinating on Afghan corpses. These are paintings about politics and power and they bring to mind what the German Jewish philosopher Hannah Arendt said about the 'banality of evil'.

Like all good artists, he draws nourishment from the greats. 'The Rembrandt thing at the National Gallery,' he said, 'I went about twelve times. Trying to get to grips with how they're made, or maybe just how they affect you. You can never put your finger on the thing, which means it's still alive. Somehow, it's weirdly compulsive, because you don't get to the bottom of it. You'll never get to the bottom of it. It's like an addiction. Is it a career? It's probably more of an addiction than a career.'

It takes, he thinks, 'a couple of decades to get some degree of quality in your work'. A couple of decades of toiling, and trying, and failing, and toiling, and trying and failing again. 'If I'm starting a large painting,' he said, 'what I'd like to do is give it four or five days in a row. If it's going badly, you try not to leave the room until you've rescued it to some extent. You might create something, you think it's great. You turn up the next day, it's bloody awful. The important thing isn't what it is, the important thing is what it could become.'

I first met Clare Higgins when I interviewed her for *The Independent*. She was starring in a play called *Mrs Klein* about the psychoanalyst Melanie Klein. She has been in *Doctor Who*, *The Golden Compass* and *Downton Abbey*, but her best work is on the stage. She has won the Olivier Best Actress award twice and has been described as 'the greatest British actress we have when it comes to communicating overwhelming tragic emotions on stage'. She is a great actor and one of the most interesting people I have met. So I was very pleased when, at the end of our interview, she offered to meet me for a drink after the play.

I saw *Mrs Klein* on the day I found out that my cancer had come back. I thought I was going to die. We are all going to die, of course, but I thought I was probably going to die quite soon. I had spent the morning at the hospital and the afternoon working out how to tell my mother the news. I didn't get round to cancelling the drink and then thought I might as well go along anyway. The play was very good indeed. Clare Higgins was brilliant, and we had a nice drink afterwards, but I'd be lying if I said that I managed to forget the shadows on that scan.

The third time I met her was after I lost my job, at a play down the road from me at the Arcola Theatre. It was a play called *Clarion*, about a tabloid paper that runs headlines like 'Fury Over Sharia Law for Toddlers!' and has upped its sales by having front-page stories about immigration every day for a year. 'Ambiguity's for cunts!' screams the editor at his terrified staff. One of them is Fleet Street veteran Verity, a former foreign correspondent who's now a columnist and one of the few people who dares to stand up to the editor. The play is funny and sad and, for any journalist, bitter-sweet. 'I never thought I'd watch our whole world disappear,' says Verity at one point. Nor, I felt like yelling out, did I.

Clare Higgins was magnificent as Verity. In the bar afterwards I told her. She gave me a hug and we agreed to meet for lunch.

'Your column was the first thing I used to turn to,' she told me as I joined her at her usual table at Joe Allen's. I felt a bit embarrassed. If I was a different kind of person, I might have shrugged and said it was water under the bridge. I might even have said that losing it was the best thing that ever happened to me. Unfortunately, I am not that kind of person. I told her that losing my job as a columnist had felt worse to me than heartbreak, worse than illness, worse almost than cancer, because at least cancer wasn't anyone else's fault. When I heard the words spoken aloud, they sounded ridiculous. 'Do you think,' said Clare, 'that that's because if you are allowed to talk about the things on your heart, you can cope with all those other betrayals, massive though they may be? But if that voice is taken away from you, you are truly in the wilderness, screaming?'

Gosh. I didn't expect anyone else to put it in such dramatic terms, but yes, I told her, that was exactly how I felt. That's the thing with actors, or at least with great actors. Like all great artists, they understand the human heart.

For her, it all started with a nosebleed. She was fourteen, and she was watching Judi Dench play both Perdita and Hermione in *The Winter's Tale*. 'For me,' she said, 'it was the beginning of a rip in the fabric of my universe. I thought: my God, there is someone else out there. I also remember thinking I wish I'd never come, because now I've got to try and do that. Nothing could stop me,' she said. 'It was willpower. Sheer, dogged, damn fucking determination. And anyone who got in the way . . . I will kill you first. I remember thinking that if I get through my three years at LAMDA, if I ever am an actress, if anyone ever pays me to do this job, how lucky would it be for me to be paid to express the love of the poets who kept me standing.'

Lucky for her? Lucky for us, I think. 'When I started to work,' she said, 'when I started to realize that I'm safe on stage in front of a thousand people, that I actually had been given the gift to say: through this text I can now give – and it's nothing to do with me. This is the thing that has blessed my life. When I got my first standing ovation, I was looking behind me going "what's going on?" It became a regular thing.'

When I first interviewed Clare, I remembered her talking about a production she had been in of *Death of a Salesman*. 'At a certain point in the show,' she said, 'there'd be this strange noise that I've never really heard in the theatre before, and it was men crying. To me,' she said, 'theatre is what church ought to be, a dark place where you're allowed to have these extreme feelings together. That beautiful silence where we can all collectively mourn.'

I remember that production of *Death of a Salesman*. I remember the crying, because I was crying, too. I was crying for Willy Loman, and his lost job and his shattered hopes and I was crying because Arthur Miller had done what all great artists do. Out of pain and failure and struggle, he had made something beautiful.

Part III

Fighting Back

'The heart is a very resilient little muscle'

Woody Allen

Sex and *Borgen* and ice cream

At a party, I met a man. He had a reputation as a serial seducer, and all through the party I kept swatting him away like a fly. When he told me that I was 'the best woman there', I gave in to flattery and agreed to go and have 'a bite'. As he slouched over his risotto, I thought he looked extremely unattractive, but our farewell peck outside Green Park Tube ended up so passionate that we almost knocked the recycling bin down.

You'd have thought, by the age of fifty, that I'd have learnt. You'd have thought, for example, that when you meet someone who's famous as a womanizer, and they tell you that you're exceptionally beautiful, and sexy, and smart, you'd realize that the reason they sound so sincere is that they say these things all the time.

It is, of course, nice to have a few nights of flattery and enthusiastic sex. We watched *Borgen* and ate ice cream in bed. We talked about books. We talked about art. I was reading a novel called *Barracuda*. He was re-reading Proust. What wasn't quite such fun was our walk on Hampstead Heath. Afterwards, he told me that he should probably mention that he had dates lined up with other women. When he left, he said that I hadn't 'heard the last' of him. I told him that he had certainly 'heard the last' of me.

I have always had a soft spot for narcissistic charmers. I think this probably started because I used to be so shy. Subtle signals of interest would be lost. I needed men with placards, men who were practically cartoons. I needed men who told me I was gorgeous – and asked me out.

My most significant relationship started sixteen years ago, at the Elephant and Castle. I was on my way home from a very bad blind date. When a tall, dark (black, in fact), handsome stranger asked me for a drink, I thought it couldn't be worse than the date I'd just left. We went to a pub under the arches. We went to the Old Gin Palace in the Old Kent Road. We walked back, hand in hand, in the early hours, to my flat. We only went out with each other for a few months, but we have both played a very big part in each other's lives. Winston is probably one of the reasons I have found it so hard to 'settle down'.

Here's how not to have a relationship. Hold out for perfection. Panic at the first flaw. Assume that a moment of awkwardness means it's time to bolt. Or, alternatively, make sure you only ever fall for men who aren't (emotionally or actually) available. That should keep your weekends, birthdays and holidays partner-free for life.

Attachment theory has a lot to teach us about how to have successful relationships. People who have a history of 'secure attachment' are much, much better at relationships than people who don't. People who are 'insecurely attached' or 'avoidant' had better find someone who's 'securely attached' if they want to have a hope in hell of making anything work. Two 'avoidants' together? That's me and Winston. Fun, but probably best to run a mile.

*

Most of my friends are, thank goodness, much better at all this than me. With my friends Emma and Tony, for example, you can still see the spark after twenty-three years. When they come round for dinner, they sometimes bicker, but you can see that they are still interested in everything the other one says. They argue, they laugh, they tease each other and they sometimes even shout at each other, but every word and gesture make it clear that they are still each other's number one.

'I think we've got a lot of interests in common,' Emma told me, 'in terms of politics, writing, our backgrounds as well, so we're comfortable with each other, but the other thing is I think we like each other. We're great friends, so we can have a laugh.' She was stretched out on the sofa in their snug sitting room. I was curled up on the armchair by the fire. 'But we also know,' she said, 'that we need our space, so we didn't actually buy a place together until we'd been going out for eight years. We've each got our own room as well. The rules are that you can't tell the other person what to do in their room. Tony wants to bring his bike to his room, and I'm really annoyed about it, but I don't have the right to tell him. You,' she said, shaking a fist at Tony, 'had better make it discreet!'

They met when she was twenty-seven and he was twenty-nine. 'I'd joined this creative writing class,' she said, 'and this wonderful guy walked in. He had a black beret on. I thought: what a poser! Thinks he's on the Left Bank, does he? And I looked at his face and thought: ooh!' For the next nine months, she 'just kind of checked him out'. And then one day she asked him out. 'He said yeah and that's how it took off. There was no drama. I just really liked him. I thought he was gorgeous to look at, he had a really nice manner and he was working class, like me. We've been together such a long time. People are quite gobsmacked, I think partly because he's white and I'm black, but we never thought of it like that. I still fancy the socks off him! I think he's the most gorgeous man I've ever seen!'

It's a cliché to talk about someone's face 'lighting up', but Emma's face really does light up when she talks about the man she loves. But, I said carefully, you do have rows, don't you? 'Oh my God,' said Emma. 'Yes!' So what, I asked, do they row about? For a moment, Emma looked as though she was struggling to remember. 'Well,' she said, 'he's very typically male, so he doesn't really say a lot, which winds me up a lot. I have been known to throw things, so there was a quiche that was thrown in here.' She laughed. 'Which I was pissed off about, because I was hungry and I'd just thrown my quiche! What else? I don't know. I think it's the living. For me, things need to be in the right place, so in my space there needs to be a sense of order. So when I'm sitting down and *somebody*'s socks pop up from the settee, that is not a sense of order, is it?'

'They're probably yours!' said Tony. Emma used to be a teacher and she gave him one of her head teacher looks. 'Or I trip over someone's shoes,' she went on. 'That,' said Tony, 'is your stuff lying around everywhere!' 'No,' said Emma. 'You're butting in. That's another thing. He talks when he wants to talk. But I think that's the main thing. His stuff. And sometimes, his organization. Tony will say he's going to do something, like in the house. We've got a broken window at the moment and every day he's been saying "I'm going to do it", but it will fall on me to sort it out.'

They have, she told me, a cleaner, to cut out rows about domestic work. They mostly get their own food, because Emma has to eat a restricted diet for health reasons and Tony doesn't 'want a lot of this gluten-free stuff, you know'. They even go on separate holidays. 'I'm not sure we travel together very well,' said Emma. 'His smoking gets on my nerves when we travel, and Tony just seems to do his own thing. When we were on our first holiday, in Morocco, a friend said to me years later, "I was watching you both." And she was going to her friend, "They're so in love! Look at him, he looks so devoted to her!" And that was a terrible holiday for us, it was our first trip away and oh my God, I thought I was going to have to kill him!'

You can see why Emma always cheers me up. I love her, and Tony, because they are both warm and funny and intelligent and kind. And because they're honest.

So what, I asked Tony, did he think had kept their relationship alive? He cleared his throat. He has a quiet voice and today it was even quieter. 'I think there are some basics you have to have,' he said. 'If you're a drunk, or a drug user, or a gambler, or you're violent or abusive, or you're just not very nice to live with, that's probably going to end badly. But I do think there's quite a lot of luck involved. I don't think most people will accept that.'

Well, OK, I said, but it's not nothing to carry on being attracted to someone for twenty-three years, is it? 'Again,' said Tony, 'you don't necessarily know what someone's going to look like.' Emma looked as if she was about to explode. 'It's *personal*,' she practically shrieked, 'what do *you personally* think about our relationship? I'm not hearing that! I hear a lot of generalizing.'

Right, I said, let me spell it out. What attracted you to Emma?

'Well,' Tony said, 'I do think it's partly that she does have quite a lot of the qualities that I don't have, which always makes somebody interesting. I'm not a very driven person. She is. I'm not a hard worker. She is. I'm not a risk taker. She is. If I'd met someone who was like me, I'd have found that quite boring. There's nothing humdrum about Emma.'

Now Emma was starting to look more cheerful. And what, I asked, irritated him about Emma? Tony looked down at his feet and then back at me. 'I do think,' he said, 'a lot of women, not just Emma, regard you as a work in progress.' Well, of course, I said. A man, surely, is just raw material? 'They want you to be slightly different to what you are,' he continued. 'Why can't you be a bit more this? Why can't you be a bit more that? If you say you're going to do something, for me that's kind of like you've done it. I am a very annoying person to live with, but I do think there's a certain amount you should just accept.'

Or, I was tempted to say, he could just make a phone call and get someone to fix that window, but you can see why I'm not the one talking about twenty-three happy years. So had they, I asked, ever got near to splitting up?

Now Emma's smile was like the light in the sky after a storm. 'No,' she said. 'I might have said "I've had enough of you", but not really. Am I right, Tone?' Tony smiled, too, and my heart gave a little jump. 'I don't think so, no.' Emma looked over at Tony and her eyes shone. 'We just think,' she said, 'nobody else will have us.'

For Emma and Tony, it all started with physical attraction. For some couples it doesn't. 'I was thirty-eight when I met Ian,' said my friend Lisa. 'At the time I was pursuing someone else. We got on well and had a good laugh, but I don't think there was much thought about anything else.' A year later, they bumped into each other at a party. 'At the end of the evening, he took my email address and I thought: this will be quite nice, because he seems like a nice person.' Not exactly Romeo and Juliet, but look what happened to them.

'About ten days or so went by and I thought "why hasn't he contacted me?" Then he emailed and we went to a comedy club. I was late. Very late.' She laughed and so did I. I remember her telling me at the time about how she had arrived in a long coat and scarf and woolly hat, breathless and apologetic, and he had told her that she reminded him of Joyce Grenfell. 'We seemed to have a nice time,' she said, 'but I bent over to pick up my handbag and hit my head on the back of the chair and nearly knocked myself out! And then I didn't hear from him for months and months.'

Ignoring 'The Rules', a dating trend at the time that encouraged women around the world, including me, to behave like passive-aggressive American teenagers, she screwed her courage to her keyboard and emailed him. 'I didn't hear anything for months,' she said. 'I went to a poetry reading and he was there and it kind of led from there, really. I always like to say that neither of us was interested in the other, but life got in the way a bit. He said he was interested, but things happened.'

They 'jogged along', she said, for eight months and then she had a shock. 'When I got home from work I thought: I'll have my usual fag and a glass of wine, and I suddenly realized I didn't want either of them and I thought: "Oh God, this is really weird."' The next day, she went to the 'well woman' clinic in her lunch hour and was told that she was pregnant. 'I remember bursting into tears,' she said. 'I walked back to work. The first person I told was the office cat. When I told Ian, his first response was "oh shit".'

Not, you'd have thought, the best start to a happy family set-up, but they both soon perked up. 'We arranged to meet in a pub,' she said. 'I had a Coke. He had a pint. We talked for about five minutes about it, and then played a game of pool. And then I said, "What about this? We don't know each other very well. We don't live together." I was looking at the practical side of what might go wrong. He was looking at the practical side of what could be right about it. I spent five months being pregnant on my own, living in a house share. And then we moved into a flat in Stamford Hill.' She smiled at the memory. 'I *loved* that first home.'

So, I told her, did I. It's just up the road from me and I remember that first visit, to see Lisa, Ian and their tiny baby, made me feel as if I should have brought some frankincense or myrrh. I will never forget the glow of happiness that seemed to shine out of all three of them – and it seems to have been there ever since. 'Ian was working nights,' she said. 'He would come home from work at nine o'clock in the morning. Ruby would be asleep by then. I would get really excited because the night before I would have taped *Father Ted* or *The Simpsons* and we would watch that, with a pot of coffee and Ruby asleep in front of us. We'd know that in our little world, everything was OK.'

Whenever I see Lisa and Ian, that's certainly how it looks to me. They have had plenty of challenges – money worries, job losses and horrible bosses – but their family unit always seems strong as a rock. When I first knew Lisa, she shared my weakness for the narcissistic charmer. She had, in fact, just come out of a relationship with a charismatic, handsome guy who had broken her heart. 'I think,' she said, 'sometimes we feel that having somebody who's perceived as more attractive, more successful, more appealing, will raise our status. But in that relationship I was always anxious. With Ian, I feel safe and confident and I like being with him. I think you should never forget how much you like that person and that's something you have to work at. You have to keep reminding yourself of whatever it is you do well.'

What I do well is panic and run away. But I'm quite good at seeing what other people do well. I was asked to do a piece about cross-cultural marriages, inspired by my own Swedish–Scottish mix. I met a fiftysomething English woman in the Cotswolds who had married a Dane. I met a twentysomething English woman who had married a *very* handsome young Italian and was living in Bari. And down the road from me in Dalston I met Veena Supramaniam, a half-Anglican, half-Hindu Sri Lankan Tamil and her Israeli-Australian husband, Nativ Gill.

Veena went to live in Botswana when she was twelve. She went to boarding school in South Africa and then went to do a degree and a PhD in Melbourne. Nativ was born in Israel, the grandson of Holocaust survivors, and moved to Australia when he was nine. He and Veena met at Melbourne when she spotted him at the gym. 'He caught my eye straight away,' she said. 'I thought,' he said, handing me a mug of tea, 'that she was very beautiful and very exotic.' But they were, they explained, friends for five years before they 'got together' and it was only after another nine years that they got married, in a Hindu and Jewish ceremony on a Sri Lankan beach.

If that sounds like a bit of a slow burn, it certainly seems to generate a lot of heat. The sliding window to their balcony was wide open. 'He always has it open,' moaned Veena, but after we'd been talking for a while, I could see why. They were so engaged with each other that the air in the room almost crackled. The day before it had been full of candles for Diwali. 'The whole house,' said Nativ, 'was a fire hazard!' A few minutes later, he was telling me that he was 'fiercely proud as an Israeli', loves to celebrate Passover and Chanukah and marks the start of the Shabbat with the kiddish, the blessing of the bread and wine. But he also said that his Judaism was 'cultural' not 'religious' and that he was 'the world's worst Jew'. 'I eat so much swine,' he confessed, 'I could support a pig farm.'

Veena, said Nativ, is a 'phenomenal cook'. But it was, he said, impossible for him to cook if she was in the kitchen 'because she's a total Nazi'. Perhaps only the grandson of a Holocaust survivor can say that to his wife.

When I tore myself away from their kitchen table, I left with the feeling that the Diwali candles and the Shabbat bread and wine really weren't the point. The point is that what it takes to have a successful cross-cultural relationship is pretty much what it takes to have any successful relationship. You have to like each other enough to put up with each other's foibles. You have to have shared interests and shared values and you have to be able to laugh. And you need enough tension to keep the spark alive. 'There is tolerance,' said Nativ, 'but there is challenge, too. I like,' and now his eyes were glittering, 'to stir things up.'

*

I once went to see a couples counsellor. I had met a man I liked and had actually managed to keep the relationship going for three months. I was worried that I would wreck it and wanted some help to make sure I didn't. The second time I saw the counsellor I had to tell her that I had already bolted. For me, breaking up isn't at all hard to do. What's hard to do is stick around.

That counsellor said she thought I was suffering from what she called a 'terrorizing idealism'. I think what she meant was that I was expecting someone like Barack Obama to turn up, perhaps with a first edition of Keats, whisk me off for dinner in Paris or Rome and beg me to make his life complete. After a simple wedding, in a white church surrounded by marguerites and wild roses, we would go off to change the world while also making time for glittering conversation and the kind of sex that makes you blush when you wake up.

She was, of course, spot on. I always thought it was about finding the right person, the right chemical and intellectual ingredients that you could chuck in a giant mixing bowl to create a massive, delicious and miraculously long-lasting cake. I didn't quite grasp that it was about effort. Not just the effort of seeking, and auditioning, and charming, but the daily effort of accommodating and listening and biting back irritation and learning that a cross word is not the end of a relationship or a world.

I wouldn't want to treat my friends as lab rats, but I can see that what they're doing confirms the evidence. Instant attraction is a very nice start to a relationship. It worked for my parents. It worked for Emma and Tony. How delicious to feel a little quickening of your pulses, a little warmth in your cheeks, a little tingling in what you might even call your loins. And how lovely – how miraculous, even – to have the trigger for that tingling sharing your bed.

My parents called it 'love at first sight', but the scientific term for it is 'limerence'. Limerence, according to the psychologist Dorothy Tennov, who coined the term, is 'an involuntary interpersonal state that involves an acute longing for emotional reciprocation, obsessive-compulsive thoughts, feelings, and behaviours, and emotional dependence on another person'. Been there, done that, got the too-tight, embarrassing T-shirt. I have driven past someone's home at night, in order to get a glimpse of the light in their window. I have stared at a Post-it note a man has scrawled, for hours and hours and hours. I have not converted any of these feelings into a successful relationship, but then there's no particular reason why anyone would. Limerence is a cocktail of dopamine, phenylethylamine (a natural amphetamine), oestrogen and testosterone. After six to twenty-four months, it generally starts to fade. It fades unless the people who have it turn it into love.

Love, according to the research, is based on friendship. It's based on thinking that you have lots of things in common. This doesn't mean that you actually need to have lots of things in common. A study of 23,000 married couples showed that similarity accounted for less than 0.5 per cent of their satisfaction. What matters, according to the psychologist John Gottman, is your emotional style. You should, apparently, emphasize similarities. You should not, as Lisa discovered, play hard to get. You should make sure you do nice things together. And you should have lots of sex. I haven't quizzed my friends on how much sex they have, but couples who have sex two or three times a week are, apparently, happier than couples who don't. But as I've said before, sex is not broccoli. If you want to kill your sex life, add it to your 'five a day'.

Space, as Emma and Tony have discovered, is good. Separate friends and interests are good. A GSOH, as the dating profiles put it, seems to be vital, and so does respect. And arguing is good. Yup, arguing is good. If you're not arguing, according to Gottman, that's probably a sign of withdrawal. If you argue, it shows that the relationship is alive.

I wish someone had taught me this at school. I wish I hadn't spent my youth with people who told me I shouldn't even kiss a boy unless God wanted me to marry him. But regret, as Katherine Mansfield said, is 'an appalling waste of energy'. So, I decided, when I said goodbye to the man who had been setting up dates with other women after our sessions of sex and *Borgen* and ice cream, are men who rely on their charm.

I sometimes worry that I've left it too late. And then something happens that reminds me that it's never too late. One of the reasons I was so happy for my friend Ros when she got married was that her new husband, Stuart, had found love for the first time at fifty-eight. 'I'd envisaged remaining a bachelor for the rest of my life,' he told me, 'probably with the occasional affair, but living that final part alone. But,' he said, and I suddenly felt a catch in my throat, 'that won't happen now.'

Madonna of the Rocks

I wanted to cook a friend a birthday meal. When I say I wanted to cook, I don't mean that I actually wanted to cook, of course, but I did want to repay Lorna for her feats, and feast, for my fiftieth. I had rented out my flat again, so my friend Dawn offered to host the meal at hers. For some reason, I thought the only way to match Ottolenghi effort was – well, Ottolenghi effort. This time it was Dawn and I who spent the afternoon toasting pine nuts, grating lemon zest and trying to follow the twists and turns of recipes that made *The Waste Land* look like *The Hungry Caterpillar*. By the time Lorna and her partner turned up, we were both so exhausted that we had drunk nearly a whole bottle of prosecco before they had even sat down.

Because I couldn't possibly drive home, Dawn and her partner Duncan offered me their spare room. In the morning, after breakfast, their daughters put on a little show. Amy, the eldest, sang Pharrell Williams's 'Happy'. Lizzie, the youngest, sang 'What a Wonderful World'. Lizzie is five. She looks like a Victorian angel. She looked like an even happier angel when I whipped out my iPad, swiped to video and tapped the red button. I think I probably have a recording of the most touching performance in history of

'What a Wonderful World'. I don't know. I've never been able to bring myself to watch it.

I had just found out I had cancer when my friend Lisa told me she was pregnant. We had both recently turned thirty-nine. I tried to smile. I started to say that I was happy for her. I *was* happy for her. Lisa is one of my dearest friends and I knew that she would be happy that she was having a baby before it was too late. But when I opened my mouth to speak, what came out was a howl.

It was two days before my forty-sixth birthday when I heard my cancer had come back. It was too late for babies. It might, I was beginning to realize, be too late for everything else. Dawn didn't want me to spend my birthday on my own, so she came round with her daughters and some little cakes they had baked for me. I gazed at her four-year-old, who looked, I thought, remarkably like my sister, and at her baby, at her skin like a peach and her clear, clear blue eyes. I didn't want to cry, because I knew Dawn would do anything to make things better, and because it wasn't her fault that she went into hospital to have babies and I went into hospital to have tumours cut out, but still this was true, and I couldn't bear it, so I cried anyway.

It does get easier. As the clock ticks, and forty passes, it definitely gets easier, particularly when you could be dead, but aren't. I love my friends' children. I'm happy to see my friends' children. But there are times when I have to protect myself from a pang.

You know how I feel about *Man's Search for Meaning*. It was bad enough when Viktor Frankl said that the only thing that kept him going at Auschwitz was the 'thought of his beloved'. Later, it gets worse. At the end of the book, he talks about a woman with a disabled son. He tells her that if she had looked back on a life that was 'full of financial success and social prestige', but with no children, she would have to say that her life 'was a failure'.

'I saw a little girl in the park the other day,' said the woman sitting opposite me, 'and I smiled because she looked so adorable. But I choose,' she said firmly, 'not to go there.' The woman sitting opposite me was Julia Stuart and we were having coffee in a London hotel. Julia is very attractive, very talented and very good company. We met when we were both working at *The Independent.* She was thirty-five and had just met the man who would become her husband. 'It was the time,' she told me, 'there was all the stuff in the papers about fertility declining once you're over thirty-five. I remember thinking "if we're going to have children, we're going to have to start now". It was really early on in the relationship and I blurted it out. We both knew it wasn't right.'

I remember that time. I remember every newspaper I opened seemed to have a giant feature on how thirtysomething women were wrecking their chances of having a family by focusing on their careers. I remember wanting to ask the people who wrote those pieces what exactly they thought we were meant to do. Where were we meant to find the sperm? And who was going to look after the child if you had to work to feed it on your own? And how were you meant to pay for that person, since you probably didn't earn all that much more than them? I even remember asking Auntie Lisbeth not to talk too much about her grandchildren in front of my mother. It was my father's funeral. It was my beloved father's funeral and I couldn't bear to add to the weight of my mother's grief.

By the time the marriage broke down, and they parted, Julia thought the chances of finding a new partner in time to have a baby were slim. 'Everyone used to say "you'd make a lovely mother",' she said, 'and now they say "you would have made a lovely mother".' And how, I asked, but I didn't really need to, did that make her feel? Julia's smile was brave. 'I could,' she said, 'burst into tears now.'

When it comes to fertility, people usually just think about women, but one in six couples in the UK has trouble conceiving, and most of these couples involve a man. Through another former colleague, I met Simon Ricketts. Simon is the son of a cleaner and an insurance salesman who both became social workers. His brother is a youth worker. He was brought up to think that life was about caring for other people, and always assumed that he'd have children to care for, too.

Like Julia, he took the traditional route into journalism, working his way up through local papers, without a degree. He has worked as a postman, a milkman and in a double-glazing warehouse. He was working 'for next to nothing' on a local paper when his girlfriend found out she was pregnant. 'We were both twenty and living with her parents,' he told me when we met for coffee in his work canteen, 'and had almost no means of our own. We discussed it a lot, but in the end she had a termination. I remember the day, clear as a bell. We went to a clinic, and were taken in and sat down. It was fairly plain I wasn't welcome during the process. I walked out of the door and I remember walking aimlessly up and down the street.'

Simon took a sip of his coffee and then looked into the distance. His kind face looked sad. 'That child,' he said, 'would now be well into its twenties. I've never thought about what gender it would be, and it's probably best not to. I just know that it was a chance for me to be a father and for her to be a mother.'

He was in his late twenties, and with a different partner, when the issue of children next came up. 'It's a decent age to be a father,' he said. 'I had a proper job by then. We tried naturally, doing all the different things you do, checking your cycles and so on. Some of it's good fun! There's a certain amount of "get home, it's a good day". But then it did become a bit like a process. The bottom line was that we weren't getting anywhere. So we started to go for tests.'

For a while, his girlfriend tried Chinese herbs. 'She had,' he explained, 'to drink all these leaves and barks and these amazing potions that smelled like the bottom of a drain.' I tried to give a sympathetic nod, but felt my mouth twist into a cartoon face of disgust. Just the mention of Chinese herbs is still enough to flood my mouth with bile. After that, he said, they tried IVF. Three cycles at £2000 a go. 'We'd done a cycle and the egg had been implanted, and they said, "We're going to give you a prescription to inject into her stomach." It was nine hundred pounds. I bought it from Boots. So I'm sitting in my bedroom with my girlfriend waiting to inject her, thinking "if I drop this, it's nine hundred pounds down the drain".'

Hope, as I know with all my medical treatments, can be very expensive indeed. But on the third cycle, she became pregnant.

'I remember clearly the day they told us the first IVF hadn't taken,' he told me. 'I can remember hardly being able to see through the tears. So we were pleased when we got the news, but cautious.' A couple of months into the pregnancy, his girlfriend came home from work in pain. 'The next day was Christmas Eve,' he said, 'so we decided to drive to the local hospital. I remember her saying, and it's a testament to her, "Let's stop at the butchers," because we'd ordered a turkey for us and our parents. We went to the hospital and yeah, she was losing it.' His voice now dropped to a monotone. 'That was very, very difficult.' I could see that he was trying hard to be matter-of-fact. 'I think it affected us both incredibly deeply.'

If I'm really honest, I think I would have liked to have been a father. It sounds like an excellent way to get the pleasures of parenthood without quite as much of the hassle. The begetting of the child, as the Bible puts it, sets the tone. A quick burst of pleasure and Bob's your uncle, or your son. After that, you can nip down to the Jolly Butchers and everyone will slap you on the back and buy you pints. You don't have to waddle round in leggings for months, wondering if some kind of alien is about to burst out of your stomach. You don't have to gaze at a bottle of Viognier, and worry that one tiny sip will turn that shrimp you saw on the scan into Saddam Hussein. You don't have to wonder how on earth that wall of muscle that can barely fit in a speculum is going to squeeze out something the size of a cat. And you don't have to go through the shock of discovering that something that looks quite easy in Renaissance paintings is actually quite painful and will leave your nipples sore and cracked.

When you're first handed a tiny scrap of wriggling flesh, you can gaze at the nose and eyes and mouth and yell 'That's my boy!' You can hold this scrap of flesh, and kiss this scrap of flesh, and cuddle this scrap of flesh and watch this scrap of flesh grow. Best of all, you can leave this scrap of flesh during the day, and strut around an office, and talk to grown-ups and do the job you had, and be the person you were, before. For you, this scrap of flesh is what a business would call 'added value'. You're the same, but now you're more. When you get home from work, you can marvel at the scrap of flesh. You might even stick photos of the scrap of flesh all over your desk, but life will carry on very much as it did before.

This is not what it's like for most mothers. It would be nice if things had changed since our mothers were young, but they don't seem to have changed half as much as we might have hoped. Mothers, as far as I can tell, are suddenly hurled from a life of work and friends and a relationship, if they have one, to life on a new planet where every part of the landscape is different. That scrap of flesh is theoretically not part of you, but why, then, does it feel as if that creature wriggling, or crying, or peeing in that baby-gro is actually a part of your heart? You can't just abandon your heart – of course you can't just abandon your heart – but you used to have interesting things to say to adult humans and now your life is all about flesh, and milk, and food, and shit, and crying, and sleeping, and crying again.

And when you leave that scrap of flesh, which you will probably have to do to keep a roof over your head, with another woman who seems nice enough, but not really good enough for your child, you will be torn in two. You will probably have to get used to that feeling. You might, for example, feel torn in two when your child goes on their first holiday without the family, and when they get their first boyfriend or girlfriend, and when they go off to university or leave home. You might well have to make some sacrifices in your career, because someone will have to dash home in time to get to the childminder, and, let's be honest, it probably won't be your bloke. And when you do get home from the office, it will be the start of a whole new working day. You will cook. You will clean. You will tidy. You will iron. You will lay things out for the morning when the whole damn caboodle starts all over again.

On top of all of this, you are now a member of a cult. In that cult, you will not gaze soulfully down at your naked toddler, in a landscape of rocks dotted with flowers, and with an angel at your side. You do not need Leonardo to paint you to know that you are now part of a clan. In that clan, you know that what redeems you is the blessed gift of parenthood. Through your children are ye saved. They are the way, the truth, the life.

In this cult, children rule. They rule the family. They rule the house. They are praised for every tiny thing they do. 'What a lovely drawing, darling!' 'What a nice, big poo!' In this cult, they get gold stars for smiling, or drawing, or just for turning up at school. I was once asked to be 'journalist in residence' at a primary school. I helped the pupils put together a little newspaper about what was going on in the school. One child wrote a report about a football match his classmates had played in. 'Well done, Husthwaite!' he wrote at the end of it, naming the school. 'But,' I said, 'I thought you lost?'

In this cult, children are ferried from one activity to the next.

They are guarded. They are coached. They are groomed. I never thought I'd be saying 'when I was a child, it was all different', but when I was a child, it was all different. On the estate where I grew up, we spent most of the time wandering into each other's houses or playing in the street. For a while, a big chunk of the estate was a building site. We treated it like a giant playground, climbing on piles of timber and running up half-built staircases that suddenly stopped. In the evenings, there was a vague system of 'keeping an eye' on each other's children, which meant that a neighbour might pop round once just to check that the house had not burnt down.

We were not chimney sweeps. We were not wolf children. We went on nice trips to National Trust houses and Royal Horticultural Society gardens, where we hoped our father would treat us to honey cake, and sometimes he did. But in the freedom we were given, we learnt how to play, to dream, to roam. We learnt how to imagine and how to tell stories. We learnt that it wasn't up to anyone else to make sure we had a nice day.

Cults are usually disappointing. I know, because I've been in something very like one, a group that talked about salvation and redemption and heaven – and also, of course, about hell. Some people find that parenthood doesn't feel much like salvation. Some people find it feels a lot more like hell. 'In my late twenties, it just came out of nowhere, this urge to have a child,' said one mother in a recent article about motherhood in *The Guardian*. 'When she was placed in my hands for the first time, it was "Oh, no. What have I done? This was a huge mistake." I hoped the feeling would go away. It didn't.' The baby was healthy and beautiful and grew into an 'awesome' girl. 'If anything were to happen to her,' she wrote in a blog post, 'I would be inconsolable. My mistake was not because I don't love her or because I don't want her or because there is something wrong with her. It is not her fault by any stretch of the imagination that I shouldn't be a parent.'

The woman in the interview was brave enough to give her real name. She is called Victoria Elder. She works for a mortgage company in Louisiana. When she answered a question on a blog, 'What's it like to regret having children?', in a matter-of-fact way, she might as well have announced that she was off to marry Kim Jong-un. She was accused of being self-indulgent and narcissistic. She was even accused of child abuse. It may or may not have been a good idea to put her thoughts in a public arena, but her daughter, according to the journalist who did the interview, didn't seem to mind. And Victoria Elder is clearly not alone.

There's a Mumsnet thread called '*deep breath* I regret having children'. 'I regret having my son,' says the mother who started it. 'While I'd go to the ends of the Earth for him, there is not a day goes by that I don't kick myself. It is not PND. I am not depressed or "down" . . . My son is perfectly lovely, and my darling husband is extremely helpful. I adore them both . . . But if there was a way to reverse time, and politely, painlessly engineer him out of existence, I would. Honestly.'

That's certainly honest. Shockingly honest. 'I miss my old life intensely,' she continues, 'and the thought that I had every right and opportunity to keep it that way makes me sick. I miss my relationship with my partner. I miss what we did together. I miss being able to walk out of the front door of my own bloody house without a second thought. I miss having the money to spend on the odd nice thing. I miss having a house full of our nice, beautiful, adult things. I miss being able to ponder freely over my career options. Honestly, truthfully, does anyone feel the same? I don't mean those who are unfortunate enough to have depression . . . does anyone actually endure cold, hard regret?'

The answer, it turns out on the thread, is yes, quite a few people do. There's a Facebook group called 'I Regret Having Children'. A French psychoanalyst wrote a book called *No Kids: 40 Good Reasons Not To Be a Mother*, which became a bestseller. In 2016, the BBC included its author, Connie Maier, in a list of the 100 most inspirational and influential women in the world. An Israeli sociologist, Orna Donath, wrote a book called *Regretting Motherhood: A Sociopolitical Analysis*, which became another bestseller. 'People were saying,' said the German blogger Jessika Rose, '"How can you admit to this?" "How can you be so ungrateful for a choice you yourself made?"' It was, Rose told the *Guardia*n journalist Stefanie Marsh, she who pressurized her husband into having a child almost as soon as they got married. 'I had a very romantic notion of being a mother,' she said, 'that I'd love going to the playground, that I would always be loving and understanding. I *hate* playgrounds. I find it extremely boring to stand there and watch the child on a swing and the helicopter mothers making sure their kids don't fall off.' She had 'never thought' about the noise, the boredom, the stress. Older generations had, she thought, repressed all their bad parenting experiences 'just to survive'.

Well, maybe. Or maybe they just didn't expect everything in

life to be fulfilling. Maybe they just had babies because that's what humans generally do, and maybe they were just grateful that they didn't have to squeeze a child out of a prolapsed womb every year of their adult life until they died. Which is, after all, if we're going to take the organic lavender oil approach to things, Mother Nature's way.

It's quite a novelty, this thing called choice. It's quite hard to know what to do with it. For my parents' generation, it was more straightforward. You got married, because everyone did, you had children, because everyone did, you stayed together, because nearly everyone did. You loved your children. You did not expect, as a suicide bomber might, that you would then be catapulted to Paradise.

Now we're all like citizens of a former outpost of the Soviet Union who are used to spending hours queuing up for a loaf and are suddenly hurled into a supermarket the size of a city. There are thousands of different types of bread on offer. Some are delicious. Some aren't. The catch is that you don't have all that long to choose your brand and you will have to stick to that one for the rest of your life. Some of us trip over, hobble around in a panic, grab the nearest thing and only find out after we have paid for it that the packet is empty. There are still lots of other things we can buy and eat and do, but that particular option has now gone.

If you don't have children, some people will think you are selfish. They think that the urge to replicate your genes, and boast about your offspring's achievements, is a noble thing, in a way that trying to be a good friend or daughter, or do a job well, is not.

Perhaps some of them protest a bit much. Everyone, as those brutally honest mothers have said, expects parenthood to make you happy, but the truth is, it often doesn't. Children, clearly, bring great joy. I have no doubt that gazing at your baby's beautiful eyes will give you a burst of joy that I'll never know. But is it actually true that children make you happy?

Professor Ruut Veenhoven is the world's only Professor of Social Conditions for Human Happiness. He has produced a World Database of Happiness, with 8000 findings from 120 countries, and the conclusions are clear. Marriage, he says, makes people happy, but when children arrive, their happiness drops. 'The presence of children', he says, 'detracts from the quality of marriage, at least to the quality of the modern, romantic, equal marriage. The situation becomes even more unhappy in modern marriages where the mother is working and looking after children.' When I think about the couples I know, I'd have to agree that some of the happiest are the ones who don't have children. They still go on adventures. They still have fun. At eighty-five, says Veenhoven, adults with children are happier than those without. But that's quite a long time to wait.

It was Julia who interviewed Veenhoven, for a feature for *The Independent*. She had just met the man she would marry and was still hoping to have a family. So how, I asked her, does she cope with the fact that she hasn't? Julia smiled. 'I deal with it,' she told me over that coffee in that London hotel, 'by accepting it. I don't believe you have everything in your life that you want. It's ridiculous to think you would. When I look back, I've had a very happy and successful life. I'm very grateful for everything I've had. I've had lots of wonderful experiences I never imagined.'

You can say that again. As a journalist, Julia won an Amnesty International press award. As a novelist, she has been a *New York Times* bestseller, and had one of her novels selected for the Obamas' holiday reading list. 'I've got good friends and a loving family,' she said. 'I haven't been able to have children, but I've had a hell of a lot of other things I didn't expect.'

Simon Ricketts takes the same view. 'I don't feel like there's a hole in my life where my child should be,' he said. 'I just think it would have been lovely to have them, but my personal situation didn't work out. There's no such thing as deserving children. Nature lets you sometimes have them, and sometimes it doesn't. It sounds cheesy, but they're a gift. I think being a parent and wanting to be a parent is about doing something for a child, not just as some accessory. Many kind people say "you'd make a great dad", and I'm sure I would have done, but that's not really what it's about. It's about would I be able to raise a good child? Would I be able to bring another human being into this world and set them off for this life? It is,' he said carefully, 'a very difficult thing.'

I agree with Simon. I agree with Julia. It would have been lovely. It could have been lovely. It could also have been awful, but that's irrelevant because we'll never know. Having children isn't meant to be about what they can do for you. It's meant to be about what you can do for them.

It's a long time since I've cried about not having children. The worst time is when it's still uncertain. When it's no longer a possibility, you adjust to the new landscape of your life. Like Julia, I feel I've had opportunities I could never have dreamt of. And like both Julia and Simon, I don't believe you get everything you want in a life. I still get the odd pang, but nowadays it really is just the odd pang. I don't need little Lizzie on my iPad to remind me that it's a wonderful world.

A life worth living

'But it's not,' said the young man sitting opposite me, 'too late for you to have a baby!' I had just told him that I didn't have children and this was his response. He was nineteen. He had a pierced chin and was wearing a baseball cap. I liked him the moment I spotted him across the room. I thought it probably wasn't worth explaining that the odds, for me at fifty, were about the same as my becoming prime minister. We weren't there to talk about the miracles of modern science. I had been asked to do a piece on teenage pregnancy and the dapper young man drinking a can of Coke, in the bar at the Southbank Centre where I had bought so many drinks for so many poets, was there to tell me what it's like to become a parent at fifteen.

Even I had to admit that work seemed to be going quite well. I was doing lots of interesting stuff for the *Sunday Times*. I was doing quite a few columns for *The Guardian*. I was still doing the press review on Sky News twice a month. I wasn't earning anything like as much as I had before, but I certainly couldn't say that the work I was doing was boring. And I was getting to meet people like lovely Leroy.

Leroy lost his virginity when he was twelve. He and his girl-friend were both fifteen when she got pregnant. 'My mum cried,' he said, 'because her baby was having a baby, do you know what I mean?' I nodded, as if I had had that very conversation with my own teenage children, but his huge smile just made me want to smile and nod along. His baby was born at the end of January. Leroy went into a young offenders' institute three weeks later. He saw him every day before he went in, and then didn't see him for a year. I was already worrying that his baby might not have recognized him when he came out, but Leroy set my mind at rest. 'Babies,' he explained, 'know you by scent.'

While he was in his young offenders' institute, Leroy decided that he wanted to be a midwife. He is now working hard to get the qualifications he needs to make his dream come true. Yvonne, who got pregnant when she was seventeen, is trying to build a career as a life coach. Lucy, who also got pregnant at seventeen, has done a business diploma and wants to study forensic psychology. 'It was quite isolating being pregnant at seventeen,' she told me. 'I lost all my friends. I would walk around in a big coat.'

I thought someone should give these young people medals because they had lost their childhood and they didn't complain. They got up every morning and did what they needed to do to make sure their children got washed and clothed and fed. None of them actively chose to be teenage parents. None of them actively chose to be single parents. With better guidance, things might have turned out differently, but they were coping with the cards they had been dealt.

The statistics on teenage parents aren't good. Their children are much more likely to grow up in poverty, end up on benefits or be placed in care than the children of older parents. Statistics on single parents aren't great either, even though nearly half of all children are now born out of marriage. Children of parents who break up are much more likely to have struggles with school, drugs and mental health than children of parents who stay together.

On the teenage parenting front, things are getting better. In recent years, the number of teenage pregnancies has dropped. On the single parenting front, they aren't. After the sexual revolution of the sixties and seventies, many people seem to think that they have a right to weave in and out of relationships as they want. Their children just need to travel light and come along for the ride.

It was the psychoanalyst W. D. Winnicott who came up with the concept of the 'good enough parent'. He didn't talk about the 'good enough child'. What is a good enough child? A child who's healthy? A child who's clever? Or a child who's kind?

Katherine was pretty sure that a child who screamed and raged and kicked and hit was not the kind of child she wanted. 'My love for him,' she told me, in such a matter-of-fact voice that I had to compose my face, 'was just negative, right from the beginning. It took a long time for me to love him properly. But,' she added, 'I never didn't have that feeling of this terrible stretch when he was away from me. I had this need to protect him and this terrible worry about what kind of life he was going to have.'

Since her son Dan was born, life, she said, has been a series of battles. There's the battle to get him up and washed and dressed. There's the battle to stop him hurting other people and himself. There was the battle to get a diagnosis of autism, which took eighteen months, and the battle to get a statement of special needs, which took another eighteen months. And there was the two-and-a-half-year legal battle to get him into a special school. 'We couldn't afford a lot of the help we needed,' she said, 'so I did a lot of the legal work myself.'

On top of all of this, when she was seven and a half months pregnant with her second child, her husband was made redundant. They had agonized about whether to have another child, but decided to do it since they both had siblings they adored. 'I was earning seventeen thousand pounds,' said Katherine. 'My husband was earning sixty thousand. I thought we were going to lose the house. We realized that he would have to be at home to look after the children because we thought Dan might harm Tom. So I had to go all out.'

Katherine did go 'all out'. She worked 'all the hours God sent' and 'got promoted up and up and up'. She is now a successful civil servant in charge of a complex policy portfolio. 'So that,' she said, 'got me through. I had this driving thing that I needed to earn more money because I thought Dan's never going to be able to support himself. That thing about keeping going because you have no choice.'

And what, I asked, about the bloke? He sounds, I said, trying to keep the envy out of my voice, pretty amazing. Retraining as an electrician and fitting his work around childcare. Offering to give up full-time work to take the hits and the kicks. Oh, and still being around. Lots of fathers of children with disabilities don't actually stick around. Katherine's smile was like the smile in the *Madonna of the Rocks*. 'We are,' she said, 'like two halves of the same thing, really. Whatever happened, I had him, and I never had to worry about him leaving me. It's above all that. Having that one thing that was good.'

Thank God they both had that. There are other good things, too. Their other son, Tom, is healthy and happy. 'He is,' said Katherine, 'a joy.' And Katherine and her husband won their legal battle to get Dan into a special school. It has changed all their lives. 'From the minute he wakes up,' she said, 'everything they do is tailored to helping him cope in the world. They're teaching him how to be a social human.'

Since Dan has been at this new school, Katherine and her husband have been able to devote more time to Tom. They go on trips. They go on long walks. Katherine has been so starved of time to do anything but work and try to deal with her son that she now leaps at every opportunity. 'I've found myself doing quite mad things,' she confessed, 'like rock climbing, things I've always been scared of. I say yes to everything. I've learnt to squeeze everything out of half an hour.' She has built up a network of friends on Twitter. She walks seven miles a day. 'I'm fitter than I've ever been,' she said. 'When you can't make your mind any better, you can try and work on your body.'

Now, when Dan comes home at weekends, or for holidays, Katherine has some of the feelings she never thought she would have. 'I came in the sitting room,' she said, 'and he was on the sofa, doing something on his iPad, and I just felt this rush of warmth. I wanted to go and hug him, but I know he doesn't like that, so I didn't. Just this simple feeling of loving him, that's so new.'

I smiled, in relief. She smiled back. 'I used to have these dreams all the time,' she said. 'In the dream, he would not be as bad as he is, and I was able to talk to him. We'd have proper conversations. I'd wake up and for a few minutes I would think it was true. When he comes home now,' she said, so calmly that I felt my heart skip a beat, 'he's almost that boy.'

There has never been any doubt about how much Mimi loves her son. When I'm round at hers, I often hear her on the phone to Tom and the love in both their voices is so clear I sometimes wish I could bottle it and give it to everyone on Twitter.

Mimi does not have the support of a loving partner. Her home is full of beautiful furniture and paintings, but she doesn't seem to have quite such good taste in men. She doesn't walk seven miles a day either. She's seventy now and has a bit of arthritis, so that would be quite a challenge to her knees. A good relationship and exercise are both things the experts say help you to deal with challenging situations, but you can't just go on Amazon and order up a lovely partner – or new knees.

But, like Katherine, Mimi works very hard. She's seventy and she still works very hard. She runs workshops, mentors people, and does poetry readings, sometimes on the other side of the world. Work, she told me, is one of the things that has kept her going. And poetry, like policy, is hard. 'For a great many years,' she told me, 'it was difficult, because I always had the sense I hadn't the faintest idea what I was doing. You're just sort of in the dark. You're aware all the time of everything you don't know. You have to work with that, and despite that.'

It sounded, I said, a bit like finding out that your son has a mental illness psychiatrists say is incurable. My mother would certainly say that that's what it was like. You're floundering around in the dark, trying this thing and that thing and just hoping that one of those things will help.

Mimi told me before about the sense of 'misplaced optimism' she had when her daughter Tara was diagnosed with a degenerative disease and then again when Tom was diagnosed with schizophrenia. Optimism, I told her, is like a snake. It can seduce, but it can bite. Optimists make promises they can't keep. Optimists let other people down. But optimism, according to the scientific evidence, can be a useful coping strategy. People who think they will get better from an illness are more likely to get better than people who don't. People with religious beliefs are likely to live longer than people without them, even if their beliefs are based on delusion or literal interpretations of ancient texts. Optimistic surgeons, on the other hand, are more likely than their pessimistic peers to do harm.

So where, I asked Mimi, did her optimism come from? Mimi took a drag of her cigarette. 'It's not something I've really thought about too much,' she said. 'I tend to be pessimistic about the smaller things. Like, if I'm commissioned to write a poem, I instinctively think "oh God, this is going to be dreadful and I'll humiliate myself". And I agree with you about optimism being annoying. I'd much rather people said "yes, there is that risk", rather than "it will be wonderful, everything will be fine".'

She paused. 'I think probably that optimism comes from the same source as the voices that say "oh, this is terrible, this is the end of the world". Because you get so frightened you can't bear to look at it, so then you just think it will be fine.' So it's optimism as a form of denial? Denial can, according to some studies, 'improve your psychological functioning' if you have something like cancer. 'It comes,' said Mimi, 'from my childhood, where I find myself in a strange country, with a strange language, in a strange school, without any family or anyone. I think I remember that feeling that it will be all right. As in, Mummy will come and get you, even though I knew she wouldn't.'

Mimi was born in Iran, but sent to a boarding school on the Isle of Wight at the age of six. She didn't speak a word of English. She saw her mother about every four years. 'I had to believe everything would be OK,' she said, 'through all my years of growing up. You can collapse, you can get totally distraught, you can have a little breakdown or whatever, but if there's nobody there, if there's no audience, there's no one who's going to comfort you, you don't do it.'

Well, exactly. Lots of people said I was 'marvellous' both times I had cancer, but if you live on your own, what choice have you got? You could, I suppose, scream at the TV, but the TV is not going to say 'poor you'. I would rather not scream at my friends, because I would quite like to keep them.

For Mimi, that sense of 'it will be all right' kept her going in the terrible years when Tom was in and out of mental hospital. 'You don't go spiralling off into months and years of panic,' she said. During the worst times, and particularly the times when Tom disappeared for months without any contact, she tried, she said, to deal with things 'in a rational way'. She would look at the 'pros and cons' of whatever she was thinking of doing, 'figure it out' and bide her time. Work got her through. Friends got her through. She has good friends, because she is a good friend. She is patient. She is kind. She is extremely good company. And she's funny. Thank God for friends who are funny. All that 'how are you really?' stuff is all very well, but can we please also have a laugh?

Most people, I told her, would feel pretty angry to have two children diagnosed with an incurable disease. Doesn't she? Mimi sighed. 'I've never really understood that question "why me?" It just seems daft. I don't like daftness! I've always been aware of how much luck I've had in my life. So, on balance, I've been incredibly lucky to have such gorgeous kids. I think they're both lovely. They're both very beautiful, they're both very bright, they're both very talented. And best of all, they're both really nice people. I think,' she said, 'that's a blessing.'

I went to see my friend Louise the day after I had given a speech in Edinburgh. I was demob happy because the speech had been an ordeal. It was a keynote speech and I had been told to time it to the minute. Just before midnight at a dinner the night before, the chairman of the organization suddenly announced that he wanted ten minutes instead of fifteen. It took me three hours to cut the text and the slides and by then I was too tired to sleep. I gave the truncated version to a thousand people on no sleep and no rehearsal. Amazingly, it seemed to go down well.

Louise picked me up from Stirling station and in her beautiful garden I opened the champagne they had handed me as I left. We clinked glasses as we watched the sun set over the Trossachs. Whenever I see Louise, I always feel like clinking glasses. She has buried a baby and spent most of the last twelve years stuck at home with a child who can't lift her head. In spite of this, or perhaps because of it, her company still feels to me like champagne.

When Louise first moved to that house, Beatrice wasn't yet a year old and Sam was four. 'I tried very hard to keep things normal for Sam,' she told me. 'I was determined to cope on my own. I did cry a lot, but then I had things to cry about. I kept washing and brushing my teeth and feeding my other child. What more,' she said breezily, 'do you want? But I don't,' she added, 'remember feeling particularly bad.'

Really? She was pretty much a prisoner, with a child who was not going to make it into adulthood, and she was basically feeling fine? Louise took a sip of her champagne. 'It's, you know, the Alcoholics Anonymous thing. God grant me the courage to tolerate the things I can, etc.' I took a sip of mine and then recited it. 'Lord, grant me the serenity to accept the things I cannot change, the courage to change the things I can, and the wisdom to know the difference.' I had, I told her, been vaguely trying to follow it since I first found the prayer in my mid-twenties, though I've never been anywhere near AA and long ago ditched any belief in any kind of a God.

'Did I,' she asked, 'really have a choice?' No, I agreed, she didn't. But she certainly had a choice about how she dealt with the whole situation, and she seems to have done it with great . . . well, what's the word? Style? Verve? Panache? 'I often think,' said Louise, 'that one of the reasons I've basically got happier – and this is not to my credit – is that I'm less different to other people. As we get older, more and more people have had really bad things happen to them. Because you do feel very separate if everyone else is having a lovely time. That's one of the pains of it.'

Tell me about it. In my twenties, I told her, I felt so embarrassed because I felt I was a walking – or rather non-walking, that was the problem – disaster. I'd been disfigured with acne. I couldn't walk more than a few yards. My sister was in a desperate state. We were all in a desperate state. My parents were desperate because we were desperate. And I was meeting people whose only trauma had been getting a 2:1 instead of a first.

'For the first few years of Beatrice's life,' she said, 'it was very, very hard work looking after her. I don't remember being acutely unhappy or repressing anything, but perhaps I was? But then, when she was eight, her airway collapsed and I got a phone call in the middle of the night saying "your daughter has crashed, do you want her resuscitated?" That,' she said with her usual lacing of irony, 'was nice. So I went in, and those were dark, dark days. I was asked over and over again whether it was a life worth living and whether there was any point in keeping her alive. And I felt it was.'

Beatrice was given a tracheotomy and now breathes through a hole in her neck. She has twenty-four-hour care. 'She has,' said Louise, 'cost you, the taxpayer, millions and millions. A lot of these severely disabled kids go to one extreme or the other. They're either very happy or very unhappy, and the ones that are very unhappy, it's a lot more difficult, obviously. But Beatrice has happiness.' How, I asked, does she know? 'Because she laughs and smiles when she sees people and things she likes. She's my happy, smiley daughter who happens to need extremely high levels of care.'

One of the things that has always struck me about Louise is her lack of self-pity. How the hell, I asked, has she managed it? Louise offered me a crisp. 'Well,' she said, 'I am a bit of a snob and I can't bear to be pitied. I want people to think I'm coping, so I can have interesting conversations with them, rather than just doom and gloom. And even your best friends get sick of misery. They do, don't they?'

Yes, I said. You have to be good company. Friends will help you get through, but you only have friends if you're nice to be around. If you have credit built up, you can sit and weep at times, but you do need to have the credit built up. You can't be miserable all the time. You have to be interested in other people. Louise nodded and we both took another gulp of champagne. 'That's crucial,' she said, 'being interested in other people. I think that's a big life lesson for everybody.'

Louise got breast cancer not long after I got it the second time. 'I remember thinking,' she said, '"well, that's fucking great"! I joined a gym around the time I was diagnosed and the people who go during the day all want to chat. I thought: I can either do the disabled child or the breast cancer, or people will think I'm a walking tragedy!'

I remember feeling pretty much the same. My sister had died, my father had died and then I got cancer and thought: enough, already. Let's talk about the weather. I told Louise about the school reunions I had missed, because I couldn't face the shiny, happy families and the glittering careers. 'I'm going to a school reunion next month,' she said, 'my first one. They had one about fifteen years ago and I thought: there's no way I'm going, they will all be successful, they'll all have healthy children, functional marriages, fabulous careers, great houses, look good, not be fat, all of that. And now I think I don't care. Things will have gone wrong for some of them.'

We clinked glasses again. 'I think one of the reasons I have coped better than some parents do,' said Louise, 'is that the baby's born, they're all happy and then someone says "oh, it's got spina bifida" and your whole world falls apart. I didn't have that situation. My two babies came into the world with a junior doctor telling me that they were both going to die, and one of them survived, and that was good. The glass is half full. When people ask me what Beatrice has done to or for me, I have to say something that sounds meaningless. She's ruined my life, and,' she said, taking one last gulp of champagne, 'been the making of me.'

A signal you send out

My upstairs neighbour keeps flooding my flat. The first time he left his bath running, what came through the ceiling was like Niagara Falls. I grabbed all the saucepans and placed them on the floor before dashing off to interview Alice Cooper. When Alice Cooper talked about performing on stage with dead chickens or boa constrictors, all I could think about was whether or not my flat had turned into the *Titanic*. When it happened the third time, I was on the phone. I heard a loud beeping and then smelled burning as water poured through the smoke alarm and on to the floor. The man I was talking to said I should call the fire brigade. Ten minutes later, six huge firemen were sitting in my hall.

Once they had stuck a label on the smoke alarm system I had already disabled, and a temporary smoke alarm in a place that meant yet another ceiling would have to be repainted, we did 'the paperwork'. How many people lived at the property? Oh right! Just one. And is it Mrs or Miss Patterson? Miss! Rightio. You could almost see them sniffing around for cats.

I don't know why single women make some people feel uneasy, but we do. In restaurants, when I have gone to eat on my own, I have been ushered to half-hidden tables at the back. Once, in a café in Stoke Newington, I was asked to leave. I had just spent a fiver on a coffee and pastry and thought I had bought myself a good hour of papers and peace. As soon as I'd taken my last bite, the manager came up to me. 'We need this table now,' he told me. Two fierce-looking young women were standing at the entrance with giant buggies. 'I'm eating my breakfast,' I said. 'You've finished it. The table,' he said, as if he'd just unearthed an obscure contract in a legal dispute, 'is reserved.' I felt the blood rush to my cheeks as I stormed out.

It's there at the gym, or on the face of the official, that pitying look when you're asked to put your next of kin and faithfully print the name of your mum. It's there when people ask you about your holiday and it gradually dawns on them that you have actually gone away on your own. 'What was *that* like?' said one political editor in the green room at Sky. I'd actually had a lovely time, reading, eating and basking in the sun, but suddenly I felt as if I'd been sent to some gulag, beaten and fed on dry crusts.

Over the years, so many people have asked me why I am single. The poet Wendy Cope, who wrote many poems about the angst of being single before she found love, at forty-nine, once told me that practically all the poets she knew had asked if anyone knew. I even once bought a book called *If I'm So Wonderful, Why Am I Still Single?*, as if the answer might be encrypted in some Da Vinci code on the last page. I think I used to think that being single was a kind of affliction, a shameful state that had been handed to me by fate. It has taken me a very, very long time to realize that I'm probably single because I really like being on my own.

'I don't think,' said a shrink once, 'that you actually want to meet someone.' I was lying on a couch. Yes, like Woody Allen,

I was actually lying on a couch. I was shocked. What do you *mean* I don't want to meet someone? What about all the dating? The bloody awful dating? What about the speed dating, and the internet dating, and the dating agency, and the blind dates arranged by friends, and the dinners, and the parties, and the sheer, exhausting and sometimes humiliating effort? I had gone to see the shrink because I didn't know what to do. It was not long after I had fallen in love, been dumped and then found out that my cancer had come back. It seemed a bit much to cope with all at once.

I saw that shrink for three years. I can't even say exactly what happened in that time, because it seemed to happen at a level beyond words. But one thing I did learn was that I don't actually need to be with somebody else.

I was thirty-five when I decided that if I was going to be single, I was going to try to do it magnificently. This may have been a slightly unhelpful self-fulfilling prophecy, but in some ways it has served me well. It was when I bought my flat. I was on my way to take some books back to the library when I suddenly saw a sign saying 'loft apartment' and a picture flashed into my head of a huge loft, full of people and parties and books. Unfortunately, I wasn't earning enough to buy a huge anything, but I did go and look at an old school in Stoke Newington that was being converted into 'lofts'. Some of them were enormous. The one I looked at was not. My father was with me. My beloved father was with me. He said, 'I think you should go for it,' so I sold my flat and did.

My flat has a small bedroom, a small study and a tiny kitchen, but it has quite a big sitting room, with a gallery I use as a dining space, and the ceiling goes up to the second floor. I can't have big parties, but I can have parties. And I can have dinners. I once served meatballs made with minced plastic, not realizing that the blender had a plastic guard you had to take off. I have dropped sea bass on the floor, scooped it up and served it anyway. I have about three recipes. The one I do most often is 'my lemon chicken', which is actually Lisa's recipe and takes about ten minutes to prepare. But people don't come round to eat gourmet food, or at least they don't come round to eat gourmet food at mine. They come to eat, drink, laugh and be with you.

Single men get called bachelors, which sounds like really good fun. Single women still sometimes get called spinsters, which makes people think of Victorian governesses wanting to cover table legs. In the Middle Ages, as Sara Maitland points out in her book *How to Be Alone*, the word 'spinster' was a compliment. It was someone who could spin well and was therefore financially independent. 'The word', says Maitland, 'was generously applied to all women at the point of marriage as a way of saying they came into the relationship freely, from personal choice not financial desperation. Now it is an insult, because we fear "for" such women – and now men as well – who are probably "sociopaths".'

I'm not sure that most people would actually go as far as thinking that single people are 'sociopaths', but I do think some people feel quite threatened by the idea that a woman can function quite well in the world on her own. She can walk! She can talk! She can have a good job! She can buy a nice flat! She can go on holiday on her own and have a really nice time! 'My view,' said Juliet Taylor, the headhunter I met when I lost my job, during one of our regular catch-ups in a hotel bar, 'is that anxiety is largely created by compliance or otherwise to social norms. Eccentrics, by definition, feel no compunction to conform. Therefore their experience of stress and anxiety is massively reduced compared to other people who are conformist.'

Juliet thinks we can all learn from eccentrics. Neither she nor I would call ourselves eccentric, but we have both, we agreed, tended to do things in our own way. 'You don't necessarily want to be a man in a caravan or someone who has fifty cats,' she said, 'but what we can all learn from eccentrics is that you can be happy without conforming. And people with a very strong character are often happier. People often regard me,' she said with a cheerful smile, 'as an eccentric, because I don't worry about the stuff other people seem to worry about. That's because my family is eccentric, my mother in particular. I've learnt from her to protect myself from the things that affect other people.'

Oh, what a gift. To stop worrying what other people think. How different our lives would be if we all stopped worrying what other people thought. In my journalism, I learnt to do this years ago. What's the point in having a platform if you can't use it to say what you think? When I go on TV or radio, I often get messages or tweets saying 'what makes you think your opinion is worth any more than anyone else's?' My response is usually: it isn't, but I've been invited to give it. And when the tweets come, telling me how ugly and old and stupid I am, I know it's mostly because they wish they could have a platform, too.

Whenever I see Patsy, my heart lifts. It always did. The moment we met, at that bookshop when I was twenty-two, we started a conversation that has never stopped. It started as we ripped open boxes of books in the tiny stock room, and continued in lunches and tea breaks, and then in the pub after work. It went on sometimes at weekends in her house, in a small village outside Guildford, a house that looked like a cottage in a fairy tale.

We talk about books. We talk about love. We talk about life. When I first met Patsy, she was separated from her second husband, Daniel. She had spent years working as a PA, then worked in the bookshop, then did a degree in English literature in her forties and then became an English teacher. I hope the boys she taught know how lucky they were.

When Patsy told me, at our usual table in the café part of the Wolesley, about her love life, I thought it sounded like a slice of social history. She was, she reminded me, a virgin when she got married for the first time, at twenty. When that marriage broke up, she moved into a little room on her own. It was 1967. 'I've never been lonely in my elder life,' said Patsy, 'but that was a lonely time, because you weren't part of Swinging London. There was something a bit sleazy about it all.'

Unfortunately, the 'swinging' ethos took quite a toll on her marriage. Her husband, Daniel, who was an artist, fitted the stereotype. He liked women. He liked drink. When she told me about some of the things he used to get up to, she laughed at the expression on my face. 'I don't think I can ever not love him,' she said. 'That person is still there somewhere. It's not like love where you feel great. I had a lover and they make you feel wonderful. I know the difference between that love and loving Daniel, who made me feel terrible.'

Once, she told me, he came back from a skiing holiday with

friends and their daughter Jane innocently announced that Patsy had managed to leave a burn mark, from a candle, on a cupboard. 'He went berserk!' said Patsy. 'I thought: hang on, you've had two weeks skiing and I've been looking after our house, our child. Then he gave me a key ring with a little ski boot hanging on it. I remember throwing it at him and saying: boots! I'll have a skiing holiday! There were so many incidents like that. You've already got the idea, haven't you,' she said, 'of why I'm happy to be single!'

Well, yes, I have, but it isn't just that. Patsy is always, always, the life and soul of a social gathering. Both men and women are drawn to her. I have seen the way people look at her, as if a crumb from her table is magic dust to be grasped and safely stowed away. Patsy loves the theatre like no one I have met. She hoovers up books. She has masses of friends. She has her daughter. She has her voluntary work. She has her grandchildren. But most of all, she likes being on her own.

A year after I left *The Independent*, she told me that her great love's wife had died and he was now trying to woo Patsy back. She had had an affair with him for years. 'With him,' she said, 'it was just the nice things. We didn't talk about the mortgage. We didn't talk about the children. The first time we met in a hotel, he put the key on the table. When I got upstairs, he had this little suitcase with champagne, two glasses. It was all fun.' The affair ended more than fifteen years ago and there had, said Patsy, been nothing but the 'odd fling' since. And now the love of her life was begging her to come back.

Her friends 'egged her on'. Her daughter was keen. Patsy agonized. I knew she would say no. You freaked out, I told her.

You didn't want to be with him. We were sitting here, at this very table, and I knew you didn't really want to be with him. 'I went home,' said Patsy, 'and he rang up and wanted to talk. I was just about to sit down and watch *Match of the Day*!' So, I said, like a judge announcing a verdict, you didn't want it. 'No!' said Patsy. 'I'm a mean old selfish person!' No, I said, you're not, but you value your independence. All that stuff you built up for yourself, your career. You were an inspirational teacher. You've had this amazing social life. 'Don't exaggerate!' said Patsy. It's true, I told her. You've had this incredibly rich, full life. And the truth is, you're a profoundly unconventional person and you didn't want to shack up with some bloke whose dinner you didn't want to cook.

Patsy gave an exasperated smile, but it was like a concession of defeat. 'I've had comments,' she said, 'like one couple who came to live with me briefly because they were between houses. The wife said, "I wish Patsy had somebody there. I wish she could get together with Tim," and her husband said, "Oh no, I don't think she'd be interested in security." He said, "She doesn't want anyone, because if she did, she would." I think,' she added, 'there's definitely a signal you put out. Daniel used to say, "You don't realize how difficult you are to approach."' I sighed. I've lost count of the number of people who have said that to me. That 'ice maiden' business among the backstage staff at the Southbank Centre was, I've gathered over the years, just the tip of a giant iceberg of male resentment about me being too cool, too independent or just too damn fierce. It is, I told Patsy, about being too self-contained, isn't it? 'Yes,' she said. 'It's also somehow not wanting anything. Because you don't!'

'The other thing I've thought,' she said, 'is when you see people and you hear what they're saying and you just think "oh God, I'd hate to be in that situation". There's someone I sometimes do some work with and she said to me recently, "I'd really love to have your life." I said, "What do you mean?" She said, "Well, you have such a lovely life." I said, "Well, it's not fun all the time," thinking what can I say that's not fun? And then I said, "Are you all right?" She said, "Yes, I'm all right, but I just don't have your exuberance." I was trying,' Patsy said with a sheepish smile, 'not to be exuberant.'

When I was asked to host a salon, by a lovely woman who runs a 'knowledge networking business', I was thrilled. I didn't have to organize it. I didn't have to cook the food. All I had to do was slap on a bit of make-up and turn up.

If it wasn't exactly Dorothy Parker and the Algonquin Round Table, it was still a lot of fun. We talked about books. We talked about banks. We talked about business and art. We talked about big issues, like unemployment and debt in the Western world, and small issues, like the rise of the twirly moustache. What we didn't talk about was our jobs. We didn't talk about our children, or where they went to school. We didn't talk about being happily married, or unhappily married, or happily single, or miserably alone. We didn't have to bother with any of this. We could, for just one evening, forget about the details of our lives, and think about ideas, and the world.

I looked up the history of the salon before I went out, and was pleased to see that one of the key women to have hosted salons was Queen Christina, after she abdicated from the Swedish throne and went to live in Rome. I felt a ridiculous surge of pride because my Twitter name is @queenchristina_, I'm half Swedish and was born in Rome. I was interested to read that Christina felt 'an insurmountable distaste for marriage' and 'an insurmountable distaste for all the things that females talked about'. I wouldn't go quite as far as that, but I would certainly rather talk about politics than fashion or shoes. And I would rather talk about current affairs than other people's families. It's one of the reasons I like parties. At a party, you're more likely to talk to someone you've just met about what's going on in the world than whether their little Amelia or Jack got into the school of their choice.

I have always been to parties on my own. It was only when I went to a garden party at Buckingham Palace, and saw eight thousand people, all in couples, that I thought perhaps it might have been a good idea to bring a guest. The only people I recognized were Cherie Blair and the Queen. They didn't, for quite good reasons, recognize me. So I marched up to a woman who looked friendly. She turned out to be the 'networking queen', Carole Stone. We had a lively conversation and she has since invited me to some of her parties. I think this kind of thing happens much more when you go to parties on your own.

It's the same with travel. If you travel on your own, you usually end up meeting nice people and having interesting conversations. You do, of course, spend a fair bit of time not talking to anyone, but who wants to talk all the time? There's the whole of world literature to get through! There's the whole of history and the whole of world news! And we all need time to stop, and muse, and dream.

Having a good life as a single person does involve more effort. If you want to see someone, you have to make an arrangement. Most single people I know make much more social effort than the people I know in couples. They also have a much richer social life. They go out more. They have more adventures and do more interesting things. When you see single people out at restaurants with their friends, they're usually having animated conversations. They're not the ones staring at their iPhones and looking – well, let's just say it, bored.

In the months after I lost my job, I met an awful lot of people to ask advice, for coffee, for lunch, for drinks. Quite a few of them were people I hardly knew. About half of them were men. After years of having more women friends than men, I've learnt that I really like the company of men. Over dinner one night, one of these men asked me how it was all going. I sighed and then told him about some of the articles I was researching, some of the books I had been reviewing and a couple of talks I had given. This man has a very big, very well-paid job. He is happily married, with a son he adores. He topped up my glass and then said something that shocked me. 'It sounds,' he said, 'pretty enviable.'

Our culture has not been kind to single women. In literature, we are portrayed as shrews and battleaxes and colourful eccentrics and tweedy detectives, or pretty young women just waiting to be picked and saved. We have a shelf life. There comes a moment when we have lost our 'bloom'. One minute we are ripe for the picking. The next, we're a Miss Bates or a Miss Havisham, struggling on with our tiny lives and rarely mentioned without the word 'pity' or 'poor'.

When *Bridget Jones* hit the bookshelves, and then the big screen, there was a big sigh of collective relief as youngish, brightish, normal-looking single women finally saw a version of themselves that didn't actually make them wince. You didn't have to knock back *quite* so much Chardonnay to be pleased that someone else was talking about the challenges of Christmas in your childhood bed.

Sex and the City followed. A world of bad dates, dry manhattans and very expensive shoes. If we couldn't quite match the lifestyle, some of us could match the bad dates, though I'm pleased to say that I have never yet been asked to pee on a man in bed. Sex was at the heart of it. These beautiful, brassy, bracingly frank women had big hopes for big homes and big lives, with plenty of money and plenty of sex. All very glitzy. All very entertaining. But this is not how most women live.

When Anita Brookner died, I looked again at some of her novels. The women in them could not be less like the *Sex and the City* girls. They are polite and self-disciplined and shy. They are not fiercely independent – they are not fiercely anything – but they work hard and do their jobs well. Like their creator, they have a clear-eyed view of the world. They would like to believe that the meek will inherit the earth, and that the mousy get swept off their feet by handsome Mr Rochesters, but they know that it's the bold and brassy who usually win.

I first read *Hotel du Lac* when I was twenty and thought it was a portrait of a miserable life. Dowdy middle-aged woman goes on holiday by a lake and faces up to a future without love. Why not, I thought, just go the whole hog and get a noose? Thirty-odd years on, it felt like a different book. Edith, the romantic novelist at the heart of it, has run away from her wedding, at thirty-nine, to a dull man she thought might be her last chance. Sent by her friends, in disgrace, on a solitary holiday at the Hotel du Lac, she meets another dull man who offers to marry her and give her the social position he thinks she needs. He doesn't love her. She doesn't love him.

'I do not sigh and yearn', she says, 'for extravagant displays of passion.' What she wants is something much more modest. 'What I crave', she says, 'is the simplicity of routine. An evening walk, arm in arm, in fine weather. A game of cards.' But you can't do this, she decides, with someone you don't love. And so she turns him down.

Anita Brookner's heroines are single not because they are too dowdy, but because they are too honest. They know that life is full of compromise, but they still see a compromise too far. They have learnt to live with quiet courage because of the choices they have made.

People don't talk all that much about quiet courage. They don't think that navigating the world on your own needs courage. They also don't understand that creating art, or writing books, or even carving out a decent career, takes time that many women who are wives and mothers don't have. Emily Dickinson knew this. Jane Austen knew this. Virginia Woolf knew this, and wrote about a woman's need to have 'a room of one's own'. Anita Brookner knew this. Starting at fifty-three, she wrote twenty-four glittering, uncomfortably truthful novels that gave voice to the unassuming, the modest and the quiet. And let's also not forget the quiet, shy, modest, single men.

Anita Brookner knew what we all learn: that life is a balance between freedom and security. Security is – well, safe. Freedom is frightening, but sometimes more fun. You can be lonely in a relationship and happy on your own. I think almost anyone can have a relationship if they really want one, but you have to be prepared to make the compromises, and put in the work.

When that fireman called me 'Miss', I almost laughed. I nearly said that yes, I was single and probably twice his age, and this was why I had ended up, after a dinner the night before, at a members' club at 2 a.m., having a fascinating conversation with a publisher, a journalist and a man who used to work with the Prince of Wales. I had a wild urge to quote Keats, who told his brother George that he didn't want to marry, because he didn't want to limit his life. 'I feel more and more every day . . .' he wrote, 'that I do not live in this world alone but in a thousand worlds.' Well, I'll raise a giant glass to that.

Shooting the breeze

When I turned up at the London Eye, I saw a few men clutching gifts. Gradually, the group grew. Then my friend Nick arrived, led by his partner, Ivan, and wearing a blindfold. It was Nick's birthday, and Ivan wanted to give him a nice surprise.

Nick's face, when he took the blindfold off, certainly showed surprise. Who wouldn't be surprised to think they were being taken off for a birthday meal and find themselves about to drink champagne with twenty-five friends in a glass capsule 400 feet above the River Thames? And then put in a cab home to find that their partner has filled their flat with food and drink for a party?

I have known Nick for fifteen years, since we both moved into the same converted school. He loves having parties. When he lived upstairs, he and his then partner, Stefano, used to have musical soirees as well as parties, where people would play the piano or sing. Stefano is still upstairs and he loves having parties, too. We all love having parties. We all love bringing together our friends.

You don't have to have parties to have friends. If you want to have friends, you just need to know how to be a friend because being a friend is an art.

I learnt it at my mother's knee. Like her fellow countrywoman

Greta Garbo, my mother sometimes mutters that she just 'wants to be alone'. This is not true. She is very happy in her own company, which is just as well since she is now on her own, but she has more friends than anyone I have ever met. She has good friends because she is good company. She is cheerful, and curious, and polite. She knows that the art of conversation is based on listening and asking questions. People sometimes say to me 'you can tell you're a journalist because you ask so many questions'. I tell them that it's nothing to do with being a journalist. It's because I was brought up to be polite.

Sometimes, I'm not polite. In all my years of internet dating, for example, I would sometimes say to the man sitting across the table, 'Would you like to ask me a question now?' Usually, I would go home exhausted, thinking that I could now write a PhD on the person I'd just met, and wondering whether they had learnt a single fact about me. The next day, I would often get a text or email saying they'd had a lovely time and would love to meet again. I sometimes felt like sending them an invoice, for therapeutic services. A man with no curiosity is not a man I want to share my bed.

I was lucky where I grew up. As I've explained, it was on an estate where we children were practically shooed out of the front door and left to roam. From the age of eighteen months I was best friends with my next-door neighbour but one, Monique. She and her brothers had been born in Barbados. My sister was born in Bangkok. My brother and I were born in Rome. I was shocked to discover that babies could be born in England, too.

Monique and I were nurses, cowboys, maids and queens. At Christmas, we were Mary and Joseph. At Halloween, we were witches, casting spells in the Wendy house and drinking Cherry-ade blood. We did magic shows in the garden. We did plays, inviting all the neighbours and acting all the parts. We played a game called 'Mary and Marion'. For this, you had to make a pile of chairs in the garden and cover the pile with blankets. Once you were inside, you could travel to the magic world in the sky. When our mothers called us in for beef burgers or Findus pancakes, we had to yell 'there's a storm coming, there's a storm coming!' and whip off the blankets, but without knocking the chairs down. Why? Goodness only knows why, but after all these years we are still in touch.

I once, by the way, chaired a panel with a writer who told me he spent quite a lot of his childhood washing grass. He and his friend picked the blades by hand, dipped them in soapy suds, rinsed them and then hung them on the washing line to dry. Another writer, a poet, told me that he jumped off a climbing frame, convinced that he could fly. He fractured both his ankles when he found out he could not.

Friends are the people you laugh with, weep with, play with, wash grass with. Friends are the people who pick you up when you leap off a climbing frame and it doesn't go quite as you planned. When I fell off the wall Monique and I regarded, for a while, as our 'camp', it was Monique who ran for help. We had fixed a broomstick in the ground to help us climb up on the wall. Unfortunately, I half landed on it, and in an unfortunate place. Luckily, Monique's mother was a nurse. She made me do a shoulder stand without my pants as she inspected the rip. I had stitches and was in hospital for several days, but am still grateful that I just managed to avoid losing my virginity to a stick.

*

When I lost my job, my friends should have won awards. At first, I couldn't speak to them. This is my pattern when something goes badly wrong. When I first discovered I had cancer, I told them by text and then didn't answer the phone. When I was told that I would need a mastectomy, chemotherapy, radiotherapy and drugs that would, at thirty-nine, make me fat and menopausal as well as bald, it was the same. My friends were mostly happily coupled up, with young families. What the fuck did they know about going through this carnival parade of horrors alone?

In fact, I managed to avoid some of the horrors. I found a surgeon who helped me avoid the mastectomy, refused chemotherapy (after looking at a graph) and found that the drugs I had to take for five years afterwards didn't make me fat or menopausal at all. My friends were wonderful, as they always are. Or perhaps I should say that nearly all my friends were wonderful. One had just met a dreadful man. She took me into hospital for my first operation and then seemed to melt into the air. For my fortieth birthday, and to thank my friends for their support, I had drinks at the Savoy. That friend didn't turn up. She forgot to send a card. I had been on holidays with her for ten years. We had shared the deepest secrets in our hearts. She is, of course, not a friend now.

When my cancer came back, my friends Jo and Lorna took it in turns to come with me to my hospital appointments. Jo was with me when the diagnosis was confirmed. Lorna was with me when the surgeon told me that it looked as though the kind of cancer I had was one that didn't have a good prognosis at all. Those were not the words the surgeon used, but they were the words I found on Google when I got home. When I went in for my big operation, Lorna sat with me in the waiting room, with coffee and cake and *Vanity Fair*. It was only recently that she told me that when she left me on the ward, she sat down on the floor of the corridor and howled.

When I went back to the hospital for a check-up, two weeks after the operation, Jo went with me. I could still hardly stand or walk. I had taken my lipstick out of my handbag, because it hurt to lift anything at all. When I saw the registrar, I told him that my reconstruction had gone a bit pink. He looked at it, drew a line in felt tip around the pink patch and told me that they were putting me back on the ward. 'We don't,' he said, 'want you to lose it.' I thought of the scar, like barbed wire, running the whole width of my hips, and the pain that kept me awake at night, and the feeling I had of being stretched on a rack and thought: not half as much as me.

I had nothing but a handbag, a tissue and a set of keys with me. Jo went back to her flat and came back to the ward with pyjamas, knickers, a bag of posh toiletries, a hairbrush and a choice of Barbara Kingsolver or Lorrie Moore. She even brought a smoothie. She had gone to her flat and made me a smoothie. A friend is a person who makes you a smoothie in hell.

In the days after I lost my job, I emailed my friends. They couldn't believe my bosses had behaved in the way they had behaved, and particularly since I was still being treated for cancer. What they said about the editor, and the managing editor, and the young man who had taken over my boss's job and decided to veto my contract for a column, was probably not kind, but it did make me feel a bit better. Friends are people who will rage when they think you have been wronged.

My friend Helen invited me down to Devon. I sat at her kitchen table and cried. I didn't weep and rage with all my friends, because weeping and raging can get boring. The other thing with weeping and raging is that it doesn't solve the problem. It might give you a temporary release, but when there's something broken in your life what you really want to do is try to fix it.

It doesn't help to talk. I know this goes against the received wisdom about distress or trauma, or whatever you want to call it, but I honestly think it doesn't help all that much to talk. If talking solved problems, or perceived problems, then I would have found a lovely boyfriend twenty-five years ago. I have moaned and moaned and moaned and moaned to friends about being single. I could have written *War and Peace* in that time. I could have built up a business empire. I could have sailed round the world or walked on the moon. What have I achieved by all that moaning? Apart, I mean, from boring my friends? Nada. Niente. Zilch.

If I'd stopped moaning I might even have noticed that I was actually having quite a nice time, and that some of the friends I was moaning to had not had their own problems wiped away, just because they had a man in their bed.

I didn't actually moan all that much about cancer, because I found there wasn't all that much to say. Get the damn thing cut out. Blast yourself with X-rays. Take the pills and keep your fingers crossed. Now can we go to the theatre? Or the cinema? Or crack open a nice bottle of wine? How do you feel? How do I feel? How does everyone feel? You know what, who cares? How you're feeling now is probably not how you're going to be feeling tomorrow. As I get older, I get less interested in how we all feel and more interested in what we all do.

When you're feeling terrible, you probably do want someone close to you to know that you're in pain. It meant a lot to me that Helen let me sit at her kitchen table and cry. It meant a huge amount to me that Jo and Lorna were with me when I thought I was probably going to die quite soon. I have wept in front of my friends Ros and Nick, when the pain in my legs came back, and when they scooped me up and took me in. Sometimes you just need a witness to your pain. But I'm not so sure about the talking part. I think it can help to talk about something once or twice, but not over and over and over and over and over and over again.

Cows have friends. A 'lecturer in animal behaviour' called Krista McLennan has shown that cows even have best friends. When a cow is put in a pen with her best friend, she has, according to her studies, a much nicer time than when she's with a stranger or on her own. Her cortisol level is lower and so is her heart rate. She may or may not whistle a merry tune. She doesn't seem to feel the need to give a blow-by-blow account of her latest upset or slight. She can just chew the cud, shoot the breeze and be soothed by her friend's smell and the sight of her lovely big eyes.

The psychiatrist Simon Wessely has done a lot of research on trauma. He has, for example, done studies on the survivors of the London 7/7 bombings. What he discovered was that getting people to talk about their trauma straight away sometimes did more harm than good. 'People,' he said in a recent interview, 'are a bit tougher than we think.' After the bombings people who were directly affected were offered counselling and the ones who got it took longer to recover than the people who didn't.

'Most people,' he said, 'will cope through normal social networks.' Normal social networks where you talk a bit, and then move on.

What I want from my friends, increasingly, is fun. I want a laugh. I want to have a nice time. When I meet my friend Lisa, for example, we sometimes laugh so much my cheeks ache by the time we part. Laughter is good for you. All the studies show that laughter is good for your health, your immune system and your general sense of wellbeing. But it's a bit like the sex-is-good-for-you thing. No one wants to do something because it's good for you. We want to do things because they give us joy.

After a column I wrote about the culture of the NHS, I was asked to give a talk. The column had been about how people do a much better job if they like their work. The headline, which I didn't write, was 'The Secret to an Effective NHS Workforce: Fun'. I was asked by the director of HR at Surrey County Council to give a talk on 'how to have fun in the workplace'. Yes, I really was asked to talk about how to have fun in the office. I thought of *The Office*. I thought of David Brent. 'How would you like to be remembered?' says one colleague to Brent. 'Simply,' says Brent, with his usual smirk, 'as the man who put a smile on the face of all who he met.' He certainly put a smile on my face for reminding me just how awful office life can be.

The most fun I had in an office was at the Poetry Society, but an awful lot of that seemed to be about margaritas in the sunshine on the roof, San Miguel in the Poetry Café, and gathering outside my office to mark some tiny victory with cava and Kettle Chips. I wasn't at all sure how I could turn this into anything that might seem like a practical policy for middle managers at Surrey County

Council, so I talked about the work of the neuroscientist Antoine Lutz, who showed that organizations that are nice to their staff are much more productive than those that aren't. And I talked about a film made by an Israeli film director, Yoav Shamir, called *10% – What Makes a Hero?* He wanted, he said, to 'identify the secret ingredient all heroes share'. He met a bloke who leapt on to the New York subway tracks to save a man who had fallen off the platform and into the path of a train. He met a woman who had hidden Jews in Belgium in the Second World War. He met a surgeon who had given away 99 per cent of his income. Shamir didn't, unfortunately, find the secret formula. What he found was that the 'heroes' he met all said that they had a lot of fun.

You can't prescribe fun. There are people, apparently, who run laughter workshops, in hospitals and workplaces, but they are probably the kind of people who do 'mindfulness for the bottom line' in banks. Count me out. Count me in if you can make some money out of it, but really, count me out. Fun is in the eye, or wobbling shoulders or stomach, of the beholder. It's that delicious sense you have when the world suddenly feels lighter because you're having a good time with people you like.

Many years ago, when I was working at the Southbank Centre, I had dinner with Gore Vidal. He was as funny and sharp as you'd expect. There have been many times in my adult life when I have thought of his line about friends. 'Whenever a friend succeeds,' he once said, 'a little something in me dies.' It would be very nice to think this was never true, but sometimes it just is.

Three of my closest friends at school got into Oxford and I didn't. I had applied to Jesus. I had given my life to Jesus. But

Jesus, it turned out, didn't want me. Balliol, Brasenose and Somerville did want them. They all had private tuition and I didn't, which may have played more of a part than God. My friends all met their partners while they were at Oxford. I had one semi-platonic relationship at Durham for five weeks. They all started having babies. I didn't. Did you *really* expect me to go to those school reunions?

One by one, my friends paired off. I would make more single friends and then they would pair off. They would do this because this, for the most part, is what people do. When they introduced me to their partners, or got married, or had babies, I would try very hard to smile. I tried to feel pleased for them, but sometimes I just wanted to stamp my feet and yell: 'But what about *me*?'

I once walked out of my friend's husband's book launch after he had given a speech about finding the love of his life. I was so eaten up by envy I couldn't stay in the room. Oh, and let's not get on to books. Why are so many of my friends successful writers? No, don't tell me it's because they actually sit down and, you know, write books. 'Writers,' said Salman Rushdie at a literary dinner I once went to, 'are people who finish books.' At the time, it seemed both obvious and profound. They are not, in other words, people who dream of writing books, but who can't be bothered and can't face the rejection.

'A man's friendships', said Charles Darwin, 'are one of the best measures of his worth.' Let's be generous and assume he was talking about women, too. I have learnt to swallow the odd stab of envy towards my friends because they are the finest people I know. And when I talk about friends, I don't mean the people you might meet for coffee or lunch or a drink. The

British anthropologist Robin Dunbar thinks we can't maintain stable social relationships with more than about 150 people. I don't think my active social circle is as big as that, but there are quite a few people I meet for coffee, lunch or drinks, just because I like them.

Friends are something else. Friends are the people who are there in the middle of the night when your heart has been broken. They are the people who will offer you a room when your flat is flooded, or when you're so exhausted that you have decided to buy yourself some time off and rented out your flat on Airbnb. Friends are the people who cook food for your parties, because they know you hate cooking, or who open their hearts and homes to you, because your weird illness has come back and the doctors can't seem to do anything about it, and nor can they, but at least they can offer you some company, some home-cooked food and some nice wine.

It goes without saying that you will do the same, or something similar, for them. Because that's the other thing about friendship: it's equal. It's reciprocal. It's give and take. When I was young, I seem to have had a sign on my forehead that said: 'Come to me, all ye who are weary and heavy laden. Come, all ye moaners, all ye slackers, all ye takers. Suck me dry.' And they would, and then they would skip off until the next time and I would be left feeling as if someone had filled my pockets with stones.

I've toughened up. I've pruned. I have a strict vetting policy now. We all sometimes slip up, of course. I've told friends off when they have hurt me or let me down and they have done the same to me. Friends are necessary critics. Sometimes they tell each other truths they don't particularly want to hear. But sometimes when I hear people talk about their friends, I wonder if they actually like them. So let's get back to basics. Friends are people you like. They are people whose company you enjoy. We should all find some space in our lives for people who can't give us as much as we give them. But they are not our friends.

The Ancient Greeks used the same word, *philos*, for a friend as a lover. Some of my friendships have been a bit like falling in love. That sense of something stirring, igniting. Sometimes, it's a sense of a shared passion, but often it isn't. Quite a few of my friends come from very different cultures and backgrounds. I have known Winston, for example, for sixteen years and in that time he hasn't mentioned a single book. Friendship isn't to do with similarity. It's to do with the spirit.

Friendship, according to the research, is one of the key factors in developing resilience. It helps you develop a stronger immune system, increases your tolerance of pain and reduces the risk of depression and early death. Those of us who are single or gay are often much better at building strong networks of friends than what Bridget Jones called 'smug marrieds'. Just don't come knocking on our door when your relationship breaks up. In friendship, you reap what you sow.

In that capsule at the top of the London Eye, I looked out at this city I love. To my left were the Houses of Parliament, that place that had, over the years, occupied so many of my thoughts and columns. Ahead of me was the National Gallery, where, three years before, I had stood in front of Leonardo's *Lady with an Ermine* and had a strange feeling that I was standing in the presence of God. On my right was Tate Modern, where I had recently seen the Matisse cut-outs with Jo. When Matisse did them, he was in a wheelchair and had just had his second operation for cancer. The pure, shining simplicity of the work had made me cry.

I smiled at Nick, and Ivan, and at their friends Amanda and Esther, who had generously offered me the use of their flat for a couple of weeks while they were away. And I remembered something Matisse once said. 'There are', he said, 'always flowers for those who want to see them.'

A charmed life

'We need,' said the academic, sitting in the Great Hall of an Oxford college, 'to re-envision money. We need to work out how much we really need.' I was meant to be chairing the seminar, on the 'philosophy of money' at a festival of ideas, but instead I felt like giving the speaker a slap. She was a Professor of the Public Understanding of Philosophy. Her job is to have big ideas. I wanted to yell out that most people didn't have the luxury of thinking about money as a philosophical concept, and that I had hardly thought of anything else since I had lost my job.

It's easy to think money doesn't matter when you have enough to pay your bills. As a child, growing up in a family where both parents worked, I barely gave it a thought. My mother certainly didn't take money for granted. Her father died when she was twelve and her mother got up at 4 a.m. to work at a post office to pay the rent. My mother grew up on jumble sale clothes and free school lunches. When she married my father, they lived in a bedsit in Earls Court, with a shared kitchen and bathroom, and my mother walked a couple of Tube stops to her job every day, to save up for a Sunday lamb chop.

When I was nine months old, my parents bought, by mail order from Rome, the house in Guildford my mother still lives in now. It was the only house still available on the estate and more expensive than the one they had hoped to get. At first, they couldn't afford carpets and my mother had to paint the floors. I was often expected to wear my sister's hand-me-downs. We went out for a meal, usually a Chinese meal, once a year. I got a Saturday job when I was fifteen to save up for the blue cheesecloth dress I'd seen at Dorothy Perkins and the tight jeans my mother said made me look like a tart. We weren't rich, but we were comfortable. I never, ever had to worry that we wouldn't have food on the table or a roof over our heads.

Until I was thirty-five, I earned around the average wage. For a while, when I had a crippling pain condition in my mid-twenties, I lived on benefits. It wasn't easy, but I knew that if I'd fallen into serious financial difficulty my parents would have helped me out. I took a pay cut to join *The Independent*, at the age of thirty-nine, and for many years earned slightly less than a teacher. In the last couple of years there I earned a fair bit more. I was extremely lucky to be able to buy my first (ex-local authority) flat when I was twenty-nine. At the time, you could still get something on three and a half times your salary. I wouldn't be able to buy an airing cupboard on what I'm earning now.

Because I own my flat (or will do, when I've paid off my mortgage), my worries about money are in a context where I would always be able to access some cash. I'm lucky. I really am very, very lucky. But having no regular income has made me think about money in a way I never have before. And I now know that people tend to think about money much more when they haven't got it.

'My friends had things I didn't have,' Ken Olisa told me, in the office of his boutique merchant bank overlooking Regent Street. 'As a child you either want something or you don't want it. You don't say "there's a normal distribution and I find myself in the top quartile". I was envious of some of the things my friends had, like a holiday for longer than a day, for example, which is what we did. But did it matter? No, I don't think so.' Ken was cheerful, as he nearly always is. If you ever try to get him to moan about anything, you'll have a challenge on your hands. So, I asked him, as the mixed-race son of a white single mother and a Nigerian father he never knew, living in a house with no bathroom, at a time when a black bus conductor was front-page news, was he *really* not aware of feeling disadvantaged?

Ken laughed. 'I can remember a few times when I got grumpy about not having a father,' he said. 'And sometimes being black was difficult. There were people asking funny questions all the time. I was once asked how I went to the loo – and they didn't mean "is it inside or in the yard?"! But I think in the scheme of things, no. I was telling our daughter – we have two daughters – about how my mother and I celebrated Christmas. We made our own decorations. She would buy one big slab of chocolate, and break it into pieces, so we'd have one in the morning and one in the afternoon, and that lasted a week. And that was part of the fun of Christmas. So,' he said, with a smile that was like a flourish, 'I had a very happy childhood.'

At the end of his first term at Cambridge, he and a friend bought an ancient car. 'I drove it back to Nottingham. My mother said, "You mustn't leave it in the road with all the stuff. You can't trust people round here." So I give my mother a lecture about society, community and all the rest of it, go to bed and have the deepest of sleeps. I wake up in the morning and it's gone! Everything,' he said calmly, 'I own in the world is in that car.'

A few days later, the police found the car, but the only things in it were Ken's textbooks, some underwear and one shoe. He needed a suit for an interview, but had no idea how he was going to get one. I had a feeling this story was about to turn around and, sure enough, it did. 'I was looking at suits,' he said, 'and the shop assistant asked me what I was looking for. I told her my sad story. She told the owner of the shop, who gives me an enormous discount on the suit – and a job.'

But the story, it turned out, wasn't over. When Ken got back to Cambridge, his tutor asked him how his Christmas had gone. 'I said, "Fine,"' said Ken, 'and he said, "I'm glad your Christmas was uneventful, because it's quite traumatic after the first term," or something like that. And I said, "Well, actually, I forgot to say, I did have everything I owned stolen." He said, "Have you got it all back?" and I said, "No, but it doesn't matter."' Ken is such a natural raconteur that he was practically acting out the part of the tutor. 'He said, "How are you going to cope with the next term?" This was hugely embarrassing in 1971, talking about money. I said, "No, no, no, I'm fine."'

The tutor asked him how he was going to buy textbooks. Ken told him he had got his textbooks back. 'Then,' he said, looking at me in the way that perhaps the tutor looked at him, 'my tutor said, "I'm going to ask you a question and I want you to think very carefully before you answer it. If you were going to buy any textbooks this term, how much would you have spent, rounded up to the nearest ten pounds?" A classic Cambridge exam question. The number was zero, but, rounded up, the answer was ten pounds. He rang up the senior tutor and said, "I'll get you a cheque tomorrow."'

In 2011, Ken and his wife, Julia, made a huge donation to the library at his old college, which is now named after him. 'When I endowed the library,' he told me, 'I pointed out that the ten-pound act of kindness had turned into two million pounds!'

Ken has been canny. There is no question that Ken has been canny. Most people from poor backgrounds do not make enough money to endow libraries at their old college. Nor, in fact, do most people from comfortable, middle-class backgrounds. Ken went to work in a field where it's possible to make money, and he has made a lot of it. He has been very focused on making a success of his business career and is now just as focused on making a success of the charities he chairs. 'There are two things about me,' he told me. 'One is that I have clearly had a charmed life. I recognize this, which is why I feel obligated to help others. The second thing I tell people is that for most of us, luck is relatively evenly distributed. The great skill is to spot it.'

'We didn't,' said my friend Dreda, 'have no money.' We were clutching our stomachs after one of her delicious and gigantic Thai meals. She had made the fishcakes. She had made the pad thai. She had even made the prawn crackers and the spring rolls. I sometimes think she can do anything. She was a teenage athletics star and East London shot-put champion. Then she read African history at SOAS, the first in her family to go to university. Then she trained as a teacher, became a deputy head and then an educational consultant and now she's a successful crime writer, broadcaster and journalist who also does work in prisons and schools.

'I grew up on a council estate one street up from Cable Street,' she told me. 'My dad worked in a chicken factory in East London, and my mum worked as a cleaner in the local hospital. She also used to give the patients tea and she loved, loved, loved her job. It was a really great community. All the mums took it in turns to wash the stairs. We used to just run around. Kids lived on the street. You went home when you were told to go home. Your mum just used to go on the balcony and shout for you.'

Dreda learnt to read at Whitechapel library. While she was there, she would go to the art gallery next door. 'We were never bored,' she said, 'and it was an outdoor lifestyle, so it seemed like we didn't really need to have more money. But I think what my parents taught me was: you have to work hard. There was never a pressure, but there was always a feeling that we want more for you.'

Like Ken, Dreda always talks about what she has, not she doesn't have. So what, I asked, did she lack? What about clothes, for example? 'We couldn't afford many clothes,' she said. 'Sometimes I went to school in trousers. I was growing and the trousers were getting shorter. I remember getting teased about that a couple of times at school and it did hurt me. My mum,' she added, 'didn't like me wearing trousers. She said it made the angels weep. I was like: what?!'

We both paused for the weeping angels. And presumably she didn't have holidays or go out for meals? Dreda laughed. 'Never! I had my first holiday when I was twenty-one.' Did she ever have days out? 'No. What my mum used to do was pack us off to Sheffield, because we had a lot of family there. She used to send us off, with a sandwich and an apple, put us on the coach and off we'd go. My dad,' she added, 'belonged to a dominoes club and every year they used to organize a trip to the seaside, so you'd have these seven coaches of black people descending and these people standing in the street,' and she opened her mouth as you would at a dentist, 'like this. We'd go to Great Yarmouth, Blackpool, Skegness and Barry Island. Everyone brought their packed lunches. There was food, there was lots of sharing.'

When her father first came to England from Grenada, he had an accident at work and lost his leg. 'I asked him years on why he didn't take any holiday,' she said, 'and he said his job made him feel strong. He didn't let what had happened to him hold him back. He said, "I've got four kids to bring up, I need to find some work."'

Dreda has always been 'a big saver'. She has always worked extremely hard. She is generous to her friends, and extremely hospitable, but she has always been careful. She bought her council flat on a discount and worked all out to pay the mortgage off. 'I think as a working-class person,' she said, 'you're really frightened something dramatic is going to happen, like you're going to lose your job. Who's that fabulous actor? Leslie Phillips. He grew up in Tottenham. He's of an age. People say, "Why do you still work?" and he says, "Because I'm really worried as a working-class person that my money's going to go kaput and I've got nothing."'

Paul Brandford doesn't worry about money. He has also never had very much, or at least not since he was a child. 'My parents had very regular nine-to-five jobs,' he told me, in the café at the Royal Academy after we had finished going round the Summer

Exhibition. 'They were lower-middle-class aspirational people. We moved to a brand-new house. I saw them getting ready for work every morning and I thought "are you crazy, why are you doing this?" I just knew that it wasn't for me.'

It's possible, I told Paul firmly, that the reason his parents did this 'crazy' thing was to feed him and his brother and sister. So when he decided to pursue art, how did he think he was going to earn a living? Paul laughed. 'I didn't think of it, and still don't! It's not that kind of involvement. I have been fortunate enough to do a whole string of art-related jobs, but my own art has never primarily been a means of making money.'

Although his art is wonderful, this is clearly true. His art jobs – largely freelance teaching – also haven't made him rich. Did he never, for example, dream of owning his own home? Paul made a face. 'I thought if it turns out I do, great, if it doesn't I'm not going to cry about it. To be honest, I don't own a lot of stuff. I own a lot of art books, but that's about it. I don't have a car any more. I've had a few third-hand cars. They got me around and that's what they were there for. I don't feel I'm defined by the things I have or the clothes I wear.'

He had, he told me, 'just enough of an income' from his freelance work. Was it, I asked delicately, less than the national average? 'What,' he asked, 'is the national average?' About £26,000, I told him. Paul looked surprised. 'To be honest,' he said, 'if I pull in twenty, that's a solid year.'

Gosh. So what gets cut out? 'We don't go on holidays much. I know someone across the table,' he said, looking at his wife, Jeanette, 'who goes on quite a few, but I don't. How old is this jumper?' Jeanette grimaced. 'Twenty years?' she said. Paul grinned. 'I don't do holidays,' he said. 'I don't do fancy cars.' Did they have their own furniture? 'At this point we haven't,' he said, 'but we have had furniture in the past. But furniture? Really?' And he giggled.

He and Jeanette rent a flat on the outskirts of London. They live there with their twenty-four-year-old son, Jake. The rent is £15,000 a year. Paul pays it out of his £20,000 income and Jeanette, who's also an artist, and also does freelance teaching, pays the council tax, electricity and other main bills. So basically, I said to Paul, you don't have any spending money? 'Look,' said Jeanette, 'at the lavish clothes he's got!' Paul half winked at his wife. 'To be honest,' he said, 'it's not something I think "oh, I'm unhappy about", or "isn't life unfair?" It is what it is and you get on with it. The whole art game is the game of a professional gambler. You take the highs with the lows. It gives you things. It doesn't give you certain other things. In a way, that's a contrast you accept.'

So did he, I asked, ever think he would make money? Paul's laugh was more like a snort. 'Of course! Everybody has dreams about their own success. Over time, those dreams are tempered by reality. Actually, weirdly, and this may surprise you, underneath it all, I'm quite happy with how things have turned out. I was fifty last year. I've spent thirty years, more or less, doing the things I want to do.'

Which all sounds lovely, but what about his wife? What, I asked, was her attitude to money? Jeanette took a sip of her tea. 'I wasn't,' she said, 'really bothered by it. Nobody thought you could earn masses being an artist.' And did her parents own their own home? Jeanette nodded. 'Yes, but we were working class.

The only reason my parents got a deposit for a house was that my mum was injured and got some money from that. Owning a house is good. I'm panicking now that we don't own anything. Now we're getting older, it does matter, because one of us is going to get ill. It used to be cheaper to rent than not, and we thought it would always be like that. I thought something would come along and it didn't.'

They had, I said, pointing out the obvious, both chosen to put their work as artists above financial comfort. Paul, it was clear, had no regrets. Did she? Jeanette looked at her husband and then back at me. 'Oh,' she said, 'I wouldn't change it. Absolutely not.'

When I first met Lisa, we were both working in the arts, on salaries that might make even Paul laugh. She had been renting a flat with her boyfriend, but the relationship had split up and she was now lodging with friends who were a couple. It was a small flat and it was awkward. I helped her find a room just up the road from me, and it was while she was there, and eight months after she had started a relationship with Ian, that she found out she was pregnant.

A month before the baby was born, she and Ian moved into a rented flat. They have had to move several times since then, and the rent on their little flats has usually been twice as much as my mortgage. They now live in a cheaper flat in Hackney. It's a lovely flat. They have made it really homely. But it's a one-bedroom flat for a family of three.

'I don't think I've been feckless,' Lisa told me, as she served up scrambled eggs in her charming kitchen, 'but I've never been a high earner. I've always been in a situation where I've never been able to buy anywhere or put any real savings behind me. It just so happens that the person I'm with has had a divorce behind him, so he's in a similar situation. I think the driving force for me has never been money. It has always been happiness, whether through job satisfaction, having a good relationship, or having a family.'

Lisa grew up in a family without much money. 'We were comfortable,' she said, 'but there were moments. I do remember being told to be quiet because the milkman had come and we didn't have money to pay him. I remember moments of looking for money, made like a game, to get enough to go to the chippy.' Unlike Dreda and unlike Ken, her family did sometimes have a few days in a caravan or a B & B, but they would also spend a few nights sleeping in the car. 'Everything,' she said, 'was always made an adventure. It was a very happy childhood and my mum was very playful.'

It's just as well Lisa had that model, because there have been times for her as an adult when things have been very tight. They got even worse when Ian lost his job. 'I suppose one of the worst situations,' she said, 'was when we hadn't paid the council tax and there's that horrible feeling of not knowing how you're going to do it. We had threats that things were going to be cut off and we were going to be taken to court. That feels quite shameful. There have been times when we've had to live really frugally, and that does feel horrible.'

After one particularly bad period, Lisa set up a home budget. 'If I know what I'm dealing with,' she said, 'I'm less scared, because I know I can manage it.' She didn't want Ruby to feel deprived, so she would check websites to find things they could do for free. 'Even in winter,' she said, 'I can remember walking through parks in the pouring rain and just making up songs and finding somewhere to eat a sandwich. Somehow, eating sandwiches in the rain, in a little shelter in the park, was exciting.'

Lisa literally learnt how to control every penny. If she had £1.60, she knew she could either get a bus somewhere, or perhaps buy Ruby a small bag of popcorn. Every day she would plan their evening meals: often baked potatoes or beans on toast. She and Ian would save up all year to take Ruby on a little holiday, a few days in Cornwall, or Paris or Amsterdam. Once, they lost their holiday because they had to move out of their flat suddenly and find a deposit. But I don't know anyone who has talked about holidays with more joy.

When Ruby was eight, Lisa got a much better-paid job. Did it, I asked, make her happier? Lisa's smile was rueful. 'No! In recent years, when the income was better, I'd get to the end of holidays or weekends and think we've not done as much. I think in some ways we were enriched when we didn't have money, because we'd be more organized about how we spent our time.'

'I suppose I'd be a liar,' she said, 'if I said there weren't times when I thought it would be easier if we had a property. In her twelve years, Ruby has already moved quite a few times, so I worry about the fact that we can't offer her that kind of security. But I think of everything else she's got. She's got a very happy home. We're always joking. We get on well. We always try to make time on Sunday morning to sit and talk about things that are happening in the world, just to make her look outwards as well as inwards.'

*

If I think of all the people I know, I'd say there's absolutely no link between happiness and wealth. Some of the happiest people I know have the least, but I don't think any of them would want to say it's fun being poor. Nobody wants to worry about having their electricity cut off. Nobody wants to feel that they could be chucked out of their home on a whim. It may not be true that money makes you happy, but if you're really struggling, it will certainly help. Once you reach a certain level, according to the happiness experts, more money doesn't make much difference. When you reach that level, which depends on where you live, what makes you happier, says the economist Richard Layard, is to earn more than your neighbours, colleagues or friends. Layard quotes the story of the Russian peasant whose neighbour has a cow. When God asks him how he can help, the peasant says: 'Kill the cow.'

In the long term, it looks as though standards of living for most people in the West are likely to stagnate or even fall. The post-war dream of having a better standard of living than your parents now seems more like science fiction. My parents had job security, automatic pay rises and index-linked pensions. They might as well have had a penny farthing. I'm probably going to have to work until I drop and so will quite a few of my friends. We are nearly all going to have to adapt our expectations of what makes for a comfortable life.

I was asked by the *Sunday Times* to write a piece about Ebola. I spoke, via a charity worker, to an Ebola survivor in Sierra Leone. He had lost all seventeen members of his family. He has no relatives, no income and no job. He eats, he told me, when people bring him food.

Before I interviewed him, I had been googling Ikea kitchens. I would like to say that after talking to him I will never google Ikea kitchens again. That would be a lie. I can watch Syrian refugees on the news and still think it would be nice to get a new sofa. We all live with these double standards all the time. I'm not sure if we need, as that professor of philosophy said, to 're-envision' the role of money in our lives, but I'm pretty damn sure that we could all learn a few lessons from Lisa.

Fortysomething millennial

'A primary job of the citizen', said the letter, 'is to earn money to pay taxes to help to support citizens whose needs are greater than our own.' The letter was from my father, and it was written on blue Basildon Bond notepaper. He wrote it when I was doing a dissertation on patterns in the novels of Iris Murdoch as part of an MA on 'The Novel', and not showing all that many signs of trying to get a job.

My father was from a Scottish Presbyterian background. My mother is a Lutheran Swede. The Protestant work ethic is etched on my genes. It started for me at school, when I treated each exam like an Olympic race. It didn't matter how many As I got or how many times I came first. However hard I worked, I knew that it would never be enough.

Not long after I got that letter from my father, when I was twenty-two, I got a job in the bookshop where I met Patsy. Since then, I have hurled myself into every job I've done. Arts administrator and literary critic? There are more books in the world than pebbles on the beach. Journalist? News and current affairs literally never stop. The only way for me to get off the treadmill is to get into other people's company and out of the house.

My parents believed in public service, not in making money. But they did believe that hard work would be recognized and rewarded, if only with a pat on the back. They didn't think you could slog your (crisp-fuelled) guts out – in my case through two bouts of cancer – and then find yourself cast out on a whim. When my mother bought me *How to Keep Your Head After Losing Your Job*, it was partly because she didn't know what to say. I, by the way, only read a few pages. I've lost my taste for self-help books. I used to like the perky tone, but now it just makes me think of people who try to sell you things, people with big white teeth and shiny suits. I'm with Aristotle. The more you know, the more you know you don't know. People who think they know a lot probably don't have much to teach.

When I lost my job, I didn't really bother with books. I just emailed everyone I could think of who might be able to help. When Grant Feller was fired by his newspaper, he did the same. 'My strategy,' he told me, 'was to see as many people as I could, and to make sure I had at least one meeting a day, to get me out of the house.' I wish I could say I followed his next strategy, but I didn't. 'I also,' he said, 'set my alarm for five thirty, because I couldn't sleep at night. The best way of sleeping was either to get drunk, which would have been easy, or to be utterly exhausted. That's the worst time, when you're lying awake. I've stuck with it. It's part of my day. I swim for half an hour and I go for a run. In fact, I ran so much in those early weeks, I completely fucked my Achilles.'

The only times I've set my alarm for 5.30 have been when I've had a flight to catch and then I've usually felt like cancelling the holiday. Like Grant, I put on my running gear most days.

Sometimes, I even go for a run. In my head, I still hate exercise, but when I do it I actually quite like it. And there's no doubt that it makes you feel better. All the studies say it helps prevent depression, heart disease, cancer, dementia and pretty much every health problem you could think of. It makes you healthier and it cheers you up. If we really wanted to solve the problems in the NHS, we would just make everyone go for a daily walk.

It isn't, unfortunately, quite so easy to resolve the challenges of an industry in decline. 'I slowly realized,' said Grant, 'that the way back I'd envisaged, into newspapers and websites, was not going to happen, or not in the way I wanted it to, which was with a job, a very good job. So I then drew up a list of about a hundred people, captains of industry and so on, who would be really interesting to meet. I also had lots of friends who were not journalists, who were really helpful. They would know someone who knew someone.'

Grant was canny. 'The key thing I did,' he said, 'was I emailed and in the guide field was "meeting", because I thought they would think to themselves "have I got a meeting?" So they would open it and then they would see in that first sentence that I had read something they had said or written recently. The other thing was advice. If you say you're looking for help, that doesn't work. If you say "I'm in the process of trying to reinvent myself and I'd like some advice" . . . I was surprised at the number of rooms I got into.'

Grant, like me, had meetings with senior journalists and realized that what was on offer was what you could really only call piecework, at a fraction of his former rate. He also started a blog and would often write something targeted at the next person he was about to meet. 'I'd walk into the room,' he said, 'and they'd say, "That was really interesting, that thing you wrote," and secretly I'd be thinking: yes, well, I wrote it for you.'

I started a blog, too, but when I discovered it was just a way to do what I did before, and not be paid for it, I couldn't force myself to do more than about one every few months. I still can't stand writing for free. When people ask me to write something, and then say 'I'm afraid we can't afford to pay you', I feel like asking them if they do the same when they ask their plumber to fix their broken loo.

For Grant, the path to 'reinvention' certainly wasn't instant. 'I suppose the first three or four months,' he said, 'I was earning nothing. The next five or six months I was earning bits and bobs. A few people from outside journalism were giving me gigs. I did some work for an events company. People realize they're giving you a bit of dignity.' Grant paused and swallowed. 'Sorry,' he said, 'I feel a bit weepy even thinking about this, because that guy who owns that events company did a really good thing.'

I felt like crying, too. I thought of all the people who had been kind to me when I had felt desperate. I thought of the literary editor of the *Sunday Times*, and the deputy editor of the *Sunday Times* and the opinion editor of *The Guardian* and the editorial director of the *Sunday Times*, and the former poet laureate, who gave me a quote for my website, and the current poet laureate, who also gave me a quote for my website. I thought of the friend who had put me in touch with several headhunters, and the former colleague who put me in touch with an eminent academic. When I had lost a bit of my faith in human nature, it helped me get it back.

Grant has now built up his own very successful consultancy, which provides content marketing, speeches, 'thought leadership' and 'storytelling' for businesses. It's all going very well, but that doesn't mean he has turned into Nelson Mandela. 'How can I say this without sounding really bitter?' he said. 'I always wanted revenge and I still do. The revenge, I suppose, is now being a success, but the feelings of revenge are always there. I *am* angry at the way people were. You can tell that by the way I remember so vividly what happened. You can't suddenly paint a smile on. There are some people who go through life and the glass is nearly always full.' Weirdos, I said, feeling a sudden sense of exhilaration. 'My glass,' he said, 'is in danger of being empty, so I fill it up and it's also a glass that I want to shatter on someone's forehead.'

We both cackled wildly. You'll have to forgive us. Once a hack, always a hack. But Grant certainly doesn't seem bitter. He's cheerful and very good company. I hope, at least most of the time, I'm relatively good company, too. Anger, we both agreed, was a fuel in picking ourselves up and driving us on. 'That's not the overriding feeling,' said Grant, 'but it's always there. At the moment, it's going well, but the complacency you have about having a full-time job, I don't have that, and complacency is not a good thing. That's why people calcify, because they've got a job and they think it's going to be OK. Millennials don't think like that. They think: "I'm going to do this and I'm going to do that." I'm a fortysomething millennial. I've learnt something and now I'm going to learn something else.'

We are all living through an employment revolution and many of us are going to be 'disrupted' out of our jobs. We missed the industrial revolution, but we're just in time for what the economists Andrew McAfee and Erik Brynjolfsson have called 'the second machine age'. According to an Oxford Martin report, *The Future of Employment*, about 47 per cent of jobs are at risk from automation. PwC think that about 30 per cent of existing jobs will be lost in the UK by 2030, and about 38 per cent in the US. Whatever the precise figure, it's likely to be a lot.

Big chunks of the working classes have already been through their revolution, with whole industries wiped out and shipped to the East. Now it's time for the middle classes to feel the squeeze. We journalists are at the forefront of this wave. Academics, legal writers and financial advisers are likely to be next. If you want to be sure of a job, become a nurse, a care worker, a barista, a construction worker, a computer programmer or a digital marketeer. Forget Martin Amis. Think Steve Jobs.

In this new world, according to the *New York Times* columnist Thomas Friedman, we will all need to act like immigrants. In this new world, we *will* all be immigrants. Passion and persistence, he says, which he calls PQ, will trump IQ. What this means, above all else, is that we will need to be flexible. Immigrants have to be flexible. Dreda's parents – a cleaner and a factory worker – did jobs they might not have expected to do at home. Winston's parents worked as a cleaner and a postman. Winston has also been very flexible. In the time I have known him, he has worked as a sound engineer, a musician, a barman, a barista, a driver, a gardener and a chef. In Italy, eight years ago, I met Joseph, who came over to Italy as a political refugee from the Ivory Coast. At first, he worked as a street vendor. Then he worked in a factory. Then he worked as a truck driver and saved enough money to buy two flats and some land. After he came to visit me, he fell in love with London and decided to move here. First, he worked as a refuse collector. Then he worked in a care home. Now he's working as a healthcare assistant and planning to train as a nurse. Now that's what I call enterprise, and what Thomas Friedman would call PQ.

'I think,' said the writer and artist Yana Stajno when I met her in a café near her studio in Wood Green, 'you have to be practical. Follow your passion,' she added, 'but just don't expect it to pay you.' Yana came to London in the seventies from South Africa. She was born in Zimbabwe to a French mother and a father who 'left Poland on the back of a lorry'. He died when she was six. 'I went to this cocktail party,' she told me, 'and marched up to this man and said, "Have you got money in the bank?"' I can just imagine it. Yana is fearless. She is also irresistible. She has big blue eyes that seem to rule out the word 'no'. 'He said yes,' she said, 'and I said, "Would you like to meet my mummy?" My mother did marry him. I hated him, though. We never got on, but my mother,' she said breezily, 'was fine after that.'

Yana was cheerful. Yana is always cheerful. I met her when my pain condition came back, just after the 7/7 London bombings. It started in my left arm and soon I was gripped with pain from head to toe. I couldn't type. I could hardly walk. Worst of all, I couldn't work. I saw pain specialists and rheumatologists and neurologists. One of the oncologists who had treated me for cancer even arranged for me to see the team who worked in palliative care. Nothing worked and then someone said 'you must see Yana' and I did.

Yana is an acupuncturist, but that's a bit like saying Matisse was a painter and decorator. Yana is a healer. I don't really know how she does it, but she is definitely a healer. She is also a writer and artist, but it's acupuncture that pays most of her bills.

She came to London with her partner, David. They had met on the steps of Cape Town University, in the middle of a riot. They were both anti-apartheid activists, doing street theatre, which was illegal, and were at constant risk of arrest. It was when they were living in the bush that they realized they would have to leave. 'An Afrikaner farmer found two children stealing from his little farm shop,' Yana explained, 'and locked them in the freezer for the night and killed them. We went to the police, but the police were friends of the farmer and that kind of did it. We thought we were either going to kill the guy or . . .' and for once the smile disappeared from her face.

She and David lived in a squat in Camden. In South Africa, Yana had worked 'in restaurants, as a life model, selling things, trading in the market' and here she got a job as a cleaner. 'I didn't actually realize you had to plug in the Hoover,' she told me. 'White Africans never used a Hoover! Rugs were beaten, not swept.' She wrote a play called *Salt River*, which did very well, but knew that writing wasn't going to pay her bills. At first she thought about physiotherapy, but then she decided to study acupuncture. 'It's very poetic,' she said, 'very interesting, and of course you never, ever get to the bottom of it. The points have such lovely names! It's a continual system of knowledge from three thousand uninterrupted years.'

It works. I have no idea why it works, but for me, with Yana, it does. Yana is an artist, in paint and words, but she is also an artist as a healer. 'The interesting thing is,' she said, 'that if I hadn't come here I would have been simply a writer and artist. It's only because I had to do something practical that I used that part of myself. And I'm really glad I did. It's such rich territory. I love my clients. Do you know? I love them all.'

I honestly think that anyone can love their job. Well, OK, perhaps not an arms dealer, or a pimp, or someone in a call centre who tells you you've had a car crash when you haven't. I believe in work. I think work is how we contribute to the wider world. Work takes us out of ourselves and into other people's lives.

I love coffee. It makes me happy to have a really good cup of coffee. In Harris + Hoole the other day, I was served by a guy with tattoos and a big bushy beard. Almost everyone serving coffee these days seems to have tattoos and a big bushy beard, but what marked this guy out was his smile. He was so cheerful and friendly that I asked him if he liked his job. 'Yes,' he said, but he didn't need to. You could see that it made him happy to add so much pleasure to someone else's day.

In a few years, perhaps we'll never meet a real person in a real shop. Supermarkets are already trying to train us all to use scanners, those horrible machines that won't let you buy a bottle of wine even when you're over fifty. I like a human to scan my Marlborough Sauvignon and Kettle Chips. I like it when they smile at me and ask me how I am. Sometimes it's the only conversation I have all day. A few years ago, some people made a big fuss about a government-sponsored scheme to support people into work that, they said, included 'slave labour' at supermarkets. They seemed to think that working in a supermarket was something that should make you feel ashamed. They could not be more wrong.

Winston changes jobs quite a lot, because he gets bored and likes to try new things. Joseph loves his work as a healthcare assistant. He can see it has a big effect on people's lives. Claire, who was made redundant from her marketing job by her horrible employers, now works with adults with learning disabilities and loves her job so much that she literally radiates joy.

The people I know who don't love their jobs are the people whose bosses talk about things like 'synergies', 'innovation' and 'low-hanging fruit'. If you want people to hate their job, just blast them with jargon, give them hundreds of boxes to tick and watch them every damn minute of the day. Bob's your uncle, or your Big Brother. George Orwell didn't need to know about the studies that link autonomy with productivity. 'Nothing was your own', he said in *1984*, 'except the few cubic centimetres inside your skull.'

It makes me angry when people sneer at other people's jobs. Most people in the world have to take what they can get. In a big city, in the Western world, you have more choice, but you are still living in a city, not in Nirvana. And it isn't just immigrants who are grateful to get any job at all.

My sister managed, through years of struggle, and while on antipsychotic medication that made her speech slurred and her mind dull, and through taking, and retaking, exams she kept failing while her siblings got straight As, to scrape four O levels and two CSEs.

She managed, after a couple of years at a secretarial college, to learn to type. She managed to get a job, in the typing pool of an insurance company, where she was, according to the reference they gave her, 'a conscientious and loyal employee'. Caroline was certainly conscientious. She was more proud of that job than anything she had ever done. The only problem was that she was extremely slow.

After three years, she got the sack. It took eighteen months, and dozens of application forms, to get another job. This time, it was as a sales assistant in a shoe shop. 'The manageress has been very kind to me,' she wrote in a letter to my brother, who was then in America. 'She is very nice, but she told me on Friday that I was too slow. The people in the shop are very nice and I enjoy dealing with the public and am good at it. It is just that I don't think I am very good at the job. I am on a six-week trial. If I don't pass it, I mustn't worry too much.'

She did not pass it. A year later, she got a two-month stint of work experience as a sales assistant at M&S. The work experience was part of a scheme to help disabled people into work. But not, unfortunately, to keep them. My mother begged the store to keep her on. They refused.

It took six years for my sister to get another job. This time, it was as a part-time cleaner in a canteen. She worked hard, and she loved it. After a year, they asked her to resign.

I have never met anyone who tried harder to get a job. I have never met anyone who wanted a job more. But employers – even nice, well-meaning employers in a world less cut-throat and slower than ours now – didn't, and don't, just want people who try. They want people who can do the job, and do it well.

In the end, we all decided that it was probably better for my sister to give up the struggle to get jobs that nobody seemed to want her to keep. She was happier without the stress of constantly trying, and constantly being told that she had failed. She lived modestly, and was grateful for her benefits. But she still wished she could work. My sister knew instinctively what the studies have shown: that people who work are happier and healthier than people who don't.

When she died, and we went to register her death, there was a box marked 'occupation'. It was eighteen years since she had worked in an office. My father paused, and then put 'typist'.

'Over the years,' said Juliet Taylor, 'I've met a lot of people whose careers have gone badly wrong in a very public way. Their professional integrity comes under assault. Their home life suffers because they've either lost their job or their reputation puts them under pressure and their finance comes under pressure. What keeps them going more than anything, in my observation, is the sense of who they are and their integrity.'

We were back in our favourite hotel bar. She was taking tiny sips of her Gavi and I was working my way through the bowl of nibbles. 'Their principles, their values, their integrity,' she continued, 'enable them to stay employable and to make the transition into other environments.'

I took a big slurp of my Viognier. That, I told her, was very interesting. So many people, I said, had told me that I had to be upbeat and say everything was fine. I didn't. I couldn't. My feeling, I said, was that people generally warm to people who are human – and anyway, they can tell if you're faking it. Juliet nodded. 'There's been a really big change in the last five or ten years,' she said. 'It's now acceptable for leaders to say it's really tough. The health service, for example, has a very high turnover of chief executives. Some continue to rise, continue to develop. But an awful lot retire early, broken, exhausted, without any hope that their skills are transferable to another setting. The ones who keep going are true to themselves, accept that problems happen, learn from it, move on.'

She's talking about leaders, because, as a high-powered headhunter, most of her work is with leaders, but the principles apply to the rest of us, too. 'Actually,' she said, 'your skills are transferable to lots of other settings. Seek advice and support that can help you keep learning. I'm such a big believer that the key to resilience is learning. And courage. And a sense of humour. Some of the most resilient people I know are agile, adaptable and entrepreneurial. They are not afraid to take risks and try new things.'

I certainly wouldn't call myself 'entrepreneurial'. I don't think anyone on either side of my extended family has ever made a penny from anything other than a job. My Scottish grandmother once told me that one of my ancestors was hung for sheep-stealing, but I'm not sure if that counts. Even so, there's a dogged part of me that feels, like Grant, that trying to get a full-time job would be a cop-out. The obvious move from journalism would be to PR. I don't want to work in PR. I would rather put together a portfolio of different things I like than spend my life promoting someone else's brand.

In the 'gig economy', you have to be flexible. I have learnt to be very flexible. If someone asks me to do something, and it's reasonably paid, I usually say yes. A man at a wedding asked me to give a talk at a conference on 'innovation in the voluntary sector'. I had no idea what it was, but I did some googling and it seemed to go fine. I've given a speech at a 'nurse of the year' award ceremony. Not as easy as you might think when the only thing most nurses know about you is that you're the journalist who slagged nurses off. I was told by a school secretary how to write a press release. I swallowed my pride and took the cheque. I've taught academics how to use Twitter. I also did a session for them on 'communicating with confidence' just after I failed an interview for a non-exec role at an NHS Trust. 'You made us all cry in response to the first question,' said the chair when I asked for feedback. 'And that,' she said, confusingly, 'got things off to a bad start.'

If you ask for career advice, many people will tell you to 'follow your passion'. They mean well, but they are mad. The world does not need all that many footballers or celebrities. It doesn't need all that many artists and poets. You might just be able to scrape a living as an artist. If you want to try, by all means give it a go. Or you can do as Yana and Maura and Mimi do, and earn your living by healing or teaching or mentoring and pursue your art in your spare time. You need to earn a living by doing something that actually pays the mortgage or rent. Garrets are now called 'loft apartments' and cost a bomb. Stefano's loft apartment is enormous, but then he's a lawyer. It's his work as a lawyer that gives him the time and money to pursue his passion for opera and art.

I do think it's a shame to do a job you hate, unless there are no other options at all. If you love banking, lucky you. If you don't and do it anyway, you might find that by the time you've racked up your millions to do the things you really want, your soul has shrivelled up. For most of us, work will be a compromise. We'll like some of it. We won't like some of it. As long as we like some of it, and have time to do some other things we like, we're doing pretty well.

I was incredibly lucky to earn a good living by doing something I loved. That's a luxury, not a right. I'm still getting this 'portfolio' malarkey off the ground, and I don't know how it's going to work out. It's knackering, but it's interesting. I like the freedom. I miss the security. It's the same with relationships. You don't often get both.

Every time someone tells me that they 'used to love' my column, I want to yell out that I used to love it, too. But I'm learning not to define myself by work. Almost every night of my life, I have gone to bed asking myself what I've achieved and concluding that it isn't enough. I'm beginning to learn that it's sometimes OK just to say: I had a nice day.

The incredible machine

The doctor seemed young. Doctors, like policemen, now seem very young. This doctor looked at my notes and told me that he was discharging me. I was, he said, 'effectively cured'.

It was about eighteen months after I left *The Independent*. I had only been at the paper for six weeks when I felt something springy in my left breast as I soaped myself in the bath. Since then, I have tried not to take a single day for granted. Since then, I have had nearly twelve extra years of life.

Through all the things that have gone wrong with my body, I have learnt a lot about being well.

I have learnt, for example, that if you are angry or sad, it might well show up somewhere in your body or your skin.

I have learnt that being 'comfortable in your skin' is not just a metaphor.

I have learnt that chronic pain usually only goes when you start to concentrate on something else.

I have learnt that if you define yourself as ill, that's usually how you stay.

And I have learnt that the body has a truly miraculous capacity to heal.

*

'I remember,' Anna told me, 'the doctor saying, "Don't worry, you won't die of it."' This was just after he had told her she had MS as she pulled up her jeans. 'I thought that was quite wise, actually, because I had seen people with MS who were just about dead.' After she got the diagnosis, she spent a weekend with a friend 'like a second mother' who also had MS. 'She made me quite quickly realize that it could be for the better. She said, "In the end, you might end up with someone kinder" – and I think that's true.'

Anna did 'end up' with someone kind. I have seen the way her husband looks at her, and the way she looks at him. What struck me, over our spaghetti in that Italian café opposite her office, was how matter-of-fact she was about everything that had happened, and how much she laughed. So didn't she, I asked, ever think 'Oh my God, I'm going to be horribly crippled and it's all going to be a nightmare'? There was a pause. 'No.' And did she think that attitude had affected the course of her illness? Anna nodded. 'Yes,' she said, 'I think mental and physical health are closely related, but if I hadn't thought that, it would have been incredibly difficult to cope.'

What, I asked, about the times when cabs wouldn't stop for her, because she looked drunk? Wasn't that upsetting? There was another pause. 'Not really, no. I think when you're in that moment, you think: "I've got to somehow get to the next place." Again, it's the practical thing kicking in.' And what about when she was in hospital, and that woman was singing 'Roll Out the Barrel' as a corpse was being wheeled out? Anna smiled. 'I've got really good friends,' she said, 'a lot of people saying "this is awful: let's just get out", but not in a woeful way, just as in "you don't belong here, this is just the worst fit ever".' She laughed. 'I think this is where you go: I actually just need a load of people round here to make me laugh.'

She had told me about the women in their fifties she used to see in the waiting room, who seemed to be crippled by their MS. That, I know, because my aunt died of MS when she was fifty-eight, is when it often gets much worse. Was she, I asked, worried about the future? This time the pause was so long I thought she had forgotten the question. 'No,' she said in the end, 'because I don't think it will happen to me. And if it does,' she said, and her smile was firm, 'then we'll handle it.'

The days following my mastectomy and reconstruction were among the worst of my life. I had expected the nursing to be good, because I was in a hospital that was meant to be one of the best in Europe. Unfortunately, it was terrible. People were screaming out and asking for help, but nobody came.

The day after the operation, Stefano sent a text and asked if he could visit me. I couldn't reach the phone to text him back, but thought I could no more talk to someone from the world outside the hospital than fly to Mars.

Three days later, Emma and Tony turned up, with a giant chocolate cookie and a bunch of orange roses. While they were there, Ros and Nick arrived, with more cakes and flowers. It was still hard to sit up, but it suddenly felt like a party. The next day, Winston strode on to the ward and up to my bed. He had gone to my flat and picked up my post. Among the bills there was a parcel. When I ripped it open, I saw it was a black knitted hat I had ordered from a 'chemotherapy head gear' site. I was still waiting to hear whether I needed chemotherapy and hated the thought of wearing a wig. Winston held out a mirror as I tried it on. We couldn't decide whether I looked more like Mussolini or a member of the IRA about to plant a bomb. The only thing to do was laugh.

The night I met Winston, at that rice and peas stall at the Elephant and Castle, he made an unusual request. We had gone back to my flat and he suddenly lay down on the floor and asked me to walk on his back. Something, he said, was out of joint and it needed to be clicked back into place.

'I broke my back falling off a roof when I was squatting,' he told me, when he finally agreed to let me quiz him on what I'm tempted to call his nine lives. We were at the Coach and Horses, just down the road from where I live now. I had offered to buy him a Thai meal in return for the poached salmon and seared beef he did for my fiftieth. 'I was,' he said, 'helping rewire a squat for a friend. I bent down and stood up really quickly and got a rush of blood to the head. I went really dizzy, in fact, and fell over the edge. It was almost like a cartoon falling.'

I couldn't help smiling. Winston loves cartoons. On the rare occasions he would stay at mine at weekends, I sometimes used to nip out for a pint of milk and come back to find him stretched out on the sofa watching *Teenage Mutant Ninja Turtles* or *Superman*. He had, he said, asked a friend who worked at an undertaker's to make him a coffin for his drum stands. 'It was purple,' he said, 'and I had it in the basement of my friend's squat. As I fell off the roof, there was a glass mezzanine. I've gone through the glass mezzanine, second floor, first floor, straight through to the basement, and landed on top of the coffin!'

If it was anyone else, I'd think they were lying, but I've known Winston for a long time. Did he, I asked, trying not to laugh, remember what he felt when he was falling? 'I don't remember falling,' he said, 'I don't remember hitting the coffin. I do remember looking up and thinking "that's weird!" and looking up at the glass, and the shape of me gone through the glass. I got up. There's a scar on my back.' He wriggled round in his chair and pulled his T-shirt up. 'A tiny scratch. Can you see it?' I peered over and could. 'I said to my friend, "I've got to go now, because I've got rehearsals." I got to the front door, fell down the stairs and that was it. Out for the count.'

He woke up in the back of the ambulance. At the hospital, they told him he had a fracture in his lower back. 'Can I feel my feet?' he said. 'No, I can't. Can I feel this? No, I can't. Couldn't feel a thing!' Bloody hell. And how did he react? 'I didn't really think about it, to be honest. I wasn't worried at all. The only time I kind of thought "whoa" was when the doctor said, "You may not recover from this, and you may not be able to walk."'

Up to this point, Winston had always been extremely sporty. He boxed for the Lynn, a boxing club in South London, and never lost a fight. He won gold medals in athletics. He had a black belt in Wadō-ryū. He did competitive cycling. He ran for miles every day. So how on earth did he feel when the doctor said this?

'I felt really annoyed,' said Winston. *Annoyed?* My voice had gone up about an octave. 'More annoyed than anything,' he said. 'I was thinking: no, that's not going to happen, because how the hell am I going to play drums and ride my motorbike? But yeah, weeks turned into months. I was in for about four months. What really motivated me, it may sound silly now, but I was busting for the toilet and there wasn't a nurse around. I just thought "right, I'm off". I'm either going to piss and shit myself, excuse my French, or force myself to go and do this. I remember it took me about five minutes to get up and out of bed. It took me ages to get to the toilet and nobody noticed.'

When he got back to his bed, a nurse asked him how he was. 'I said, "I'm all right, I've just been to the toilet." It was like a delayed reaction, and she went, "Oh my God! Nurse! Get the doctor! He's walking!" And that was it. From that point, I was on the road to getting up and walking.' It was, I told him, like a scene from the Bible. Was it agony? 'Oh yeah,' said Winston, 'it was absolute agony. The kids used to come and stay with me in the squat and they used to help me bathe.'

It took Winston about a year and a half to get back to normal, or something like normal. Three years later, he broke his back again. 'I'd just got a motorbike,' he said, 'really nice, a 750. I was dispatch riding. I'd just been to see my mum.' He was at the roundabout at the Elephant and Castle, just opposite the rice and peas stall where we met, when a car zigzagged first to the right and then to the left, and then slammed into the back of his bike. 'I'd had my hair cut,' he said, 'I'd had my dreads cut off. I just had a new crash helmet, which kind of saved my life. I broke the barrier, like three tiers of metal barrier. I've gone through the railing. Half my body is hanging through it. My head and back is, like, over the barrier and my legs are the other side. I looked up and all I could see was my bike coming towards me. I thought: "oh fuck".'

He was taken to Guy's Hospital. 'I remember waking up in

ER,' he said, 'and all these doctors and nurses are running around me, and blood here and there. My neck was in a brace. I had these brown leathers, really sexy brown leathers. They were so cool! They were starting to cut them and I said, "Don't cut my leathers, take my pants off." I got a fractured neck, broken collarbone, broken jaw, knocked out five teeth.' He opened his mouth and showed me the gaps. Why, I asked, didn't he replace them? 'I'm fine,' he said.

When his girlfriend came to visit, he didn't know who she was. He was in and out of consciousness for days. This time the recovery took nine months. 'And the third time,' he said, 'was in France.' *Third time?* I didn't know anything about a third time! 'I was working up in Courchevel,' he said, 'round about Christmas. Not a lot of snow, and it was very icy. El Stupido here went up on the piste. I got on the snowboard. It was like the *Titanic* coming down the slope, it hit the tiniest of rocks and it just went over. I kept on going over and over and over. The run is about fifteen hundred metres long. All I heard was,' and he made the clicking noise of a bone breaking, 'on my neck. The doctor said, "You're going to die if you don't stop."' Don't stop what? I said. 'Being an arse!' Well, I said, exactly.

When I first met him, I reminded him, he was very fit, but he did have problems with his back and with his nerve. 'Sciatica,' said Winston, 'that's caused by all the back injuries.' Did he still have it? 'Yeah, it's happening now, just along there, on the outside of my foot.' Does he have it all the time? 'Yes, pretty much, but it's manageable now.' Has he, I asked, basically been in pain all the time? Winston shrugged. 'Not all the time. It's as I've gotten older it's gotten worse.' In all the years I've known

Winston, he has never complained about it. 'What's the point?' he said. 'There are other people who've got much more serious things than I have. I'm up and I'm alive.'

Gosh. Where did he think that lack of self-pity came from? Winston smiled. 'It's my mum,' he said. 'My mum's tough, man, she was tough. She'd say, "If there ain't no blood, don't bother crying."' But there was blood! 'I couldn't see it,' said Winston. 'If you've got a reason to moan, moan, but make sure there is a reason to moan, you don't moan because you wanna.' What, I said, counts as a reason to moan? 'I don't know,' said Winston, 'because I haven't got a reason to moan.'

Winston joined the Territorial Army when he was thirty-six. 'When I first joined,' he said, 'I joined the medical section of the Paras, because it was the closest regiment. But then I smashed my knee. I didn't know until about six weeks later. They said, "The break's healed nicely," and I said, "What break?"' Then he was transferred to a different regiment, but went back to the Paras and got his 'wings' just before my forty-seventh birthday. I remember, because he was doing the food for my party when he went to pick them up. Seared beef and poached salmon, again.

And then, a couple of years later, he had a stroke. 'I cooked some breakfast,' he said, 'had a nice pot of fresh coffee, sat down, about ten o'clock, next thing I know it's half past four. I couldn't get up. I was really dizzy. I was slumped over the coffee table. My eye had gone, my lip and nose and this and that. I thought, "Who the hell come and kicked the shit out of me?" That's what I thought.' So how, I tried again, did he feel? 'Well,' said Winston, 'I've had a stroke, how are you supposed to feel? My hand doesn't work as good as it did, but it works. I can write, I can cook, I can chop up food.'

And then, I said, you developed epilepsy as a result of the stroke. 'It was annoying,' said Winston. 'To be honest, the epilepsy was really annoying. I've had fits when I'm sleeping, fits when I'm awake. I don't really care to count them. You just get on with it.' Winston now wears a tag around his neck. For a while, he couldn't work, but now he does. Does he *really* never feel sorry for himself? 'Nah,' he said. 'It's pointless. You've got a hand and that's what you've got. You've got to go out and pick the aces.'

I would love to be able to say that this was how I responded when I got lupus and cancer and when my skin was so ravaged by acne that you could hardly see it because of the weeping pustules and throbbing red lumps. It wasn't. I was desperate. I was furious. I felt I could blast the surface off the earth with my rage. There were times when I thought it would be easier to die. Both times I got cancer, I thought about suicide. I couldn't face what I had to go through. I thought if I lost my breast and hair, I would no longer feel like a woman. I thought men would see me as damaged goods. I thought I had never even managed to find a man to have regular sex with and now I never would.

I didn't actually want to die. I have never wanted to die. I have only ever wanted to avoid more pain. But both times I got cancer I soon learnt that I would do pretty much anything to hang on to my life.

The first time, I got a second opinion, had a second operation and managed to keep my breast. I turned down chemotherapy.

I was the new girl at work and I didn't want people to know I had cancer and I knew they would if I was bald. I kept my job. I kept my hair. I had radiotherapy before work every day for five weeks. In a year of treatment, I had two and a half weeks off.

The second time, I couldn't avoid a mastectomy. I didn't want to see myself without a breast and made sure that when I had it removed, I had something made to fill the gap. The plastic surgeon was like Michelangelo. He took a chunk of my stomach, and the blood vessels, and moved them to the place where the breast had been. For months after, I felt as if my body had been squeezed into someone else's skin and muscles, skin and muscles that were far too tight. But you honestly wouldn't know that my left breast isn't real.

I didn't, in the end, have to have chemotherapy. I kept my hair. The drugs I took for several years afterwards didn't make me fat or sick. And I now have a nice, flat stomach. Whatever I eat, I have a nice, flat stomach. My flat stomach is the silver lining in a big, black cloud that passed.

The first time I got cancer, I went to a 'holistic' cancer centre in Bristol. A doctor there told me not to have radiotherapy. Someone else told me to do meditation. Someone else told me to eat a lot of carrots. I nearly bought a book with what I still think is the saddest title in the world. It was called *Vegan Cooking for One*.

You do this if you want to. I think cancer is not for dilettantes. Slice it out. Blast it out. Stuff me with drugs. Just get the damn thing gone.

But I do think there are plenty of other illnesses that need a different approach.

If I hadn't seen a psychotherapist when I was twenty-six, I think I would probably be in a wheelchair now. I don't know why I got ill. We can never really know why we get ill. I don't think it helped to have a sister who had a serious illness and to feel guilty for being well. But I do know that medicine doesn't always work, and when it doesn't it can help to see a counsellor or shrink. It's not necessarily the talking that helps. It's what the talking unlocks.

In his book *Why Do People Get Ill?*, the psychoanalyst Darian Leader says that 'between 25 and 50 per cent of GP visits are for medically inexplicable complaints'. Physical symptoms, he says, 'are frequently signs that something is being communicated'. The challenge, I have found in all my years of illness, is to work out what the hell that message is.

This doesn't mean that ill health is all in the mind. A lot of it, I've discovered, is in the gut. When I first saw Yana, and told her about my symptoms, she told me she thought I had a condition called 'leaky gut'. What it meant, she explained, was that the gut wall sometimes becomes more porous and allows some un-digested food particles into the bloodstream and that this can trigger an immune response. I thought it sounded disgusting and unlikely, but when I got home I looked it up. Some of the things that often go with leaky gut, Google told me, were acne, insom-nia, migraines, Raynaud's syndrome, vitiligo, lupus and cancer. Everything, in fact, that I've had.

I recently read a bestselling book by a German scientist, Giulia Enders, called *Gut*. It's funny and clever and makes the argument that the gut is as important to human function as the brain and heart. I am not, of course, a scientist, so I don't know if she's right. All I know is that when my pain comes back, I go and see Yana and she tells me to keep off the booze, and gluten and sugar and yeast, for a while, and she sticks needles in me, once a week for a while, and I get better.

I don't like fussy eating. I live in a part of London where everybody seems to be allergic to gluten and I feel like telling them to get a grip and get a life. But sometimes I'm the one peering at labels and paying a fiver for a loaf of what isn't really bread. I can't say that my body is a temple, but I have learnt that you can't treat it as a cesspit and expect it all to work just fine.

I still drink, because although the studies say it isn't good for your health, I think it's very good for your mood. I know some medics call it a 'depressant'. Maybe it is for them, but that happiness professor Julia interviewed says that having two or three glasses of wine a day makes people happy. I think the studies assume that you're drinking them with other people, and that's usually true for me. When I read this, I felt quite proud. I felt as if I'd discovered the secret of happiness on my own.

Positive thinking does not get rid of illness. We all get ill and we all die. But I've learnt that the best way to keep healthy is to be happy, and active, and curious, and to be grateful for the incredible machine we all live in, on the face of this incredible earth.

Because I could not stop for Death

It's fourteen years since my sister died. On the anniversary of her death, my mother always goes to visit her grave. She and my father are in the same grave. One day, my mother will be in it, too. I can't think of anything in life that I dread more.

My mother believes in ritual. She goes to light a candle and bring flowers. I think she's right to do these things. Rituals, according to all the anthropologists, are one of the things that help us deal with death. My approach to bereavement has been more British. Not just keep calm and carry on, but try to push it right out of your head.

When my sister died I felt as if I was suddenly on a different planet and trying to behave like the natives of that planet, but finding it very hard because the planet and its natives all seemed to be part of a ridiculous game. One night, I dreamt that Caroline and I were walking on a giant causeway made of clouds. There were flamingos on either side of the causeway. All around us, the sky was pink. My sister and I were holding hands. When I woke up, I was crying. I don't believe in life after death, but I couldn't shake off the feeling that after all her struggles she was finally at peace.

With my father, it was different. He had had colon cancer for two years. They were terrible years. In the end, it went to his brain. In the end, he could hardly talk. When the news came that he had finally died, it was almost a relief.

Before I drove down to Guildford, I took ten minutes to wash the car. When I'd told my father that I was thinking of buying a Mazda MX-5, he said he thought it was important to 'cut a bit of a dash'. He, by the way, had never had anything smarter than a Morris Marina. The first time I washed my Mazda, I used a scourer. You don't really know the meaning of the word embarrassment until you've sat in the waiting area of a garage and someone yells out 'woman who washed the car with a scourer!' My father, my beloved father, offered to pay for it to be resprayed. I thought, in one of the mad flashes you get when everything has changed, that he would be pleased that I had stopped to wash my car.

My sister died seven months after I took over as director of the Poetry Society. My father died two years later. I had to rush back from the funeral preparations to give a speech at a leaving party for someone who had worked there for thirteen years. I cried in the car all the way back to London, then went to Pret a Manger to get a grip and wipe my face. Work kept me going. Work has always kept me going. There has to be something to keep us keeping on.

Morag and Mike were two of the people who kept my mother going, after Caroline, and then Dad, died. They have, as I have explained, had plenty of practice at grief. They never wanted to be experts, but they are.

'We supported each other through the ups and downs,' said Morag, that afternoon I met them at my mother's for tea. 'It's funny how we took it in turns,' she said. 'One would wake up in a terrible state, and the other one would make cups of tea and so on, or vice versa, you know. Every so often, it just hits you.'

She picked up her list, the list she had prepared that said, at the top of the page in large print, 'Living with and overcoming the grief of losing a loved one'. Number one on the list, she said, was 'a happy marriage'. It 'gives one', she read, 'the strength to carry on'. Number two was her 'caring parents', aunt, uncle and many friends. 'One friend,' she said, 'phoned me up every Monday morning after Mike went back to work, for a year. That's the sort of thing. It's a small thing. I've never forgotten her for that.'

Number three on her list was their six-year-old daughter, Emma. 'We were having a cup of tea,' she said, 'and Emma said, "Oh well, Grandpa, you'll be the next one to die, then Granny, then Mummy, then Daddy." Children accept death in such a matter-of-fact way. I suppose it helps you, in a way.'

Number four on her list was 'our own new baby boy', the boy Morag describes as their 'miracle baby'. The boy who, thirty-two years later, climbed into a car after a party and never made it home. 'Our second loss,' she had written on the next page, 'was much harder and has left us with a lasting sadness. We are lucky to have so many memories of happy times together, which never fade. Time,' she added, 'helps.'

Mike's list was more like a short essay. 'In surviving this,' he wrote, 'people were all-important to us: the in-laws who came to stay to support us, friends who invited us to stay. Contrary to what some of our friends thought, we did not want to be left on our own.' Mike looked up from his piece of paper and then carried on reading. 'The only way to get through this period,' he said, 'was to stick together to support each other, but I felt it was vital as far as possible to be as positive as possible in the circumstances, otherwise this tragedy was going to finish us off.'

It was, said Mike, important to keep 'frantically busy' by trying to keep family life going for Emma. 'When Anthony died,' he read, 'the awfulness of a double tragedy hit us hard. The feelings were just as severe, even if we could not feel the guilt that we did with Patrick.' What helped, he said, was talking about Anthony, both to each other and to Anthony's friends. For some years they would all get together on Anthony's birthday.

'If you're understanding this,' he said, 'you'd really have to think about the dark period that one goes through and that's really the only way to describe it. I think it takes about three years for that to lessen. And that's what people are contending with.'

He and Morag still talk a lot about Anthony. 'We still have a laugh,' said Morag, 'about things Anthony said. Memories we've got of him now. We talk about him still, but Mike doesn't like talking about their deaths. Moving house helped. Since we moved, we've got over that terrible waking up in the morning. But our house is full of photographs of Anthony just as yours is of dear Caroline.' We both looked around the room. All the bookshelves have family photographs on top of them. Between two armchairs is a little table with photographs of my father and Caroline. It has a vase Caroline loved and a candle. It is, to be honest, a kind of shrine.

'The best thing I've heard about grief,' said Angela, 'is that there are waves and you can be on a beach, and it can be very, very gentle, but it's always lapping at your feet.' We were at the Troubadour, a coffee house and bar in Earls Court where Bob Dylan has played, and Paul Simon, and Jimi Hendrix, and Elton John. That night Maura was reading, with her brothers Tim and Terence Dooley, who are also both poets. Yes, three siblings who are all poets. They all have curly hair, and we joked that they should also all be wearing tight satin suits.

'Grief,' Angela continued, 'is always lapping about your feet. But there's always the possibility a very big wave will come over you. It is,' she said, in her usual wry way, 'very unexpected. Most peculiar timing.'

So what, I asked, helped her ride out those waves, when her husband John died and she was left a widow with two young sons at the age of forty-two? Angela speared her fishcake. 'I didn't find many people I could go and talk to,' she said, 'but peculiarly enough, even though I was brought up a Catholic, I went to see our local rector at a C of E church. He was a great believer in diversions, and so am I.'

She told him that she was exhausted, after two years of watching John get ill and die, and wanted to go on a retreat. 'He said, "No, that's the last thing you want to do."' He told her to do things she liked instead. 'Going to see a play,' she said, 'or a film and losing yourself. I always recommend this to people. Give yourself time out. I know exactly what it's like to howl, and I think it's very good to go and do something and for two hours you're caught up in someone else's life. That gradually builds up.'

So when, I asked, did she start to feel better? Angela sighed. 'That's hard to answer, because obviously I had two sons and we had to. I want to say it was a very, very long time. For ages, it was hard for me to win through, but I did.'

One day, when she went to see the rector for a pot of tea and one of their chats, she saw that the daffodils were coming out. 'I said, "It's a beautiful day, isn't it?", and he said, "Oh good, you can see it." That, to me, was the thing. Some days you can't even see it's a beautiful day. If I think about my husband, I think about him laughing. For some reason, he used to find Mr Bean incredibly funny. He was a very thin tall man and he would just be like a shaking thin tall man with tears running down his face.' She smiled at the memory, and there was a faraway look in her eyes.

And did she, I asked, write off the thought of meeting someone else? Did her heart close? 'It must have,' she said, 'because for a long time I never did. I remember this Indian lady saying, "You must want a man," and, do you know, no English person has ever said this to me. It stopped me, because she was right. I knew that people were putting me in a box of "oh well, that's it then, for her". I get a lot of comments: "But you've got your boys."'

Her social circle, she said, was entirely made up of 'suburban couples' and suddenly she was shut out of it. 'I'd been a part-time teacher, whose husband had a very good career and had fallen into all of the traps. There's a certain kind of script and it all changes, and you haven't been given many lines it.' Or, she said, with a dry laugh, 'you've been written out of it completely!'

When divorced men started to approach her, she just felt irritated. 'There was,' she said, 'an idea of "you're on your own, you must be interested".' So when, I asked, did she start feeling open to the possibility of romance? 'I think,' she said, 'somebody asked me out and I did go, four or five years after John died. I had two relationships with men, neither of whom were that suitable.' How long did they last? Angela laughed. 'Quite a few years, actually, which is surprising, but I think I'm a "quite a few years" sort of person. I thought, "This is as good as it can get."'

It turns out it wasn't. Angela gave up her part-time teaching job, where she was treated like 'pond life', moved to London and started a PhD in politics. One New Year's Day her younger son suggested she try internet dating. The first man she met was 'perfectly nice' and gave her lots of advice about internet dating. The second man she met was even nicer and also a very handsome lawyer. I know because I've met him. Angela has now been with him for four years. 'I've been very lucky. It's very weird that I was so fortunate. I think when you meet someone, you find what you need if you're lucky. It will not be everything you would have wanted, but it *is* what you need. I think what I have found,' she said calmly, 'is more than I need.'

'I lost,' said Frieda Hughes, 'my father, my mother, my brother and my half-sister. Two of my grandparents went at an early age – and, of course, they're all dead now. Last year I lost the last of my father's siblings; my aunt and uncle. They went within months of each other. I've lost various best friends. I lost two of my dearest friends in Australia within two years of each other, both from brain tumours, which was a bit odd, not to mention all the animals. We can't love something without having loss at some point.' Would I, she added, like more coffee?

You can see why she's matter-of-fact about it. If Sylvia Plath was patron saint of depression and suicide, it would be easy to cast Frieda into the role of patron saint of grief. It's so much loss.

It's too much loss. But here she is, smiling, glowing, almost exploding with energy. She has, she told me, just finished a project that involved doing a painting a day for more than a year. She had, in fact, done more than four hundred. She showed me some of them. They are like jewels. I cannot begin to imagine how she managed to do it.

Work, it's clear, has been the driving force of her life, the creative work that helped her recover from serious illness in her thirties and that has enabled her to speak and paint and write, against all the odds, in her own clear voice. Her father's death was bad enough. We were both, we discovered, the same age when our fathers died, both of cancer, also at the same age.

And then, eleven years after her father died, Frieda got the news that her brother, Nicholas, had hanged himself, at home in Alaska, at the age of forty-seven. He was a year old when their mother gassed herself in the kitchen of that flat in Primrose Hill while he and Frieda slept in the next room. In 1998, shortly before he died, Ted Hughes wrote a letter to his son, describing the mental scars that Plath's death had left on the family. 'I tell you all this,' he said, 'with a hope that it will let you understand a lot of things . . . Don't laugh it off. In 1963 you were hit even harder than me. But you will have to deal with it, just as I have had to. And as Frieda has had to.'

'When my brother died,' Frieda told me, 'there were a couple of friends who were really brilliant, and they used to phone all the time. I became very unsociable for a while, obviously. I remember in the early days I used to sit on the sofa on the middle floor landing.' She had just shown me round the house and I had just seen it. 'There was a mirror facing the sofa and I used to sit on the sofa on the phone, and I remember looking at my face once. I was weeping myself into a little wreck, and I looked at my face and I didn't recognize myself. I thought: right, that's enough now, I have to get on with life.'

There are a number of poems in *Alternative Values* about Nicholas's death. 'There's a poem in there,' Frieda told me, 'that just encapsulates all that pain, because his death was attached to my mother's death. It just gathers all the deaths together and becomes a big mourning fest.' The poem is called 'Transition' and it talks of 'this new wasteland where nothing stopped the bitter wind'.

'This person phones up,' said Frieda, 'and said, "I'm so sorry to hear about the loss of your brother," and she says, "Have you got help?" I said, "What do you mean, what kind of help?" And I'm thinking: she means a psychiatrist. I don't need a psychiatrist! My brother died. My husband and I have broken up. One thing happened just after the other, and I was very, very sad and that was normal. It turned out that what she actually wanted to know was whether I was getting the right medication. Why would I want to medicate against sorrow? If I can't feel it, then how can I process it? Address it? Digest it? Understand it? I was simply very sad and it would wear off one day, as a natural process. Part of the process of living.'

Yes, it's 'part of the process of living'. It's normal to be sad. I prefer not to use the word 'depressed' because I think depression is an illness, and I have not suffered from the illness called depression. But there have been times in my life when I, like Frieda, have been very, very, very, very sad.

'I don't,' she said, 'want to feel anything that isn't natural, because I want to know the size, the shape and how painful the shadows I'm boxing are. I know the one thing that's calculated to get me off my backside is the passage of time I cannot get back. It's a real driver. The year my brother died I was seeing someone briefly and he said, "Are you dying?" I said, "Everybody's dying," and he said, "No, I mean are you dying now, do you have cancer or something?" And I said, "Why do you ask?" He said, "Because you do everything at a hundred miles an hour, you've got to get things done and you're always so driven." And I said, "But I've been like that all my life and it's called living."'

We are all going to die. It doesn't matter if you're ready, or if you want it. 'Because I could not stop for Death,' as the poet Emily Dickinson put it, 'He kindly stopped for me.' You don't have to have seen Bergman's *The Seventh Seal* to know that we are all playing chess with Death.

Most of us don't think all that much about dying. I have to admit I don't even have a will. This is partly because I don't want to face up to the fact that I haven't got anyone obvious to leave my stuff to. Property, if you have any, usually goes to children, or perhaps to nephews or nieces. It usually goes to blood. Or, of course, to charity, but when you see some of the salaries paid to people who work in charities, it does make you wonder if you really want the sweat of all your book reviews to give those people the kind of pension nobody you know will get.

But when I got cancer the second time, I had a sudden feeling that I needed to sort some things out. I went through my papers. I sat on the floor of my study and gazed at the piles of paper and felt as if I was stuck in *Bleak House*. I got about halfway through and then thought that if I died at least someone else would sort it all out. Then I thought it would probably have to be my mother and I thought it would be too much for her to have to do that, too.

I decided to sort out my books. I don't really know why. My flat has always been like a sort of petri dish that breeds books instead of mould. My cousin Robin generously offered to help. He thought the books should be alphabetical and in categories, perhaps because he's a man. It was so hard to choose which books had to go. I was picking up books, and wondering if I would ever read them again, and wondering if I would ever get the chance. I thought I couldn't bear to leave some of those books unread. In the end, we made sure that the books on the mezzanine were all poetry, the books in my study were nearly all fiction and the books in my hallway, which is two storeys high, were non-fiction. The books that Robin sorted were in alphabetical order. The books I sorted weren't, because I felt overwhelmed by all the books and because I was tired.

I sent away for one of those wills you can get for £25 and filled it out the night before my operation. I left half my stuff to my friends and my brother and half to a charity called Kids' Company. The charity has since gone bust, so it's just as well I didn't die, though the will wouldn't have been legal anyway. The administrator on the ward refused to witness it, so I went down to the operating theatre thinking that if I didn't come out, what I had would go to HMRC. In fact, it would have gone to my mother, but I don't think it would have done all that much to cheer her up.

A week before the operation, I went to meet a friend in

Trafalgar Square. When I saw the lions and the fountains, and the lights on the fountains, and the buses going past, and the people walking through the square, the feeling that I didn't want to die hit me so strongly that it was like a spasm running through me. And I don't. I don't want to die because I really, really like being alive.

Almost half of us will get cancer. We all know people who have it, and if we don't now, we soon will. Some of those people will be old, but quite a few of them won't. Old is bad enough. Old can break your heart. But if they're not old, you feel cheated. You feel as if someone has torn up the contract that guaranteed your three score and ten. In the West, we all think we're entitled to our three score and ten. What we forget is that the mortality rate, in East and West, and even in countries like Denmark, is always 100 per cent.

If we don't die of cancer, we'll die of something else. 'Being brave', said Philip Larkin in his poem 'Aubade', 'Lets no one off the grave.' Death, he said, 'is no different whined at than withstood'.

'I feel,' says Diana Athill, who is still going strong at ninety-nine, 'that we all have a duty to try and develop sensible attitudes to . . . death and remind ourselves that it is a part of life.' She wrote her book about old age, *Somewhere Towards the End*, when she was ninety. 'The difference between being and non-being', she says at the end of it, 'is both so abrupt and so vast that it remains shocking even though it happens to every living thing that is.'

I don't know if Diana Athill is prepared for death. I don't really know how you prepare for death, apart from making sure that the people you love know you love them. Diana Athill doesn't have children. She does have lots of younger friends, a very nice room in a very nice care home, and generally seems to have a lovely time.

If I make it to old age, and I'm stuck in one of those care homes they film on secret cameras and put on *Panorama*, and if my friends are too old and frail to visit me, I may come to the point where I've had enough of life. In the meantime, I don't want to waste a minute. In the meantime, count me in.

Stick your face in the sun

Italians know about *la dolce vita*. They have plenty of practice in doing it well. Perhaps it's because I was born in Rome that the Italian view of *la dolce vita* is pretty much mine. Give me sunshine, give me good coffee, give me delicious food, give me delicious wine. Give me all of these things and I, too, will think that life is sweet.

Seven years ago, on a press trip to Seville, I got talking to a journalist from the *Corriere della Sera*. She talked about the house in the country that she went to when she wasn't in Rome. I asked her how a journalist could afford a second home, and she told me that she'd bought it for 8000 euros. I don't know exactly what happened, but I heard the words '8000 euros' and something went off in my head.

When I got back to the hotel that night, I sat by the computer in the foyer, looking at Italian properties on the internet until 3 a.m. Unfortunately, there was nothing for 8000 euros. There were things for 80,000 euros, but I didn't have 80,000 euros. I started thinking about friends who didn't earn any more than me, but who were somehow managing to pay for child minders for their children. I remembered something I'd read that said it cost £250,000 to bring up a child. I didn't know how the sums would work out, but I thought that if they could pay to bring up a child then maybe I could increase my mortgage to get something that cost about the same as a child's leg.

Within five days of getting back to London, I had found, on the internet, and made an offer on, a tiny flat in a fourteenth-century watchtower in Tuscany. I didn't tell my friends, or even my mother, what I was doing, because I thought everyone would tell me I was mad. I was on a course for a new computer system at work when someone called from the estate agent to say that my offer had been accepted.

I tried not to panic as I asked my boss if I could take a day off, and booked an early-morning flight from Stansted and an evening flight back. I drove to Stansted, parked the car, got the flight, and arrived at Pisa at 11 a.m. feeling as if I was about to take an exam. A woman from the estate agent met me. She asked if I'd been looking for property in Tuscany for a while and I had to tell her that until two weeks before the thought had never entered my head.

When I saw the watchtower, which was made of bricks that were partly a kind of pink colour and partly grey, I felt my heart jump. It was like when you're at a party and you suddenly lock eyes with someone very handsome, and you feel your heart beating faster until someone tells you they've got a wife. First, we walked out to the little piece of garden in front of the watchtower. The view made me gasp. There was a hill, covered in fields. Some of them were a golden colour, and some were different shades of green. Some of the trees had leaves that looked as if they were floating, like little green clouds, on their trunks. Some, which I thought were probably cypress trees, were tall and pointed. In front of the cypress trees, and the trees that looked like clouds, there were olive groves. In the distance, on another hillside, you could see a village and a church spire. The pool, which was built on a slope, had one of those edges that make it look as though the water is part of the landscape, like an upside-down sky.

My flat, or at least the one I had made an offer on without seeing, had its own front door at the top of a steep flight of stairs. It opened straight into a small room that was completely empty, without even a sink or kitchen cupboards. Off it there was another small room that was completely empty, and off that was a shower room. The floor was made of terracotta tiles that looked hundreds of years old. The ceiling was high, and supported by ancient oak beams. In each room there was a big window. From the main room and the bedroom, you could see the patch of garden and a walnut tree. From the bathroom, you could see the terracotta roofs and stone houses of the next village.

When I looked out of the main window, I remembered a conversation I'd had four years before. It was just after I had the results of my lumpectomy, and been told that there was still some cancer left behind. I had a session with a counsellor. She said she thought it was a good idea to have a picture of something in your head to keep you going through what you had to face. The picture that came to my head was of me in an Italian village, sitting by a window, writing and looking out at terracotta roofs. I had completely forgotten this till now.

The woman from the estate agent drove me to the nearest town, which had a thermal spring and a pretty square, and in the Gran Caffè of the square we met her boss and the architect. We talked about contracts and payments, and we had a Spritz, which is an Italian aperitif made from prosecco and Aperol or Campari, and clinked glasses and said '*salute!*' After that, she drove me to a furniture shop, where the other people in the watchtower had bought their furniture and their kitchens. By the time I got to Pisa airport, where I ate gnocchi and drank red wine, and chatted to a couple of English guys at the next table, and felt so happy I thought my heart would burst, I had bought, or committed myself to buying, a flat in Tuscany, and a kitchen.

Since then, Italy has been my other world. When I signed the contract, six weeks later, and picked up the keys, I slept on an airbed from Argos, and used a torch from Argos, because there was still no furniture or electricity or gas. Two days later, Winston turned up with the furniture I'd bought in London in a van. It was quite hard to get the sofa up the stairs, and to squeeze the furniture into those two tiny rooms, but when we did, and were finished, it looked like what it was: a tiny, beautiful home.

The first time I was out there, I met Norbert and his wife, Josephine. They live in a nearby village and since then they have kept an eye on my flat when I'm not there. When I am there, I see them, and sometimes their daughters Christine and Jessica, and Christine's daughter, Lucia. A few months after my big operation, I went over for Lucia's First Communion. I have spent Easter and Christmas at their home. They have become my second family.

I go to Italy to write, read, look out at a sun-drenched hillside, and dream. I go to sip Vermentino in the local bar, and eat pasta with sweet, ripe tomatoes, flecked with fresh basil. I go to wander around crumbling cities and to practise my Italian, which always makes me feel as if I'm in a country that speaks in song. I go to lie in a pool and gaze up at a blue, blue sky.

In Italy, as the sun sets, you have an *aperitivo*. This could be a glass of prosecco. It could be a glass of the local wine. It's often a Spritz, which is the colour of a jewel, either dark orange or dark pink. You usually have it with a bowl of peanuts and a bowl of crisps. In many bars now, even the bar at the local supermarket, they have a whole *aperitivo* buffet, of crisps, peanuts, little bits of focaccia with ham or pecorino, little squares of pizza, little chunks of cheese. The Italians have, in fact, taken a collection of my favourite things and made it into a daily ritual that feels like a celebration.

The summer after I lost my job, I didn't go. I was too worried about money and thought I needed every penny from rent I could get. The following summer, I rented out my flat in London for five weeks and spent two and a half of them in Tuscany. I was trying to get a writing project off the ground, but couldn't do it in London as I seemed to spend all my time sending emails or lurching from one deadline to the next.

When I woke up the first morning, and looked out at the fig tree, and the olive trees, and the cypresses, I thought of Marvell's poem 'The Garden'. He talks about withdrawing to a garden, a place of quiet and solitude where 'luscious clusters of the vine' crush his mouth with their wine, and where the whole world turns into a 'green thought in a green shade'. Having cast 'the body's vest aside', he says, his 'soul into the boughs does glide', where 'like a bird it sits and sings'.

I wouldn't put it quite like that, but I would certainly say that I go to Italy to feed my soul.

We all need to feed the soul. We all need to have those moments when the noise in our head falls away and we can see the beauty in the world and just stop and breathe it in. We need them to get us through what Marvell called the 'uncessant labours' and what some of us might be tempted to call the crap.

You don't need a poet to tell you that it's a kind of miracle to watch a bud turn into a flower. For Morag and Mike, the flowers they have grown in their gardens have sometimes been like candles in the dark. For my father, I think it was the same. When I saw him kneeling by his roses, I sometimes thought it was as if he was taking Holy Communion.

It was the same when he listened to music. I often saw him wipe away tears when he listened to Handel or Bach. I often wipe away tears when I listen to them, too. 'Where words fail,' said Hans Christian Andersen, 'music speaks.' And words, as we all know, fail a lot. For my cousin Robin, music has played a big part in keeping what Churchill called the 'Black Dog' away. Robin has been in the BBC Symphony Chorus for twenty-two years. 'The commitment,' he told me, 'is as professional as it could be. It's hard work. You don't always feel like turning up after a day at the office, but it's a great privilege. It has been a retreat when work or personal life hasn't been going so well.'

Stefano also sings in a choir. Singing in a choir, according to the studies, is good for your health and good for your brain. It is also, apparently, one of the best ways of making you feel happy. There's something about getting together with other people, and drawing in air, and expelling that air to make a harmonious sound, that lifts the spirits and touches the soul. So much better than drawing in air and counting to six.

The purple coffin that might well have saved Winston's life when he broke that glass ceiling (but not in the way HR managers tell you to if you're a woman or you're black) was there to store his drum stands. Winston has been in bands for most of the time I have known him. He has been playing drums since he was five. He is, to use his words, a 'shit hot' drummer. He has even played with Michael Jackson. It was because he wanted to play his drums that he was 'annoyed' when a doctor told him he might not walk. That, and the fact that he wanted to get back on his bike.

I once went on a motorbike in the Austrian Alps. It was for a travel feature for *The Independent*. I had to borrow someone else's leathers and they were so tight that the words 'hung, drawn and quartered' sprung into my head as I zipped them up. I finally managed to swing one taut leg over the seat and could feel myself blush as I looped my hands around the waist of the man whose bottom was inches away from my crotch. It had rained all weekend and the rain was still coming down in slabs. I was meant to be looking at the mountains so I could write something nice and descriptive, but all I could see, through the rain-splashed visor of my borrowed helmet, was blurred lines.

I pulled the visor up and then the rain was like needles on my face. I was cold. I was wet. The bumping against my crotch reminded me of the time I went down Mount Sinai on a camel. Biking, I discovered, is not my glass of Aperol Spritz. But it's Frieda Hughes's Veuve Clicquot. Like Winston, she's hooked on the buzz. She even met her current partner through biking. He was surprised to find a fiftysomething woman who did track days and who, like him, thought that maybe one motorbike wasn't enough.

I've never really got into any kind of sport, but my father and brother were both sports mad. My father played rugby, cricket and squash. My brother played football, rugby and volleyball. For them, going to a football or rugby match, or even watching one on TV, was a shared and sacred rite.

For Rolien, stuck in her miserable job, sport was part of her escape. 'I went cycling one afternoon,' she told me, 'and went past a field where they were playing softball. Softball,' she added, 'is a great passion.' She googled the field, found the team and within a couple of years was captain of it. 'It opened a massive new network and support system,' she told me. 'Through those connections I went on fantastic holidays. There were baby showers and weddings and endless, endless memories.' And through one of those connections she found the job she now has, and loves.

For Grant, swimming, running and football have helped keep hovering clouds at bay. Katherine's seven-mile walks kept her feet literally on the ground when she sometimes thought the tantrums at home might send her reeling over an edge. Maxine, too, is a walker. She says the rhythms of walking clear her head. Even I, who have tended to take my mother's view that there's not much point in walking down a road that isn't lined with cafés or shops, find that I miss exercise if I don't do it. When I was lying in my hospital bed, wondering if I would ever be able to stand straight again, I decided that if I ever could, I would run. I don't run marathons. I don't want to run marathons. I trot round the park and then often stop for a cup of tea and a scone.

I've only been to one football match – at White Hart Lane, to write about a poet in residence at Spurs – but I understand why, for many people, going to a football match is like going to a church. It doesn't matter if it's on a football field or in a theatre. It *is* a spiritual experience to see human beings performing at their peak.

People often talk about their 'hobbies'. Rolien would probably say that hers are music, theatre and film as well as sport. When she was living in her miserable shared house – a house she hated so much that the words 'West Ruislip' still, she says, trigger 'a physical reaction that crawls over me' – she would save up to go to the theatre. When she couldn't afford to go, she would 'rent a bunch of DVDs' and spend the whole weekend on a 'movie marathon'. Being swept away to another world gave her strength to cope with her own.

Since Melanie's husband left her, she has started to discover the power of the arts. 'I think,' she told me, 'I was diminished in that relationship. I'm finding who I am at forty-eight and I'm not finding the person I was before. I feel there are things bubbling away in the background and I really enjoy that. They're about connection, also about valuing aesthetics. They are what I need for my flourishing.'

And for Laura, stuck in her abusive marriage, dreams of interiors helped her imagine a life beyond the one she was in. 'I've always loved home stuff,' she told me. 'I had an idea of studying interior design. Home had completely ebbed away. Our bedroom, there was no colour to it. It was all white. I had no choice in what we ate, or how we had the home, how our money was spent. So I had a little fantasy of a pink room, a dusky pink, and of my own space, where I could just do what I wanted, and have all my favourite books around me. I started buying little things for my new home and hiding them in this cupboard we had in the attic. That,' she said with a dry laugh, 'was my way of coping, creating a mini home in hell.'

The word 'hobby' comes from 'hobi', the Anglo-Latin word, from about 1400, for a 'small, active horse'. The modern use of the word, as 'a favourite pursuit, object or topic', is from 1816, a shortening of 'hobbyhorse', which was a wooden or wickerwork figure of a horse, used as a costume in a morris dance or a child's toy. It was, to put it another way, a horse that's going nowhere, an activity that has no obvious use. It is also described in the dictionary as a 'sideline', a 'diversion', a 'divertissement'. But I don't think we're talking about things that pass the time. I think we're talking about things that can save a life.

It was the psychologist Mihály Csíkszentmihályi who came up with the idea that people are happiest when they are in a state of 'flow', a state where they are so absorbed in what they are doing that they hardly notice anything else. In this state, he says, 'the ego falls away' and 'time flies'. It is, in other words, the exact opposite of a pastime or a 'diversion'. It's when there aren't enough hours, minutes, seconds to do this thing that allows you to forget your worries, your ego and your self.

For my acupuncturist, Yana, it started when she was clearing out the loft. 'I was bringing out the summer things, putting away the winter things,' she told me, 'and I suddenly felt my heart break.' This was when she was forty-eight. Her father had died when she was six. It was only when she was writing Christmas cards that she found out he was dead. 'I would write "love from Mummy, Daddy and me",' she told me, 'and my mother said, "You've got to cross out Daddy." That's got to be the worst possible way of getting to know that somebody was dead! I only knew that he'd gone to hospital and that my mother couldn't stop crying.'

For years, she had carried the pain around without knowing what she was carrying. She went to see a shrink, the same shrink she later recommended to me. 'Then I realized,' she said, 'that this is actually what I've been feeling all my life. There must have been a memory of clearing things or packing them away, heart-break that I'd never been able to express. I sobbed and howled. I do,' she added, 'howl like a wolf if I ever howl. There was this howling heartbreak and then I never had it again.'

It was after that that she started to paint. First she went to classes, where she learnt to draw. Once she started, it just poured out of her. 'I felt I'd woken up the next morning and had wings. I didn't have to walk, I didn't have to do anything. I could fly and I'd be immediately there.'

Yana has taken her heartbreak and created paintings that are bursting with colour and life. Maddy Paxman has written a memoir and given her grief a searing voice. Mimi Khalvati has channelled her pain into deceptively delicate poems that pack a fierce emotional punch. Frieda Hughes has created landscapes and poems of blistering bleakness and savage beauty. 'If I can't paint or I can't write,' she told me, 'then nothing's happening. It's how I process everything.'

Laura held on to her vision of a dusky pink room. She got through the court cases. She got through the cornflakes for dinner.

She now has a job she loves and has created a beautiful home where her son visits her. 'When I say goodbye to him,' she told me, 'I know that for two days I'm going to be really sad. Before, I used to try and fight it. I actually plan a day off after he's gone. The first thing I do is wash his bedding. I sniff his pillow and have a good cry. I give myself two days and after that, usually it's fine.'

When Laura lost custody of her son, she did not think that one day it would be 'fine'. When they were parted, he was five and a half. 'He was,' she said, 'still clinging to my legs. It does get easier. He's fourteen. Our relationship is good. I think he sees me as a strong woman. He knows that I'm always there for him, and that I did everything I could to make sure our relationship stays strong. He doesn't,' she added, 'see me as a victim.'

When I go to my Italian bolthole, the first thing I do is look at the guest book signed by people who have rented the flat. I'm always pleased that so many people seem to love it as much as I do. Some of the couples who stay there are on honeymoon. When there's a honeymoon, I always leave champagne. I sometimes think that I've created a little love nest and that I'm the only person who stays in it on my own.

I'd be lying if I said I didn't sometimes feel a stab of envy. I would also be lying if I said I was lonely or bored. Even on my own, I'm hardly ever lonely and I honestly can't remember feeling bored. I often get the feeling Mihály Csíkszentmihályi describes when I write. I've had it from reading all my life. Books are my food, my drink, my canapés, my Casanova. Ever since I was a child, I've felt that books understand me in a way sometimes other people don't. Books have made me. Books have taught me that you are never in a place that someone else hasn't been in before.

Nine years ago, just before I found Yana, I went to the Red Sea. I thought I had won my battles against my body, but the pains had come back and I was in a state of screaming rage. Somehow, I hobbled on a plane. A coach took me to a hotel that was a slab of concrete in a desert. That week I stuck my face in the sun and read *War and Peace*. I didn't know how to get rid of the pain that racked my body, but something inside me said that as long as I could read and find a way to stick my face in the sun, I would be OK. Then I got back and found Yana, and I was.

I have learnt that there is nearly always a way to stick your face in the sun. I hope that I'll be able to hang on to my little chunk of the watchtower, but there was sunshine before I found it, and there will be sunshine after it has gone.

In the nearest town to my village, there's a statue of Dante. In my first year of learning Italian, as a subsidiary subject to my main degree in English, I had to translate some chunks of his *Divine Comedy*. '*Nel mezzo del cammin di nostra vita*,' it begins, '*mi ritrovai per una selva oscura, / ché la diritta via era smarrita.*' Or, as Clive James puts it, in his translation: 'At the midpoint of the path through life, I found / Myself lost in a wood so dark, the way / Ahead was blotted out.'

As I sat and looked out at the olive trees, and the cypresses, and the terracotta roofs of the houses on the other side of the valley, I allowed myself to write what was on my heart. I thought of all the times that I felt I had been lost in dark woods. And I thought that the darkness had always cleared, as it was clearing now.

A big cone

It was my birthday. A year since the Ottolenghi recipes, and the beef that set off the smoke alarm. A year since the leather-bound *Sentimental Journey*, with its open ending and its promise of a world that is not 'barren'. I had been invited to a conference run by a think tank on 'character'.

Resilience, said the chair of the conference, is not enough. Resilient people can join the mafia. What the organizers of the conference wanted was for people not just to have 'grit' but to 'flourish'.

The shadow health secretary said that schools throughout the world were looking at how 'character skills' could help raise standards of achievement. A man called Paul quoted Churchill. 'Failure,' he said, 'is not fatal, it is the courage to continue that counts.' A woman from an exam body said that some skills that help build character can be taught. She said that when thinking and reasoning skills were taught in prison, rates of reoffending dropped. A Paralympian who had won gold medals for swimming said that you build quite a lot of character when you do 8000 metres a session and when your alarm goes off at 4.40 a.m. every single day. A man called James said: 'We know how important the development of character is, but we're still not clear how it happens.'

I'm not sure how it happens either, but I'm pretty sure where it all starts. It starts with your parents. It starts with love. And it starts with the shock of finding out that you are not the centre of the universe, after months as a tiny baby feeling like a god.

William Blake saw the world in a grain of sand. I once saw it in an ice cream. It had swirls of vanilla rising out of a cornet, swirls that had been dipped in chocolate and brushed with nuts. It was called a *Storstrut*, which means a 'big cone', and it cost one Swedish krona. My father said that that was too much. I could, he said, have a Zoom, which was an orange ice lolly, but I didn't want an orange ice lolly. You could almost say that the next seventy-odd years are about how you deal with the fact that you want a *Storstrut* and sometimes get a Zoom.

Jean Piaget studied the behaviour of children for more than sixty years. He started off with molluscs, and then moved on. Children, he worked out, partly from studying the three he had with his wife, moved from a position of 'egocentrism' to 'sociocentrism'. They start off by sucking everything in reach. They literally suck the world and see. He called the first stage of development 'the pre-operational stage'. During this stage, he said that children were able to form 'stable concepts' as well as 'magical beliefs'. Their thinking at this stage is still 'egocentric', but from seven to eleven they move into the 'concrete operational stage', where they learn that not everything is about them. He called this a process of 'assimilation' and 'accommodation'.

It's fine to avoid the 'accommodation' stage of development if you're going to run Zimbabwe or North Korea. If you're going to do anything else, it isn't.

There's a book that has become very fashionable recently. It's by an American social scientist called Angela Duckworth and it's called *Grit*. In the book, she talks about how her Chinese father would yell at his children that they were 'no genius' or 'no Picasso'. Duckworth's response was to forge such a successful career that she has been awarded a MacArthur fellowship, which is also known as 'the genius grant'. She has spent years studying how people overcome setbacks, with passion, persistence and what she calls 'grit', to achieve success.

There are an awful lot of books about success. These books tell you how to work hard. They tell you how to believe in yourself. They tell you that what matters most in your life is what you achieve.

In my first week at university, I met a young woman on the same course as me. 'The important thing,' she said, as if she was making an obvious point, 'is to get on in life.' I was shocked. It seems ridiculous now, but I honestly was shocked. I had always been told by my parents that the most important thing in life was to be a decent person and to try to put other people first.

My father believed in public service and he did it so well that he had what most people would describe as a very successful career. After a double first at Cambridge, he worked in the diplomatic service and then transferred to the civil service when I was nine months old. He ended up running the Department of National Savings. He ended up being made a Companion of the Order of the Bath and being given an award by the Queen. He still wouldn't use the office phone for personal calls. He was sometimes offered a car, but he would always take the bus.

When he retired, he volunteered for the Citizens' Advice Bureau, spending several days a week giving advice to people who were down on their luck. In the instructions he left for his funeral, he said that there were to be 'no personal comment or tributes'. He wanted 'the main point of the address to be that the greatest rewards come not from being in charge of thousands of people, but in trying to help individual vulnerable people'. The occasions, he said, 'when I was able to help sad people in the Godalming Citizens' Advice Bureau were the most fulfilling of my life, and my many years of trying to help my daughter Caroline to cope with mental illness were my most challenging task, supporting my heroic wife'.

I have never been in charge of thousands of people. I have tried to help 'individual vulnerable people', but I have not tried nearly hard enough. I had my parents' example. I don't need a conference to tell me that the most important thing in life is to be kind.

After the conference, I went and bought a dress. I bought a red dress because I like the colour red, because it's energetic and passionate, and because it was my birthday and I was going to a party. It was not a surprise party organized by a lover, in a pod on the London Eye. It was the *Sunday Times* books desk Christmas party. It was a very nice party. I saw quite a few people I like and quite a few people whose writing I admire. I was still thinking about the conference when I left and remembered something John Ruskin once said. 'The greatest thing a human soul ever does in this world is to see something, and tell what it saw in a plain way.' I'm not sure it's 'the greatest thing', but I do think it's worth a lot.

Afterwards, I went to a pub round the corner for dinner with some friends. We had steak and chips and delicious red wine, and when they raised their glasses to wish me a happy birthday I had a sudden urge to cry because I thought I was so lucky to have such lovely friends.

I told them about something that had happened a few weeks before. It was in the green room at Sky. I was on with Matthew Syed from *The Times*. We were meant to be choosing articles to talk about from the next day's papers, and he had picked out a comment piece in *The Independent*. It was by the young man who had taken over my boss's job, the young man the managing editor told me had vetoed my contract for a column. I saw the name on the piece, yelled 'I don't think so!' and then told Matthew about my last day on the paper, and how I had shouted at the editor and never been back. Matthew touched me on the arm. 'Do you mind,' he said, 'if I give you some advice?' I suddenly felt nervous. Even I could hardly hear my whispered 'no'. 'You need to let go of your anger,' he said, 'or it will eat you up.'

When I walked into the studio, I could feel my cheeks burn. I had to talk about the next day's front pages, but I just wanted to tell Matthew that he was wrong. It was all very well for him, I wanted to say. He still had his nice fat *Times* contract. He still had his column. He wasn't the one who was having to get used to hearing himself described as 'former' or 'ex'. Anger, I wanted to tell him, was an energy. I wouldn't have managed to do half the things I had managed to do since leaving the paper if I hadn't been fuelled by that energy. And how the hell was I meant to 'let go' of my anger when the people who had wronged me weren't even sorry? Look at all the things, I wanted to say, that have been achieved through anger! Slavery was abolished because of anger! Children weren't chimney sweeps because of anger! Don't fucking tell me not to be angry!

We didn't talk about slavery, or chimney sweeps, or even how humiliated I felt when I walked in front of those TV cameras and sat down on that sofa. I hardly ever watch myself on TV, so I don't know if any of this was caught on my face, but I think it probably was. A friend once saw me reviewing the papers with a man who had gone silent on me after several dates. She said he looked as if he was waiting for the guillotine. That, I told her, was a really good idea.

A few months ago, I was asked to take part in a TV discussion on forgiveness. There was an archbishop, a pastor of a Pentecostal church, a columnist who used to be a colleague, and me. The archbishop said forgiveness is what enables you to let go. The pastor said that he had learnt to forgive many people who had done him harm. The columnist, who is Muslim, said she thought forgiveness was a beautiful part of the Christian faith, but that it wasn't part of hers. I said I thought forgiveness was irrelevant. I said that 'to forgive', according to the dictionary, was to 'stop feeling angry or resentful', but that if you were feeling angry you couldn't just pretend you weren't. I said that when people ask you for forgiveness, they usually just want you to make them feel better. Why, I said, would you want to forgive them when they hadn't even asked you to? When, in fact, they might never even have thought that they had done anything wrong?

As I told my friends about that evening at Sky, I suddenly had the answer. You forgive people who have wronged you to make yourself feel better. It doesn't matter whether or not they think they have done anything wrong. Resentment, I finally realized, and as Carrie Fisher once said, 'is like drinking poison and waiting for the other person to die'.

I once went on a 'positivity' course. It was after my sister had died, my father had died and I'd had cancer and I was trying to get over a broken heart. In a central London hotel, with cream walls and a blue carpet, and tables with pump-top coffee flasks of sour filter coffee, the hypnotist Paul McKenna tried his best. He had learnt, he told us, to 'turbo-charge' his brain with 'the Power of a Positive Perspective'. Now it was up to us to learn how to do the same.

He told us to make pictures in our mind. He told us to laugh when he gave us the sign. He tried to teach us how to 'Master Your Emotions and Run Your Own Brain'. I sat through the weekend, and drank the coffee, and ate the biscuits. I even bought the CDs. It didn't make any difference. When I thought of my sister, and my father, and the man I loved and couldn't be with, I just felt sad.

It was a relief to stop trying, just as it had been when I had told friends the results of my biopsy and they had looked me in the eye and told me it was bloody awful. That was so much better than the people who told me not to worry because it would be fine. I wanted to ask them if they had suddenly discovered they were psychic. Or if, perhaps, they had gone away and secretly trained as oncologists. Or if, perhaps, they were just trying to cheer themselves up.

There's a lot to be said for negative thinking. 'Whereas positive mood seems to promote creativity, flexibility, co-operation and reliance on mental shortcuts,' says Professor Joe Forgas in *Aus-*

tralian Science magazine, 'negative moods trigger more attentive, careful thinking, paying greater attention to the external world.' People 'in negative mood', he concludes, can cope with more demanding situations than their sunny neighbours and are 'less prone to judgmental errors, are more resistant to eyewitness distortions and are better at producing high-quality, effective persuasive messages'.

Well, I could have told him that! Who started the Iraq War? A man who told *Vanity Fair*, after he first took office, that he was 'not really the type to . . . go through deep wrestling with my soul', a man who picked the rug in the Oval Office to reflect his 'optimism'. Who decided to hold the referendum on whether or not to stay in the EU? A man who was sure he could win it, and who told his first party conference that he wanted to 'let sunshine win the day'. Who was the key player in making sure he lost it? A man who promised the British people that they could 'have their cake and eat it', because he always had.

And who caused the global economic crisis? Men and women (but mostly men) who sold mortgages to people with no credit rating, or savings, or sometimes even income, and then wrapped those debts up and sold them on, and thought it would all be fine. David Hare wrote a play about them, which ran at the National Theatre. It was called *The Power of Yes*.

The trouble with positive thinking is that it confuses the world with your head. It puts you back in the mind of a baby who has only to cry to summon a breast. It tells you that if you think like a baby, you can will your way to health, wealth and success. You can try it, until something goes wrong.

I am not against optimism. That would be like being against

the sky. I'm with Gramsci. Not politically, because in the places Marxism has been tried and tested it doesn't seem to have gone all that well. But I'm with Antonio Gramsci, from beautiful Sardinia, in his belief in 'pessimism of the intellect, optimism of the will'. Pessimism of the intellect means that you see the world as it is, not as it would be if you were king of it. You understand that the laws of gravity, economics and cancer reproduction are not subject to your whims.

Optimism of the will means that you have the courage to do difficult things, because you can probably do more than you think. It means that when your world has fallen apart you get out of bed anyway.

If people want to know about courage, I could tell them about my sister. As a child, I had no idea of the demons that haunted her. I had no idea, when I was nine and she was fourteen, why she was suddenly sent away or why, when she came out of hospital, she looked so hunted and hunched. More than anything else, she wanted to be ordinary. She didn't manage it. She didn't have an ordinary life or manage to keep a job. She did manage to be a great friend and to find pleasure in many small things. My sister was not ordinary. She was the bravest person I knew.

I could tell them about my father, who fell in love for the second time when he saw the baby with a full head of hair the same colour as his. Caroline was his firstborn. When she was sent to what we all called 'the unit', he did a three-hour round trip every night to visit her. As soon as the psychiatrists would let him, he got up at five every morning to drive her to the hospital before he started his long commute to work, so she could spend the nights at home. For the rest of her life, he took her for long walks. I think they both saw those walks as a kind of prayer.

I could tell them about my mother, my beautiful, brilliant mother, who wrote a letter to her mother-in-law just after Caroline was born. 'Caroline is the best thing that has ever happened to me,' she wrote, but as she watched her daughter's struggles over the next forty-one years there must have been times when she was tempted to change her mind. In all this time, and in the years since then, my mother has continued to lavish her children with love.

And I could tell them about some of my friends. I could tell them about Louise, who buried one of her twins, and has spent the last fourteen years looking after a child who can't speak or lift her head. I could tell them about Mimi, whose son has schizophrenia and whose daughter is probably going blind. I could tell them about Winston, who has broken his back three times, had a stroke and now has epilepsy, but says he hasn't 'got a reason to moan'. I could tell them that I picked them as my friends because of their courage. But that would be a lie. I picked them as my friends because I love their company and they make me laugh.

I believe in laughter. I believe in friends. I believe in wine. I believe in crisps. I believe in coffee. I believe in beauty. I believe in art. I believe in grace. I believe in kindness. I believe in wit. I believe in doubt. I believe in cake. I believe in moving your body, since it's the only one you get. I believe in hard work. I believe in lie-ins. I believe in candles, and canapés, and champagne. I believe that the world works an awful lot better if people are nice. I believe there are usually some reasons to be cheerful, but sometimes it would be weird not to feel sad. I believe in learning. I believe in curiosity. Oh my God, I believe in curiosity. I believe it's the best way to remind ourselves that we're tiny specks in a big world. And I believe in anger. Yes, I do believe in anger, but the kind of anger that gives you the energy to fight back.

Abraham Lincoln said, or is said to have said, that 'most people are about as happy as they make up their minds to be'. If I'd read that when I was younger, I'd have wanted to smash a glass in his face. Now I think he's right. Not if you have depression. Depression is not the same as misery and you can't just will it away. But I have learnt, through my bouts of misery, that happiness is largely a choice. 'I believe,' said Frieda Hughes, who has lost every member of her family and lived her whole life in the shadow of suicide, 'that happiness has to be worked at. I believe it has to be earned. It's like a marriage or a friendship, or any kind of relationship. We can try and we can fail. We do not,' she added, and her smile was dazzling, but also fierce, 'always succeed.'

No, we don't. And anyway, what is success? A marriage that lasts for life? Healthy, employed children? A career that glides gently upwards towards a peak? If so, I've failed. If so, many of us have failed.

I do not think that we have failed. We are here. We are fighting. We are learning. We are laughing. We are getting up in the morning and trying to earn a living and trying to learn how to be better daughters, sons, partners, lovers, colleagues, neighbours and friends.

On the way home from my birthday dinner, I thought about Yana. The shrink I saw for a while, the one she saw for a while, told me that he had 'never managed to cure her of her optimism'. I laughed. When I told her, she laughed too. I don't mind Yana's optimism. Unflagging optimism often irritates me, but hers, for some reason, does not.

Once, when I was lying on her couch covered in needles, she told me of the time she met a Holocaust survivor. She told me carefully, because she knows what I think of Viktor Frankl. The woman she met was called Alice Herz-Sommer. She was 104. 'I was fazed by her optimism,' Yana said. 'I couldn't believe it! I said to her, "Alice, the sun will die," and do you know what she said?' I shook my head, in as far as you can when you're lying on your front and feeling like a porcupine. 'She said,' Yana told me, and I could hear the smile in her voice, '"Then we will find another sun."'

Epilogue

I don't like books that end in clichés, but it seems churlish not to mention that I found love. Two years after losing my job, at the age of fifty-one I found love.

I'd just started to dip a toe back into the shark pool of internet dating and had had a couple of nips that had left me nursing wounds. One guy had cooked me a very nice Sunday lunch at his house in Sussex and invited me to a Rembrandt private view at the National Gallery the next day. He had, in fact, asked to see me three times in one week and then travelled all the way to Stoke Newington to have Sunday lunch at my flat. Perhaps it was my cooking, but when he left he said he hadn't had the 'coup de foudre'. I did not tell him to fuck off and die, but kept my promise to drive him to Finsbury Park.

My lovely bloke popped up a few months later. I don't want to tempt fate by saying too much about him, but I will say this: he's everything all those narcissistic charmers aren't. He's modest. He's quiet. He's reliable. If he says he'll do something, he'll do it. He doesn't make grand promises. He just gets on with things. If something's broken, he'll mend it. He'll go online and order a spare part and – hey presto! – I'll have windows in my car that actually go up and down. He prefers to make things happen than be in the limelight. He is a gentleman. He is a gentle man. He is polite. He is thoughtful. He is kind.

And he's romantic. I didn't think it would be possible to meet anyone so romantic. He brings me flowers and chocolates and delicious wine and also, of course, delicious crisps.

We have been to the Cotswolds. We have been to Norfolk and Cambridge and Oxford and Devon. We have had pub lunches in the sunshine. We have walked in the rain. We have been to Italy. We have been there in the spring sunshine and the summer heat and the sparkling frost of Christmas Day. Now I can wake up in my lover's arms and open the shutters and look out at the fig tree in the garden and drink coffee with him in bed as we gaze out at the bright, beautiful day.

My love has taught me that love is something that has to be renewed every day. He has taught me that love really is like a garden. You can't just plant the seeds and hope they'll grow. You have to water them. You have to cherish them. You have to make sure they get some sunshine. You have to treat them well.

On our second date, which was the day after our first date, I had a strong feeling that I would never again meet a man who was capable of loving me as much. I still think this is true. I don't know if we'll ever live together. I don't know if I want to live with anyone. If you ask me, it's just too many damn meals. And I don't know if it will last. We can't know if anything in life will last. I'll be grateful for whatever time I have with him, but I have also learnt that I am actually pretty happy on my own.

You can probably imagine what my mother thought. I think she had got to the point where any male with a pulse would have done just fine. When she met him, she looked so happy that I honestly thought she might clap her hands. We had tea in the garden. We sat near what used to be the Wendy house, where Monique and I once set our Halloween decorations on fire. My mother had laid the table for tea, with a tablecloth and nice china and the home-made cakes she had bought. As always, she took tiny bites of her cakes. As always, I took big bites of mine. Between the bites, her smile was like the sun.

My mother was very excited when I told her that my lovely bloke was helping me make some changes to my flat. In recent years, it had got dark. The trees had grown so much they were blocking out the light. He had come up with a plan to turn the main windows in my sitting room into French windows, opening out into the communal garden, and to create an extra bull's eye window to let more light in from the south. He's an architect. He's an award-winning architect, in fact, and he knows how to make changes to old buildings that don't interfere with the original design. We got planning permission from Hackney Council. My friend Arifa told me about her brilliant builders. I made plans to empty my so-called savings account of what was left of my redundancy pay. I couldn't think of a better thing to do with the financial fruits of all that pain than turn it into light.

I couldn't wait to show my mother the finished work and arranged to have the grand unveiling on her birthday. Unfortunately, one of the bolts for the French windows didn't arrive in time, so the giant hole in my sitting room wall was still covered in plywood when the date loomed. The bolt, as it happens, was from a Swedish manufacturer, not all that far from where my mother was born. But phone calls to Gothenburg couldn't summon it, and so the birthday lunch was postponed.

Two days before her birthday, my mother tripped on the stairs. She lay on the hall floor for several hours before she managed to reach the phone. In the hospital, they told her she had broken her hip. She spent the morning of her eighty-second birthday having it replaced. When I walked on to the ward, I didn't, at first, recognize the frail woman with wild white hair.

For the next five weeks, either Tom or I visited her every day. Sometimes the drive from London would take three and a half hours. Often the parking machines at the hospital didn't work. One Sunday morning, when I had planned to spend a day at home in London, Tom called to say that she was in a bad way. When I finally got to the hospital, the parking machines swallowed all my coins. I queued up at the parking office and tried to work out how much parking you had to pay for when it looked as if your mother might die.

When I arrived at her bed, her eyes were half open, and you could only see the whites of her eyes. Tom was there already. The curtains round her bed were closed. I clutched my mother's hand. I told her that I loved her and that having her as my mother had been the biggest blessing of my life. I asked her what had given her the most pleasure in hers. Suddenly, she opened her eyes. For the first time in days, she smiled. 'My children,' she said.

When she first went into hospital, I thought that if my mother died, it would be the end of the world. But when the nurses began to talk about her needing twenty-four-hour care, I began to wonder if I was wrong. One day, my mother told me that she had

had enough. 'You know what to pray for,' she said as I kissed her goodbye. A few days later, I was running round my local park. Even though I don't believe in God, I was mouthing a kind of prayer. 'OK, Mum, you can go now,' I said. 'I don't want you to go, but if you want to go, then I want you to go. Please God,' I added, 'let her go.' Ten minutes later, I got a call from the hospital. 'Your mum,' said the ward sister, 'is very, very sick.'

I think she was already dead. When I was sitting in traffic in Green Lanes, and pulled into a side road to answer my phone, Tom told me she was dead. I stopped to get some petrol on the North Circular. I asked the man at the garage if I could use their loo. 'My mother's died,' I said, but he still told me to go to the pub across the road. Please help me, I wanted to say, because the person I have always loved most in the world is dead.

That night, my brother and I sat at the kitchen table, in what has always been our family home. We tested what it was like to talk about our mother in the past tense.

There have been moments when I think my heart will break. There was a moment at Starbucks, at the Sainsbury's nearest to my mother's home, when I saw a sign, next to cinnamon buns, saying 'a taste of Scandinavia' and thought I was going to break down. There was a moment at Euston when I saw a suitcase just like one of my mother's, blue with pink flowers, and wanted to yank it off the escalator and hug it to my heart. There was a moment when I found a voicemail from her on my phone and thought I might go mad because I would never hear that voice again.

But really, I feel lucky. I started my mother's eulogy by saying, 'My mother always said she was lucky.' And she did. In spite of it all, she did. I think I'm the lucky one to have had her as my mother. I'm lucky to have had such loving parents. I'm lucky to have had so many opportunities. I'm lucky to have been born in a peaceful nation in the Western world. I've been to a refugee camp in Jordan. I've met Syrian refugees who have lost everything. I really do know how lucky I am.

And I'm very, very lucky that when my mother wanted to go, she did. When she was in hospital, I brought her flasks of good coffee and china coffee cups and Swedish cakes. I brought her gin and tonic and crisps. I brought my laptop and subscribed to Netflix so my mother, who loved the Queen, could watch *The Crown*. But she couldn't really eat and she couldn't really swallow and she couldn't really follow all that much of what was going on. And so I thank the sun, the moon and the stars that when my darling mother wanted to go, she did.

We had pink roses on her coffin, pink roses like the ones she had in her wedding bouquet. After the funeral, I placed them in a vase by my new French windows. It was very hard to throw them out.

On a sunny day I sit on the sofa opposite the French windows that my beloved has designed. I look out at the silver birches, which remind me of the silver birches my father planted. One, he said, for each member of the family. That house is going now, and those silver birches have already gone. But the ones in my garden, the garden I share with my neighbours, are still here and still strong. When I look at them, I think of my father, and my sister and my mother. And I think that Larkin was right. What will survive of us is love. Our love for the family members we have lost and also our love for the living family of our friends.

It's spring now. The trees, as Larkin said, are coming into leaf. And I can almost hear them whisper: 'Begin afresh, afresh, afresh.'

Acknowledgements

I had eight good years at *The Independent* and two that were a lot less fun. But we hacks know the power of regime change more than most. During my time on the paper I worked with many brilliant journalists who were also supportive bosses or colleagues. In particular, I would like to thank Simon Kelner, Katherine Butler, Adrian Hamilton, Arifa Akbar, Mary Dejevsky, Boyd Tonkin, Chris Schuler and Roger Alton for their kindness and the benefit of their experience and brains.

Since leaving the paper, I've had the opportunity to work for other brilliant editors on other papers. In particular, I would like to thank Andrew Holgate, Sarah Baxter and Eleanor Mills at the *Sunday Times*; Katherine Butler (again!), Hugh Muir, Joseph Harker and David Shariatmadari at *The Guardian*; Liz Hoggard and Celia Duncan at the *Daily Mail*. I'd like to thank Oli Foster at Sky News, Matthew Syed, my most regular sparring partner on the press preview, and Alison Hanning, Sue Black and the other women in make-up who wreak regular miracles with Touche Éclat.

I'd like to thank Peter Robinson for the conversation that sparked the book, and for nursing me through its gestation, Toby Mundy for the title and Karen Duffy at Atlantic for taking it on.

I would like to thank my friends, for coffee, cake, wine, crisps, critical feedback and life support.

I would like to thank my brother, for being a brick.

I would like to thank all the people who agreed to talk to me for the book: for opening up, cheering me up and offering a glimpse of their hearts.

And darling, I think the epilogue speaks for itself.